TextGraphs-16: Graph-based Methods for Natural Language Processing

Held online due to COVID-19

Gyeongju, South Korea
12-17 October 2022

ISBN: 978-1-7138-6196-6

Printed from e-media with permission by:

Curran Associates, Inc.
57 Morehouse Lane
Red Hook, NY 12571

Some format issues inherent in the e-media version may also appear in this print version.

Printed with permission by Curran Associates, Inc. (2023)

For permission requests, please contact the Association for Computational Linguistics at the address below.

Association for Computational Linguistics
209 N. Eighth Street
Stroudsburg, Pennsylvania 18360

Phone: 1-570-476-8006
Fax: 1-570-476-0860

acl@aclweb.org

Additional copies of this publication are available from:

Curran Associates, Inc.
57 Morehouse Lane
Red Hook, NY 12571 USA
Phone: 845-758-0400
Fax: 845-758-2633
Email: curran@proceedings.com
Web: www.proceedings.com

COLING

International Conference on Computational Linguistics

Proceedings of the Conference and Workshops

COLING

Volume 29 (2022), No. 16

Proceedings of TextGraphs-16: Graph-based Methods for Natural Language Processing

The 29th International Conference on Computational Linguistics

October 12 - 17, 2022
Gyeongju, Republic of Korea

Preface

Welcome to TextGraphs, the Workshop on Graph-Based Methods for Natural Language Processing. The sixteenth edition of our workshop is being organized on October 16, 2022 in Gyeongju, Republic of Korea, in conjunction with the 29th International Conference on Computational Linguistics (COLING 2022).

For the past sixteen years, the workshops in the TextGraphs series have published and promoted the synergy between the field of Graph Theory (GT) and Natural Language Processing (NLP). The mix between the two started small, with graph-theoretical frameworks providing efficient and elegant solutions for NLP applications. Graph-based solutions initially focused on single-document part-of-speech tagging, word sense disambiguation, and semantic role labeling. They became progressively larger to include ontology learning and information extraction from large text collections. Nowadays, graph-based solutions also target Web-scale applications such as information propagation in social networks, rumor proliferation, e-reputation, multiple entity detection, language dynamics learning, and future events prediction, to name a few.

The target audience comprises researchers working on problems related to either Graph Theory or graph-based algorithms applied to Natural Language Processing, Social Media, and the Semantic Web.

This year, we received 19 submissions and accepted 10 of them. Similarly to the last years, we organized a shared task on natural language premise selection. This task takes as input a mathematical statement, written in natural language, and outputs a set of relevant sentences (premises) that could support an end-user finding a proof for that mathematical statement. The shared task attacted four teams; their participation reports along with the shared task overview by its organizers are also presented at the workshop.

We would like to thank our keynote speaker and we are also thankful to the members of the program committee for their valuable and high-quality reviews. All submissions have benefited from their expert feedback. Their timely contribution was the basis for accepting an excellent list of papers and making the sixteenth edition of TextGraphs a success.

Dmitry Ustalov, Yanjun Gao, Alexander Panchenko, Marco Valentino, Mokanarangan Thayaparan, Thien Huu Nguyen, Gerald Penn, Arti Ramesh, and Abhik Jana

TextGraphs-16 Organizers

October 2022

Program Committee

Amir Bakarov, Behavox
Flavio Massimiliano Cecchini, Università Cattolica del Sacro Cuore
Mikhail Chernoskutov, Krasovskii Institute of Mathematics and Mechanics
Hejie Cui, Emory University
Stefano Faralli, University of Rome Sapienza
Michael Flor, Educational Testing Service
Natalia Grabar, Université de Lille
Aayushee Gupta, International Institute of Information Technology, Bangalore
Rima Hazra, Indian Institute of Technology, Kharagpur
Dmitry Ilvovsky, National Research University Higher School of Economics
Rohith Gowtham Kodali, ambientone
Andrey Kutuzov, University of Oslo
Ping Li, Soutwest Petroleum University
Suman Kalyan Maity, MIT
Gabor Melli, Sony PlayStation
Enrique Noriega-Atala, The University of Arizona
Damien Nouvel, Inalco (ERTIM)
Jan Wira Gotama Putra, SmartNews, Inc.
Leonardo F. R. Ribeiro, TU Darmstadt
Minoru Sasaki, Ibaraki University
Viktor Schlegel, University of Manchester
Mark Steedman, University of Edinburgh
Mihai Surdeanu, University of Arizona
Adrian Ulges, RheinMain University of Applied Sciences
Vaibhav Vaibhav, Apple
Mariana Vargas Vieyra, Inria Lille Nord Europe
Xiang Zhao, National University of Defense Technology

Organizing Committee

Dmitry Ustalov, Toloka
Yanjun Gao, University of Wisconsin-Madison
Alexander Panchenko, Skoltech
Marco Valentino, University of Manchester & Idiap Research Institute
Mokanarangan Thayaparan, University of Manchester & Idiap Research Institute
Thien Huu Nguyen, University of Oregon
Gerald Penn, University of Toronto
Arti Ramesh, Educational Testing Services
Abhik Jana, University of Hamburg

Table of Contents

Multilevel Hypernode Graphs for Effective and Efficient Entity Linking
David Montero, Javier Martínez and Javier Yebes 1

Cross-Modal Contextualized Hidden State Projection Method for Expanding of Taxonomic Graphs
Irina Nikishina, Alsu Vakhitova, Elena Tutubalina and Alexander Panchenko 11

Sharing Parameter by Conjugation for Knowledge Graph Embeddings in Complex Space
Xincan Feng, Zhi Qu, Yuchang Cheng, Taro Watanabe and Nobuhiro Yugami 25

A Clique-based Graphical Approach to Detect Interpretable Adjectival Senses in Hungarian
Enikő Héja and Noémi Ligeti-Nagy 35

GUSUM: Graph-based Unsupervised Summarization Using Sentence Features Scoring and Sentence-BERT
Tuba Gokhan, Phillip Smith and Mark Lee 44

The Effectiveness of Masked Language Modeling and Adapters for Factual Knowledge Injection
Sondre Wold 54

Text-Aware Graph Embeddings for Donation Behavior Prediction
MeiXing Dong, Xueming Xu and Rada Mihalcea 60

Word Sense Disambiguation of French Lexicographical Examples Using Lexical Networks
Aman Sinha, Sandrine Ollinger and Mathieu Constant 70

RuDSI: Graph-based Word Sense Induction Dataset for Russian
Anna Aksenova, Ekaterina Gavrishina, Elisei Rykov and Andrey Kutuzov 77

Temporal Graph Analysis of Misinformation Spreaders in Social Media
Flora Sakketou, Joan Plepi, Henri-Jacques Geiss and Lucie Flek 89

TextGraphs 2022 Shared Task on Natural Language Premise Selection
Marco Valentino, Deborah Ferreira, Mokanarangan Thayaparan, André Freitas and Dmitry Ustalov 105

IJS at TextGraphs-16 Natural Language Premise Selection Task: Will Contextual Information Improve Natural Language Premise Selection?
Thi Hong Hanh Tran, Matej Martinc, Antoine Doucet and Senja Pollak 114

SNLP at TextGraphs 2022 Shared Task: Unsupervised Natural Language Premise Selection in Mathematical Texts Using Sentence-MPNet
Paul Trust, Provia Kadusabe, Haseeb Younis, Rosane Minghim, Evangelos Milios and Ahmed Zahran 119

Keyword-based Natural Language Premise Selection for an Automatic Mathematical Statement Proving
Doratossadat Dastgheib and Ehsaneddin Asgari 124

TextGraphs-16 Natural Language Premise Selection Task: Zero-Shot Premise Selection with Prompting Generative Language Models
Liubov Kovriguina, Roman Teucher and Robert Wardenga 127

Conference Program

9:00–9:30 **Opening Remarks**

9:30–10:30 **Keynote Speaker**

10:30–11:00 **Coffee Break 1**

11:00–12:30 **Oral Session 1**

11:00–11:18 *Multilevel Hypernode Graphs for Effective and Efficient Entity Linking*
David Montero, Javier Martínez and Javier Yebes

11:18–11:36 *Cross-Modal Contextualized Hidden State Projection Method for Expanding of Taxonomic Graphs*
Irina Nikishina, Alsu Vakhitova, Elena Tutubalina and Alexander Panchenko

11:36–11:54 *Sharing Parameter by Conjugation for Knowledge Graph Embeddings in Complex Space*
Xincan Feng, Zhi Qu, Yuchang Cheng, Taro Watanabe and Nobuhiro Yugami

11:54–12:12 *A Clique-based Graphical Approach to Detect Interpretable Adjectival Senses in Hungarian*
Enikő Héja and Noémi Ligeti-Nagy

12:12–12:30 *GUSUM: Graph-based Unsupervised Summarization Using Sentence Features Scoring and Sentence-BERT*
Tuba Gokhan, Phillip Smith and Mark Lee

No Day Set (continued)

12:30–14:00 Lunch Break

14:00–15:30 Oral Session 2

14:00–14:18 *The Effectiveness of Masked Language Modeling and Adapters for Factual Knowledge Injection*
Sondre Wold

14:18–14:36 *Text-Aware Graph Embeddings for Donation Behavior Prediction*
MeiXing Dong, Xueming Xu and Rada Mihalcea

14:36–14:54 *Word Sense Disambiguation of French Lexicographical Examples Using Lexical Networks*
Aman Sinha, Sandrine Ollinger and Mathieu Constant

14:54–15:12 *RuDSI: Graph-based Word Sense Induction Dataset for Russian*
Anna Aksenova, Ekaterina Gavrishina, Elisei Rykov and Andrey Kutuzov

15:12–15:30 *Temporal Graph Analysis of Misinformation Spreaders in Social Media*
Flora Sakketou, Joan Plepi, Henri-Jacques Geiss and Lucie Flek

15:30–16:00 Coffee Break 2

16:00–17:20 Oral Session 3 TextGraphs Shared Task

16:00–16:20 *TextGraphs 2022 Shared Task on Natural Language Premise Selection*
Marco Valentino, Deborah Ferreira, Mokanarangan Thayaparan, André Freitas and Dmitry Ustalov

16:20–16:35 *IJS at TextGraphs-16 Natural Language Premise Selection Task: Will Contextual Information Improve Natural Language Premise Selection?*
Thi Hong Hanh Tran, Matej Martinc, Antoine Doucet and Senja Pollak

16:35–16:50 *SNLP at TextGraphs 2022 Shared Task: Unsupervised Natural Language Premise Selection in Mathematical Texts Using Sentence-MPNet*
Paul Trust, Provia Kadusabe, Haseeb Younis, Rosane Minghim, Evangelos Milios and Ahmed Zahran

No Day Set (continued)

16:50–17:05 *Keyword-based Natural Language Premise Selection for an Automatic Mathematical Statement Proving*
Doratossadat Dastgheib and Ehsaneddin Asgari

17:05–17:20 *TextGraphs-16 Natural Language Premise Selection Task: Zero-Shot Premise Selection with Prompting Generative Language Models*
Liubov Kovriguina, Roman Teucher and Robert Wardenga

17:20–17:30 Closing Remarks

Multilevel Hypernode Graphs for Effective and Efficient Entity Linking *

David Montero and **Javier Martinez** and **J. Javier Yebes**
NielsenIQ
{david.montero, javier.martinezcebrian, javier.yebes}@nielseniq.com

Abstract

Information extraction on documents still remains a challenge, especially when dealing with unstructured documents with complex and variable layouts. Graph Neural Networks seem to be a promising approach to overcome these difficulties due to their flexible and sparse nature, but they have not been exploited yet. In this work, we present a multi-level graph-based model that performs entity building and linking on unstructured documents, purely based on GNNs, and extremely light (0.3 million parameters). We also propose a novel strategy for an optimal propagation of the information between the graph levels based on hypernodes. The conducted experiments on public and private datasets demonstrate that our model is suitable for solving the tasks, and that the proposed propagation strategy is optimal and outperforms other approaches.

1 Introduction

Information extraction (IE) from documents has become a hot research topic over the last few years (Jaume et al., 2019; Wang et al., 2020; Carbonell et al., 2021; Dang et al., 2021). It is a challenging problem that requires combining Computer Vision (CV) and Natural Language Processing (NLP) models in order to locate and parse the information segments, understand the document layout, and extract semantic relations between the segments.

This problem becomes especially complex when dealing with unstructured documents, such as purchase receipts, where the layout of the documents can highly vary, making it hard for the models to learn how to extract semantic information. At this point, Graph Neural Networks (GNNs) seem to be a promising approach to overcome these difficulties and to solve the semantic information and relation extraction tasks, as they work over flexible graph-based representation capable of adapting to complex layouts, and they provide efficient and effective mechanisms for learning the relations between the segments (Carbonell et al., 2021; Davis et al., 2021; Hwang et al., 2021b; Baumgartner et al., 2021; Papagiannopoulou et al., 2021; Luo et al., 2020; Khalife and Vazirgiannis, 2019).

Nevertheless, semantic IE still remains a challenging task. In fact, due to its complexity, it is usually split into three subtasks:

- Entity Building (EB): refers to the task of connecting text segments together that are related semantically and are spatially close in the document, also known as word grouping.
- Entity Tagging (ET): classify each of the built entities attending to their semantic meaning, e.g., product description, store name, etc.
- Entity linking (EL): connect the semantic entities to form higher level semantic relations, e.g., a product description is connected to a quantity and a price.

Thus, we can distinguish between three levels of information containers:

- Text segment: lowest level information, usually given by an Optical Character Recognition (OCR) engine at word level.
- Entity: intermediate level generated by grouping the text segments during the EB task.
- Entity group: highest level container that groups entities resultant from the EL task.

For a solution based purely on GNNs this leaves two options. One is trying to solve all the tasks using a single graph at segment level (Hwang et al., 2021b). The second option is splitting the problem into two graphs: one graph based on segment nodes for performing EB, and another one composed of

*A patent has been applied for that covers the subject matter described in this article.

Proceedings of TextGraphs-16: Graph-based Methods for Natural Language Processing, pages 1–10
October 16, 2022.

entity nodes for performing ET and EL tasks (Carbonell et al., 2021). We believe that the second one is more effective for the following reasons:

- The model can work on extracting node-level relations only, which reduces the complexity.
- The information learnt by the segments nodes during the message passing can be used to generate optimal features for the entity nodes.

Nevertheless, the multi-graph approach has more complexity, as it requires designing the way the output segment features and the entity features are related, and it has not yet been studied in depth. Thus, in this work we focus on optimizing this propagation of information between the two stages using a novel approach within the IE field based on hypernodes. These are the main contributions:

- A multi-level GNN-based model that performs EB and EL on unstructured documents. The model is purely based on GNNs, using as inputs for each segment the bounding box and the entity category, and it is extremely light (0.3 million parameters).
- A novel strategy for an optimal propagation of the information from the segment nodes to the entity nodes, where the latter are generated as hypernodes over the base graph and connected to their child segment nodes using relation edges. Then, the subgraph resulting from the relation edges (relation graph) is used to propagate the features with Graph Attention Layers (GATs) (Veličković et al., 2018).
- An ablation study on different feature propagation strategies, evaluating among others the one proposed in (Carbonell et al., 2021), and comparing them with the single graph approach (Hwang et al., 2021b).

The conducted experiments demonstrate the effectiveness of the proposed method over highly unstructured documents in terms accuracy, processing time, and resource consumption.

2 Related Work

The growing interest in IE is patent in the number of recent publications. Attending to the input data, most of the methods rely on the text and bounding boxes of an OCR engine for extracting the input features (Jaume et al., 2019; Carbonell et al., 2021; Hwang et al., 2021b; Prabhu et al., 2021; Zhang et al., 2021; Hong et al., 2022; Wang et al., 2022). Other approaches enrich these OCR predictions with image features (Wang et al., 2020; Dang et al., 2021; Xu et al., 2021; Tang et al., 2021). However, the results reported in public IE benchmarks like FUNSD (Jaume et al., 2019) or CORD (Park et al., 2019) suggest that the image features are not so relevant. Finally, there are also a few models that purely rely on image features (Hwang et al., 2021a; Kim et al., 2021). The model proposed in this work extracts features from the OCR bounding boxes, but does not use the text, as it gathers the necessary information from the entity category input.

Attending to the model architecture, most of the methods are based on Transformers (Vaswani et al., 2017) and Convolutional Neural Networks (CNNs) (Jaume et al., 2019; Wang et al., 2020; Dang et al., 2021; Xu et al., 2021; Hwang et al., 2021a; Li et al., 2021; Prabhu et al., 2021; Zhang et al., 2021; Kim et al., 2021; Villota et al., 2021; Hong et al., 2022; Gu et al., 2022; Wang et al., 2022). Nevertheless, GNNs are gaining importance thanks to their flexibility and capacity of adapting to complex layouts, along with their effective mechanisms for learning relationships between the nodes. In (Carbonell et al., 2021), the authors propose a two-stage GNN model. First, they generate a k-nearest neighbor (KNN) graph to solve EB using text and bounding box features. Then, the entity features are computed by aggregating the output features and processing them with a linear layer, and they are used to solve the ET and EL. In (Hwang et al., 2021b), the authors propose a single-stage GNN model: EB and ET are solved via rel-s edges where each seed entity-type node links to its entity parts in sequence (solving also ET as a consequence), EL links the entities via rel-g edges, finally all mentioned edges are decoded at once. Other GNN approaches solve only the ET and EL tasks, as they rely on the entity regions detected by the OCR engine (Tang et al., 2021; Wan et al., 2021; Zhang et al., 2022), or by a previous CNN model (Davis et al., 2021).

As it can be seen, there are few approaches based on GNN solving both EB and EL. We aim at contributing to this line of research following an approach based on a two-stage GNN model, related to the one presented in (Carbonell et al., 2021), but with important modifications in the feature extraction, edge sampling, feature propagation, GNN architecture, and postprocessing.

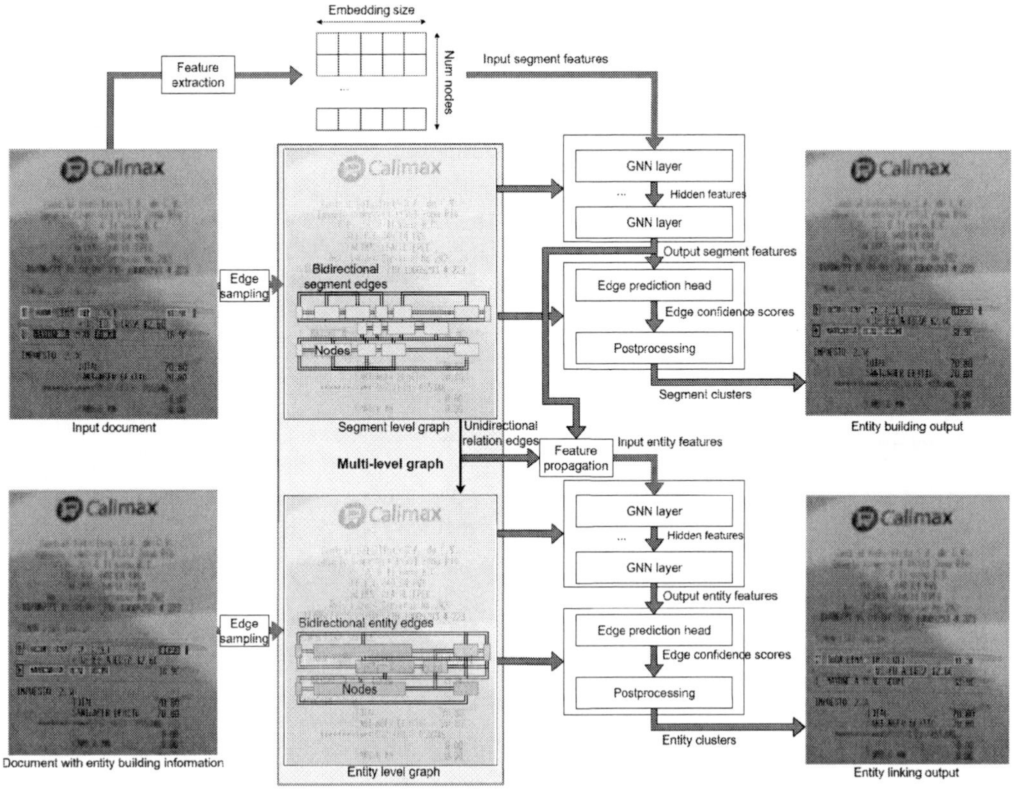

Figure 1: High level diagram of the proposed solution for the EB and EL tasks.

3 Methodology

We aim at solving the entity building (EB) and entity linking (EL) tasks for a given list of documents. Each document is composed of a list of semantic entities, that can be linked together to form entity groups. Each entity can also be divided into smaller text segments. Thus, given a list of text segments from an OCR engine, the goal is to group the text segments by their entity and then link together all the entities that belong to the same entity group. We propose to use GNNs as the best approach:

- Graph-based representations can adapt to complex layouts in unstructured documents.
- EB and EL can be modeled as link prediction tasks between pairs of segments, where GNNs have been demonstrated to be highly effective.
- The number of connections that need to be evaluated can be limited based on the coordinates, limiting the time and resource consumption. GNNs are suitable for this type of highly sparse data structure.

Figure 1 illustrates the proposed solution. From the incoming list of segments, the system performs the edge sampling and generates the base graph level. In parallel, the features for the nodes are extracted. The input features are passed through the segment GNN layers and used to generate the segment clusters (EB output). For each generated cluster, an entity hypernode is created and connected to their child segment nodes using relation edges. Then, feature propagation uses the subgraph of relation edges (relation graph). Finally, these entity features are processed in the same way as in the previous stage to generate the entity clusters (EL output).

3.1 Feature extraction

We consider the three sources of information available: the bounding box, the text string and the entity category. We discard the text, as we have empirically observed that all the necessary information is contained in the entity category. Also, we remove the impact of the OCR text errors.

We select the following features from the bounding box: left and right center coordinates, and the angle in radians $(\frac{-\pi}{2}, \frac{\pi}{2})$. Notice that using the left and right center we are losing the information related to the height of the bounding box. We do this on purpose, as we observed that the model tended to overfit using this feature. We normalize both centers using the width of the document, the most stable dimension, as the height can highly vary. For extracting the information from the entity category we use a one-hot encoder, and then a linear layer to adapt the features and map them to an embedding of length 8. Finally, the category embedding is concatenated with bounding box features to generate the node feature embedding (with 13 float values).

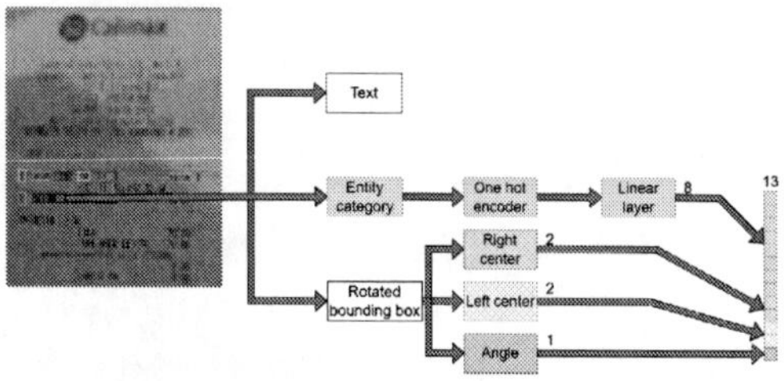

Figure 2: Feature extraction stage.

3.2 Edge sampling

The message passing involve the edges and also they are used by the edge prediction head to generate the final predictions. Hence, it is crucial to select an appropriate sampling function that covers all the possible true positives.

Moreover, we are dealing with highly unstructured documents and we cannot trust the usual sampling functions, such as k-nearest neighbor or beta-skeleton (Carbonell et al., 2021; Wan et al., 2021; Zhang et al., 2022), as they are prone to miss connections between segments that are far away from each other.

Thus, we developed a custom sampling function to ensure that all the segments in the same line are connected: an edge from segment A to segment B is created if the vertical distance between their centers (C) is less than the height (H) of segment A by a constant (K) (see Equation 1). In our experiments we set this constant to two, as we want to generate connections also between the segments of adjacent lines for the case of multi-line entities, and to consider the possible rotation of the document. This sampling function is also used to generate the edges for the entity level graph.

$$edge_{A-B} = |C_A^y - C_B^y| < H_A * K \quad (1)$$

3.3 GNN

Selecting the most appropriate type of layer is another important step in the model design. Most of the GNN layer implementations require an additional scores vector for performing a weighted message passing, for deciding the contribution of each neighbor node. This implies adding more complexity to the design of the network for computing the weights.

In our case, the information needed for that computation is already embedded in the node features. Taking advantage of this, we select Graph Attention Layers (GAT) (Veličković et al., 2018) as the best suited. In the GAT layers, the weights for the message passing are computed directly inside the layer using the input node features. In addition, they have been widely used and demonstrated their efficiency in document understanding tasks (Carbonell et al., 2021; Zhang et al., 2022). In order to avoid 0-in-degree errors (disconnected nodes) while using the GAT layers, we add a self-loop for each node.

The proposed GNN architectures for the two graph levels are illustrated in Figure 3 and they both use GAT layers. All the layers are followed by SiLU activations (Elfwing et al., 2018) except for the last one. This activation seemed to work better than ReLU and other variants. We also add residual connections in all the layers to accelerate the convergence of the model.

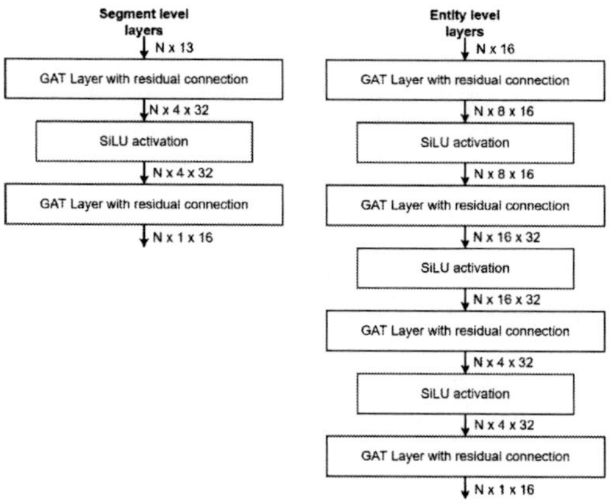

Figure 3: Proposed GNN architectures.

Another introduced enhancement is the use of a global document node, inspired by (Zhang et al., 2022). We use one global node per graph level, and we connect it bidirectionally to the rest of the level nodes. Its feature embedding is initially computed by averaging all the level node embeddings. It has a double function in the network: it provides context information to the nodes, and it acts as a regularization term for the GAT layer weights. These global nodes are only considered during the message passing.

3.4 Feature propagation

The feature propagation strategy is one of the critical parts of the model, as it defines the connection between the two stages and how the entity features are generated.

First, we analyze the strategy followed in (Carbonell et al., 2021), where the features of the nodes belonging to the same entity are added and processed by a linear layer. We believe that this strategy is not optimal for two reasons. First, as the number of nodes of an entity is variable, adding their features will lead to variable magnitude embeddings, which might impact on the stability of the model. This could be mitigated by using a mean aggregation. Second, they assume that all the segment nodes contribute equally to the entity. We believe that this is an erroneous assumption, as there might be key segments (maybe those which are bigger, or which have a strategic position) that should contribute more.

We propose a new approach where the entity nodes are built as hypernodes on top of the segment level graph and connected to their child segment nodes using unidirectional relation edges (from segments to entities). Then, the features propagation is conducted by GAT layers that operates on the subgraph of the relation edges (relation graph). The feature propagation model is composed of 2 GAT layers with a SiLU activation between them. In this case we do not use residual connections, as we want to maximize the information shared by the segment nodes. See below:

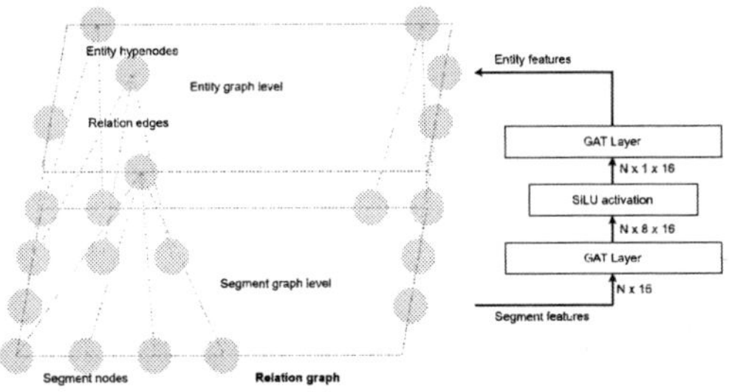

Figure 4: Feature propagation strategy.

3.5 Edge prediction heads

After each GNN level, the node features are used to solve the corresponding task (EB or EL). For each pair of connected segments, we extract the confidence that they belong to the same higher-level container. The strategy we follow is concatenating the output features of the pair of nodes and processing them with an MLP (see Figure 5). After the first layer, we apply another SiLU activation. Finally, we apply a sigmoid function to the output logits to obtain the confidence scores.

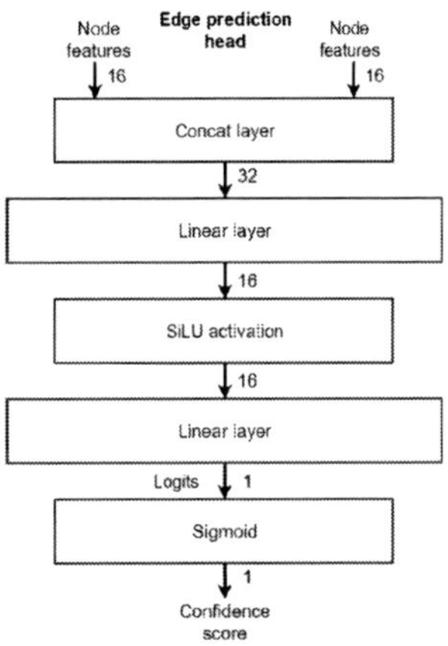

Figure 5: Diagram of the edge prediction heads.

3.6 Postprocessing

Once the confidence scores for a task are computed, we apply a postprocessing function to generate the final clusters. For edge prediction tasks, a commonly used function is Connected Components (CC) (Carbonell et al., 2021). However, due to its simplicity, it highly suffers from any link error, it usually struggles when dealing with complex data distributions, and it depends on a threshold parameter which might be biased to the dataset. For these reasons, we propose to use a different method based on Graph Clustering made of 2 blocks (Equation 2): 1) number of clusters estimator and 2) node grouping. The former, 1), is based on the eigenvalues of the normed graph Laplacian matrix computed from the adjacency matrix (A), by taking first differences (D1) of the sorted eigenvalues and getting the maximum gap + 1. The latter, 2), is based on recursively merging pair of clusters, using the number of clusters estimated (nc) and as the linkage criteria the average of the distances (1 minus the adjacency matrix), being a highly efficient method.

$$\lambda = EigenValues(NormGraphLap(A))$$
$$n_c = argmax(D_1(sort(\lambda))) + 1 \quad (2)$$
$$c_i = FeatAgglom(avg(1 - A), n_c)$$

The benefits are: no need to optimize any parameter avoiding concept drift impact, estimating the number of clusters dynamically for each new data distribution, no need of handcrafted heuristics, and efficient and accurate as the CC approach.

3.7 Training details

Only during the training stage, the entities are constructed using the ground truth (GT). This accelerates the convergency of the model, as it reduces the dependency of the EL task and the EB task. The model is trained for 100 epochs using a batch of 4 graphs on each iteration. The selected optimizer is Adam, with an initial learning rate of 0.001, with a reduction factor of 0.1 in epochs 70 and 90. We use binary cross entropy for computing the loss for the two tasks, and then we sum both losses. Finally, we finetune the model using the predicted entities instead of the GT, so the second part of the model adapts to the real data. The benefits of finetuning the models are demonstrated in the experiments section. The model is finetuned for 10 epochs, with an initial learning rate of 0.0002, being reduced to 0.00002 at epoch 7.

4 Experiments

4.1 Datasets

4.1.1 Private dataset

We have built an internal challenging dataset composed of 8729 purchase receipt images from 5 countries: Germany, Italy, France, Mexico, and Brazil. Receipts vary widely in height, density, and image quality. They may contain rotation and all kinds of wrinkles. Each receipt has annotated all the text segments related to purchased products. The available annotated information for each text segment is the rotated bounding box, the text, the entity category, and the product ID.

There are 9 types entity categories: *unit_type*, *value*, *discount_value*, *code*, *unit_price*, *tax*, *quantity*, *discount_description*, *description*.

The dataset also contains the receipt region annotation for each receipt, so we have preprocessed the dataset for all the models by cropping the images, filtering the segments that are outside the receipt, and shifting the coordinates of the remaining segments to the cropped pixel space. Finally, we split the dataset in training, validation and test sets using a ratio of 70/10/20.

In Figure 6 we present some examples of the dataset after cropping the receipt region. We also include in the images the GT information for the entity building (bounding boxes) and the entity linking (bounding boxes with the same colors and linked by lines). Note that this dataset is more challenging than other IE datasets, such as FUNSD (Jaume et al., 2019) or CORD (Park et al., 2019), as the number of entities can vary from several to hundreds, layouts are highly diverse, and the quality of the receipts and images has a bigger amount of noise.

4.1.2 CORD

Consolidated Receipt Dataset (CORD) (Park et al., 2019) is composed of 1000 Indonesian receipts which contain images and box/text annotations for OCR, and multi-level semantic labels for semantic parsing and relation extraction tasks. In the ground truth, each segment is associated with the *category* field (our entity level) and the *group_id* field (our group level). It contains more entity categories (30), but with significantly fewer instances. It can be observed that the difficulty level is lower but it is the only public dataset we have found for benchmarking. In this dataset, the receipt region annotations are available only for a subset of receipts, so we are not considering them. The samples are split into 800 for train, 100 for dev(validation), and 100 for test.

4.2 Metrics

4.2.1 Group F1 Score

This metric is very restrictive and aims at evaluating the number of groups that are perfectly formed, highly penalizing the groups that are split or merged with others. We compare the predicted groups with the ones from the ground truth. For each predicted group in a document, we only consider it as a true positive (tp) if it matches exactly the ground truth group. Otherwise, it is considered a false positive (fp). Ground truth groups not found in predictions are considered as false negatives (fn).

4.2.2 ARI

The Adjusted Rand Index (ARI) (Halkidi et al., 2002), is more focused on analyzing the quality of the segment clusters rather than checking if they perfectly match the ground truth ones. First, the Rand Index (RI) computes a similarity measure between two clusters by considering all pairs of samples and counting pairs that are assigned in the same or different clusters in the predicted and true clusters. Then, the raw RI score is "adjusted for chance" into the ARI score.

Figure 6: Examples of successful predictions from different countries and retailers. Each box is a predicted entity, and the ones with the same color (and connected by lines) belong to the same group.

4.3 Results

In this subsection, we present and discuss the experimental results with the aim of demonstrating the effectiveness of the proposed method and the contribution of our novel feature propagation. These are the considered approaches:

- Relation graph: described in Section 3.4.
- Without feature propagation: the features of the entities are generated from scratch, in the same way as the text segment features. The entity bounding box is computed using the minimum rotated rectangle and the entity category is computed using the mode.
- Sum aggregation + linear layer: the procedure followed in (Carbonell et al., 2021).

Besides, we include in the comparison the results of a single-stage version of the model, following the approach proposed in (Hwang et al., 2021b). The GNN architecture for this model is the same as for the entity GNN of the proposed model.

Model	EB		EL (E2E)	
	F1	ARI	F1	ARI
ours	0.974	0.966	0.925	0.960
w/o feat prop	0.9756	0.971	0.914	0.955
sum+linear	0.971	0.965	0.915	0.955
Single stage	0.979	0.973	0.913	0.950

Table 1: Results of the proposed model on the purchase receipt dataset and comparison against different feature propagation strategies. We present the results for EB and EL (using the entities predicted in EB).

For all the variants, the model is trained under the same conditions, following the training details specified in Section 3.7. The results of the experiments are gathered in Table 1. It can be observed that the proposed model is achieving impressive results for both tasks (0.974 F1 Score for EB and 0.9252 for EL) considering the challenges of the proposed dataset. Some examples of successful model predictions are shown in Figure 6.

Also the proposed strategy for the entity features generation outperforms the others in the end2end metrics by more than 1%. The strategy without feature propagation achieves slightly better results in EB (less than 0.2%), but we believe this is because in this case the two tasks are more independent from each other, and the model can focus on optimizing better the first task (but at the cost of sacrificing accuracy in the end2end). The same happens with the single stage strategy.

Additionally, we want to measure the impact of the finetuning stage described in Section 3.7, where, instead of using the GT information to construct the entities, we use the predictions from the EB task, and train the model in an end2end manner for 10 epochs. Thus, we compute the end2end metrics for all the model variants before and after the finetuning. The results, presented in Table 3, show that in all the cases both the F1 Score and the ARI metrics are improved. This improvement is less noticeable for our approach, as even if we are using GT information for constructing the entities, the two tasks are still strongly connected by an optimal feature propagation strategy.

Next, we conduct an experiment to test the proposed model under a public benchmark, using the CORD dataset. For this experiment we consider all the annotated segments, using the *category* field as the entity annotation and the *group_id* field as the group annotation. Again, the model is trained following the procedure specified in Section 3.7.

Model	EB Link F1	EL Link F1	EL Group F1	ARI	Params
Rel graph (ours)	0.975	0.988	0.943	0.983	0.3M
Spade(Hwang et al., 2021b)	0.969	0.896	-	-	-
BROS w/o order(Hong et al., 2022)	0.968	0.905	-	-	340M
BROS w order(Hong et al., 2022)	0.966	0.974	-	-	340M

Table 2: Results on the CORD dataset evaluated at link level and at group level.

Model	Before FT		After FT	
	F1	ARI	F1	ARI
Rel graph (ours)	0.917	0.957	0.925	0.960
w/o feat prop	0.903	0.948	0.914	0.955
sum+linear	0.901	0.948	0.915	0.955

Table 3: Impact of the finetuning removing the GT information for the entity generation.

The results are presented in Table 2. To the best of our knowledge, there are no published works that address exclusively the EB and EL tasks, since they are usually combined with the entity tagging task. Consequently, although they are not fully comparable, we decided to include the results of two state-of-the-art end-2-end models that perform ET, EB, and EL, Spade (Hwang et al., 2021b) and BROS (Hong et al., 2022). It can be observed that the proposed model outperforms the others especially on the EL task, while massively reducing the number of parameters if we compare it with BROS. Notice that for BROS we present the results with and without the text order information, as it is dependent on it. We also include the Group F1 Score and the ARI metrics so other future works can fairly compare against our model.

Finally, we also measure the processing time and the resource consumption for our model. The experiment was conducted on a machine with one NVIDIA Tesla V100 GPU, 64 GB of RAM, and 1 Intel(R) Xeon(R) Gold 6142 CPU. For the time calculation, we infer all the dataset samples using batch 1 and compute the average time. We take into account also the preprocessing time since the input files are loaded, including the parsing, feature extraction, and graph generation. The resulting time per image is 0.25 seconds (0.15 for preprocessing and 0.10 for inference and postprocessing), with a low GPU memory consumption of around 1300 megabytes.

5 Conclusions and Future Work

In this work we have addressed the automation of information extraction on unstructured documents, given as inputs the predictions from an OCR engine and an entity tagging model, and focusing on two tasks, entity building and entity linking. We have justified the suitability of GNNs for the considered use case and proposed a model based on this approach. This model tackles the problem in two stages that are strongly connected by using the concept of hypernodes. We have also proposed a novel strategy of propagating the features from the segment nodes to the entity nodes in an optimal way. The results of the conducted experiments demonstrate that the proposed model is suitable for solving the tasks, and that the proposed feature propagation strategy is optimal and outperforms other approaches. In addition, we have compared our model with other state-of-the-art methods that perform the EB and EL tasks using the public benchmark CORD and, although the models are not fully comparable, it can be observed that our model achieves state-of-the-art results with an extremely lower number of parameters.

Future work will focus on expanding the application of the model to address also the ET task. To this end, new types of features could be considered, based on text or image, as we believe that the layout information is not enough to solve ET task. In addition, we will keep enhancing the current capabilities of the model, exploring new ways of propagating the features, improving the postprocessing, and optimizing the GNN architectures.

References

Matthias Baumgartner, Daniele Dell'Aglio, and Abraham Bernstein. 2021. Entity prediction in knowledge graphs with joint embeddings. In *Proceedings of the Fifteenth Workshop on Graph-Based Methods for Natural Language Processing (TextGraphs-15)*, pages 22–31, Mexico City, Mexico. Association for Computational Linguistics.

Manuel Carbonell, Pau Riba, Mauricio Villegas, Alicia Fornés, and Josep Lladós. 2021. Named entity recognition and relation extraction with graph neural networks in semi structured documents. In *2020 25th International Conference on Pattern Recognition (ICPR)*, pages 9622–9627.

Tuan Anh Nguyen Dang, Duc Thanh Hoang, Quang Bach Tran, Chih-Wei Pan, and Thanh Dat Nguyen. 2021. End-to-end hierarchical relation extraction for generic form understanding. In *2020 25th International Conference on Pattern Recognition (ICPR)*, pages 5238–5245. IEEE.

Brian Davis, Bryan Morse, Brian Price, Chris Tensmeyer, and Curtis Wiginton. 2021. Visual fudge: Form understanding via dynamic graph editing. In *International Conference on Document Analysis and Recognition*, pages 416–431. Springer.

Stefan Elfwing, Eiji Uchibe, and Kenji Doya. 2018. Sigmoid-weighted linear units for neural network function approximation in reinforcement learning. In *Neural networks: the official journal of the International Neural Network Society 107*, volume 107, pages 3–11. Elsevier.

Zhangxuan Gu, Changhua Meng, Ke Wang, Jun Lan, Weiqiang Wang, Ming Gu, and Liqing Zhang. 2022. Xylayoutlm: Towards layout-aware multimodal networks for visually-rich document understanding. In *Proceedings of the IEEE/CVF Conference on Computer Vision and Pattern Recognition (CVPR)*, pages 4583–4592.

Maria Halkidi, Yannis Batistakis, and Michalis Vazirgiannis. 2002. Cluster validity methods: part i. *SIGMOD Rec.*, 31:40–45.

Teakgyu Hong, Donghyun Kim, Mingi Ji, Wonseok Hwang, Daehyun Nam, and Sungrae Park. 2022. Bros: A pre-trained language model focusing on text and layout for better key information extraction from documents. In *Proceedings of the AAAI Conference on Artificial Intelligence*, volume 36, pages 10767–10775.

Wonseok Hwang, Hyunji Lee, Jinyeong Yim, Geewook Kim, and Minjoon Seo. 2021a. Cost-effective end-to-end information extraction for semi-structured document images. In *Empirical Methods in Natural Language Processing (EMNLP)*.

Wonseok Hwang, Jinyeong Yim, Seunghyun Park, Sohee Yang, and Minjoon Seo. 2021b. Spatial dependency parsing for semi-structured document information extraction. In *International Joint Conference on Natural Language Processing (IJCNLP)*, pages 330–343.

Guillaume Jaume, Hazim Kemal Ekenel, and Jean-Philippe Thiran. 2019. Funsd: A dataset for form understanding in noisy scanned documents. In *2019 International Conference on Document Analysis and Recognition Workshops (ICDARW)*, volume 2, pages 1–6. IEEE.

Sammy Khalife and Michalis Vazirgiannis. 2019. Scalable graph-based method for individual named entity identification. In *Proceedings of the Thirteenth Workshop on Graph-Based Methods for Natural Language Processing (TextGraphs-13)*, pages 17–25, Hong Kong. Association for Computational Linguistics.

Geewook Kim, Teakgyu Hong, Moonbin Yim, Jinyoung Park, Jinyeong Yim, Wonseok Hwang, Sangdoo Yun, Dongyoon Han, and Seunghyun Park. 2021. Donut: Document understanding transformer without ocr. In *arXiv preprint arXiv:2111.15664*.

Yulin Li, Yuxi Qian, Yuechen Yu, Xiameng Qin, Chengquan Zhang, Yan Liu, Kun Yao, Junyu Han, Jingtuo Liu, and Errui Ding. 2021. Structext: Structured text understanding with multi-modal transformers. In *Proceedings of the 29th ACM International Conference on Multimedia*, pages 1912–1920.

Chuwei Luo, Yongpan Wang, Qi Zheng, Liangchen Li, Feiyu Gao, and Shiyu Zhang. 2020. Merge and recognize: A geometry and 2D context aware graph model for named entity recognition from visual documents. In *Proceedings of the Graph-based Methods for Natural Language Processing (TextGraphs)*, pages 24–34, Barcelona, Spain (Online). Association for Computational Linguistics.

Eirini Papagiannopoulou, Grigorios Tsoumakas, and Apostolos Papadopoulos. 2021. Keyword extraction using unsupervised learning on the document's adjacency matrix. In *Proceedings of the Fifteenth Workshop on Graph-Based Methods for Natural Language Processing (TextGraphs-15)*, pages 94–105, Mexico City, Mexico. Association for Computational Linguistics.

Seunghyun Park, Seung Shin, Bado Lee, Junyeop Lee, Jaeheung Surh, Minjoon Seo, and Hwalsuk Lee. 2019. Cord: a consolidated receipt dataset for post-ocr parsing. In *Workshop on Document Intelligence at NeurIPS 2019*.

Nishant Prabhu, Hiteshi Jain, and Abhishek Tripathi. 2021. Mtl-foun: A multi-task learning approach to form understanding. In *International Conference on Document Analysis and Recognition (ICDAR)*, pages 377–388. Springer.

Guozhi Tang, Lele Xie, Lianwen Jin, Jiapeng Wang, Jingdong Chen, Zhen Xu, Qianying Wang, Yaqiang Wu, and Hui Li. 2021. Matchvie: Exploiting match relevancy between entities for visual information extraction. In *International Joint Conference on Artificial Intelligence (IJCAI)*, pages 1039–1045.

Ashish Vaswani, Noam Shazeer, Niki Parmar, Jakob Uszkoreit, Llion Jones, Aidan N Gomez, Łukasz Kaiser, and Illia Polosukhin. 2017. Attention is all you need. In *Advances in neural information processing systems*, volume 30.

Petar Veličković, Guillem Cucurull, Arantxa Casanova, Adriana Romero, Pietro Lio, and Yoshua Bengio. 2018. Graph attention networks. In *arXiv preprint arXiv:1710.10903*.

María Villota, César Domínguez, Jónathan Heras, Eloy Mata, and Vico Pascual. 2021. Text classification models for form entity linking. In *arXiv preprint arXiv:2112.07443*.

Qian Wan, Luona Wei, Xinhai Chen, and Jie Liu. 2021. A region-based hypergraph network for joint entity-relation extraction. In *Knowledge-Based Systems*, volume 228, page 107298. Elsevier.

Jiapeng Wang, Lianwen Jin, and Kai Ding. 2022. Lilt: A simple yet effective language-independent layout transformer for structured document understanding.

Zilong Wang, Mingjie Zhan, Xuebo Liu, and Ding Liang. 2020. Docstruct: A multimodal method to extract hierarchy structure in document for general form understanding. In *Empirical Methods in Natural Language Processing (EMNLP)*, volume abs/2010.11685, pages 898–908.

Yiheng Xu, Tengchao Lv, Lei Cui, Guoxin Wang, Yijuan Lu, Dinei Florencio, Cha Zhang, and Furu Wei. 2021. Layoutxlm: Multimodal pre-training for multilingual visually-rich document understanding. In *arXiv preprint arXiv:2104.08836*.

Yue Zhang, Bo Zhang, Rui Wang, Junjie Cao, Chen Li, and Zuyi Bao. 2021. Entity relation extraction as dependency parsing in visually rich documents. In *Empirical Methods in Natural Language Processing (EMNLP)*.

Zhenrong Zhang, Jiefeng Ma, Jun Du, Licheng Wang, and Jianshu Zhang. 2022. Multimodal pre-training based on graph attention network for document understanding. In *arXiv preprint arXiv:2203.13530*.

Cross-modal Contextualized Hidden State Projection Method for Expanding of Taxonomic Graphs

Irina Nikishina[1,2], **Alsu Vakhitova**[2], **Elena Tutubalina**[3,4], **and Alexander Panchenko**[2],
[1]Universität Hamburg, [2]Skolkovo Institute of Science and Technology,
[3]Sber AI, [4]Kazan Federal University
irina.nikishina@uni-hamburg.de, alsu.vakhitova@gmail.com,
tutubalinaev@gmail.com, a.panchenko@skoltech.ru

Abstract

Taxonomy is a graph of terms organized hierarchically using is-a (hypernymy) relations. We suggest novel candidate-free task formulation for the taxonomy enrichment task. To solve the task, we leverage lexical knowledge from the pre-trained models to predict new words missing in the taxonomic resource. We propose a method that combines graph-, and text-based contextualized representations from transformer networks to predict new entries to the taxonomy. We have evaluated the method suggested for this task against text-only baselines based on BERT and fastText representations. The results demonstrate that incorporation of graph embedding is beneficial in the task of hyponym prediction using contextualized models. We hope the new challenging task will foster further research in automatic text graph construction methods.

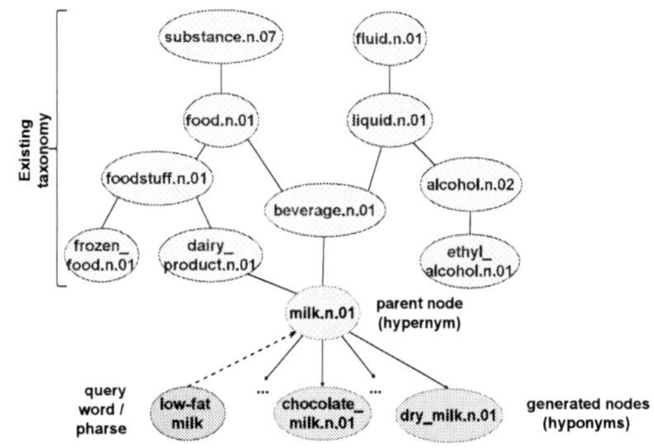

Figure 1: Two types of taxonomy enrichment task: attaching provided candidates (red, prior art) and generating nodes in place without candidates (green, our work).

1 Introduction

In this paper, we focus on taxonomic structures which are quite relevant in many Natural Language Processing (NLP) tasks such as lexical entailment (Herrera et al., 2005) and entity linking (Moro and Navigli, 2015; Sevgili et al., 2022) to represent the relations between products or employees.

Taxonomies are tree-like structures where words are considered as nodes (synsets) and the edges are the relations between them. Such kinds of relationship is called a hypo-hypernym relationship. For instance, let us consider two words: "apple" and "fruit". The former word is *hyponym* ("child") to the latter and the latter is *hypernym* ("parent") to the former.

Many approaches have been proposed to automatically update existing taxonomies (Schlichtkrull and Martínez Alonso, 2016; Arefyev et al., 2020; Nikishina et al., 2020b). However, we argue about one crucial limitation of the existing setups questioning their usefulness in real-world application. In the traditional Taxonomy Enrichment task setting the system is provided with the candidate (orphan) to add and the task is to find the correct place for it in the existing taxonomy. Compiling lists with the new words to add is extremely important but inherently challenging: it might be not clear to which of the multiple sources we would give our preference: neologisms, teenage slang from the Internet or professional jargon.

On the contrary, large pre-trained language models such as BERT (Devlin et al., 2019), ELMo (Peters et al., 2018), GPT (Brown et al., 2020) already contain information about the majority of terms in a language. For instance, many probing studies (Rogers et al., 2020; Jawahar et al., 2019; Ettinger, 2020) show that a vast amount of linguistic information is encoded inside large transformer networks, e.g. syntax or lexical semantics.

In our study, we assume that the huge amount of knowledge from pre-trained models can be leveraged to predict new words missing in taxonomic resources. We suggest a novel candidate-free task formulation for taxonomy enrichment, arguing that compiling word lists may be redundant. Information about new words is already present in the large

Proceedings of TextGraphs-16: Graph-based Methods for Natural Language Processing, pages 11–24
October 16, 2022.

pre-trained networks. There would be not need in compiling lists of "parents" to predict hyponyms either, as language models should be able to predict words only if necessary.

Furthermore, we propose a Cross-modal Contextualized Hidden State Projection Method (CHSP) for candidate-free taxonomy enrichment. The approach includes several stages: (i) learning embeddings of WordNet taxonomy, (ii) projecting them into the hidden states space of BERT, and (iii) decoding them back to text candidates.

Thus, the contribution of our work is three-fold:

- First, we formulate a novel task of candidate-free taxonomy enrichment and present a new dataset based on WordNet 3.0 taxonomy (Miller, 1995);
- Second, we implement baselines for this task based on BERT and fastText (Bojanowski et al., 2017) models, demonstrating the difficulty of the task;
- Third, we propose a method for incorporating graph information into pre-trained language models, based on hidden contextualized state projection yielding superior performance in comparison the baselines.

2 Related Work

There has been two major competitions that have introduced the task of taxonomy enrichment: SemEval 2016 (Jurgens and Pilehvar, 2016) and RUSSE-2020 (Nikishina et al., 2020a). However, their formulations both required a predefined list of candidates. A detailed overview of taxonomy-related papers is presented in Jurgens and Pilehvar (2016); Nikishina et al. (2022).

At the same time there exists a lot of research on how suitable is BERT for capturing and transferring information about hypo-hypernym relationship Ravichander et al. (2020); Hanna and Mareček (2021); Schick and Schütze (2019). For instance, Ravichander et al. (2020) examine hypernymy knowledge encoded in BERT representations. In their experiments BERT demonstrated the ability to correctly retrieve hypernyms, however, they argue that it does not necessarily follow that BERT is capable of systematic generalisation.

Another paper about BERT's knowledge of hypernymy (Hanna and Mareček, 2021) applies several patterns to predict possible hypernym candidates: "[MASK], such as x" and "My favorite [MASK] is x". Such prompts often elicit correct hypernyms from BERT. However, BERT still fails in 43% of cases, therefore, the authors claim that BERT has limited understanding of hypernymy. There exist many more Hearst patterns (Hearst, 1992) that aim to identify hypo-hypernym relationship in unlabeled texts (Snow et al., 2006; Pantel and Pennacchiotti, 2006). We compare baselines with some of them in Section 6.

Anwar et al. (2020) examine the influence of context-aware word representation models for lexical units and frame role expansion task. This task is related to our setting in a sense of generation of meaningful substitutes with preservation of content. We adopt their context-aware methods for our task. In our case the meaningful substitute will be generated for a masked hyponym with preservation of meaning represented in projected embeddings (see Section 4).

3 Taxonomy Enrichment Task

We formulate taxonomy enrichment in a new way avoiding the need of pre-supplied candidates (cf. Fig. 1) making it more challenging yet realistic. Given a taxonomy $T = \{h, r, t\} \subseteq E \times R \times E$, the task is to predict new nodes $n \in N, N \not\subseteq E$, which are not yet included in the taxonomy T, starting from the current node $h_i \in E$.

3.1 Dataset

We provide subgraphs sampled from the existing taxonomy as input to predict hyponyms at a certain place (see Fig. 1 as the example). In this research, we perform experiments on WordNet 3.0 (Miller, 1995) nouns (82,115 synsets, 117,798 lemmas). We suggest using synsets 2 hops away from the target node, as further located synsets may not be semantically related.

From this taxonomy we randomly select 1,000 nodes out of 15,646 nodes which children are leaves, i.e., the children do not have hyponyms of their own. We also take into consideration the distance length from the root to the leaf which should be more than 5 hops. This allows us to exclude the case of predicting very abstract or broad concepts. For each "parental" hypernym all its hyponyms (leaves) were replaced by a single "masked" node, e.g., *handwear.n.01* had hyponyms *glove.n.02* and *muff.n.01* that were replaced by a single *ORPHAN_100000243*. This place in the taxonomy was then considered for extension and the candidates predicted for the masked node could be compared against true hyponyms. All in all, we masked 4,376 leaves out of 65,422 noun leaves to 1000 "[MASK]" tokens.

We limit our experiments to leaves only, replacing all children with one mask in order to be able to compare with a wide range of possible answers, as one synset might have several hyponyms. We leave node injection to future work on the topic.

3.2 Evaluation metrics

The generated candidates will be compared against the true candidates from the existing taxonomy. We utilize Precision@k (P@k), Recall (R@k), and Mean Reciprocal Rank (MRR): $Precision@k = \frac{\text{relevant items @k}}{\text{recommended items @k}}$, where k is the number of candidates at each step; $MRR = \frac{1}{|Q|}\sum_{i}^{|Q|}\frac{1}{rank_i}$, where Q is the sample of queries, $rank_i$ is the first position of the relevant candidate in the ranked list for the query i. Intuitively, MRR looks how close to the top of the list the correct answer is. Both metrics are commonly employed in the Hypernym Discovery and Taxonomy Enrichment shared tasks, which require systems to produce ranked lists of potential hypernyms (Camacho-Collados et al., 2018; Dale, 2020). Furthermore, numbers for both metrics are multiplied by 100 for clearer presentation.

4 Cross-modal Contextualized Hidden State Projection Method

The main idea of the paper is to predict new words using knowledge preserved in BERT and enhance the word generation process with graph information. Fig. 2 demonstrates the overall architecture of the CHSP approach that we use to solve the task. First, we train a graph representation model to compute graph embeddings. Furthermore, we learn a projection layer to transform target graph embeddings to the BERT vector space. Then we apply the projected embeddings as input to the masked language modelling part of BERT model. The prediction head generates new lemmas that are treated as candidate hyponyms for parent nodes. This process results in gradual joining of graph and textual modalities.

4.1 Graph Embedding Computation

In this section, we study various graph embedding representations to integrate into BERT. In Fig. 2, it is the Graph-BERT model that is depicted, however, it could be any model for representing graph structure. We evaluated several inductive and non-inductive embeddings such as Graph-BERT (Zhang et al., 2020), node2vec (Grover and Leskovec, 2016), GCN (Kipf and Welling, 2016), GAT (Velickovic et al., 2018), TADW (Yang et al., 2015), and Poincaré (Nickel and Kiela, 2017) embeddings. We also tested directed and undirected structures of Graph-BERT, node2vec and Poincaré. We performed both intrinsic and extrinsic evaluation of the computed embeddings.

As for the intrinsic evaluation, which was conducted on the unmasked WordNet, we generated the top-10 nearest neighbours and computed Precision@k and Recall@k scores (k=1, 2, 5, 10) metrics that assess the amount of hyponyms presented in the top-k list. We assume that the more "children" are presented in the list, the more suitable embeddings are for the tree-like structures and hyponym prediction. From Table 1 we can see that the best inductive embedding model is Graph-BERT on the directed graph and non-inductive node2vec on the undirected graph. We observe that node2vec and Poincaré show much higher scores than other methods. We speculate that this can be explained by the fact that these two algorithms are the only ones that do not incorporate textual features into the learned embeddings. Intuitively, similarity in textual features is not equal to similarity in graph. Additionally, degradation of node similarity in models that aggregate information from graph structure and node features is a known issue (Jin et al., 2021) and is linked to the over-smoothing problem. We believe that this could be one of the reasons why the approaches, which demonstrate promising results on traditional taxonomy enrichment task (Nikishina et al., 2022), like GAT, GCN, TADW do not perform well on predicting nearest neighbours. Moreover, we hypothesize that it also might be explained by the fact that such models better represent co-hyponymy or hypernymy, rather than hyponymy. Graph-BERT is known for avoiding over-smoothing problem, thus, performs much better than GAT, GCN and TADW.

For the extrinsic evaluation (evaluation of the downstream task) we have used two models: the best non-inductive and the best inductive embeddings. It is either a Graph-BERT (Zhang et al., 2020) that accepts a sequence of node representations and their positional embeddings describing their local and global positioning in the graph, or a node2Vec (Grover and Leskovec, 2016) that

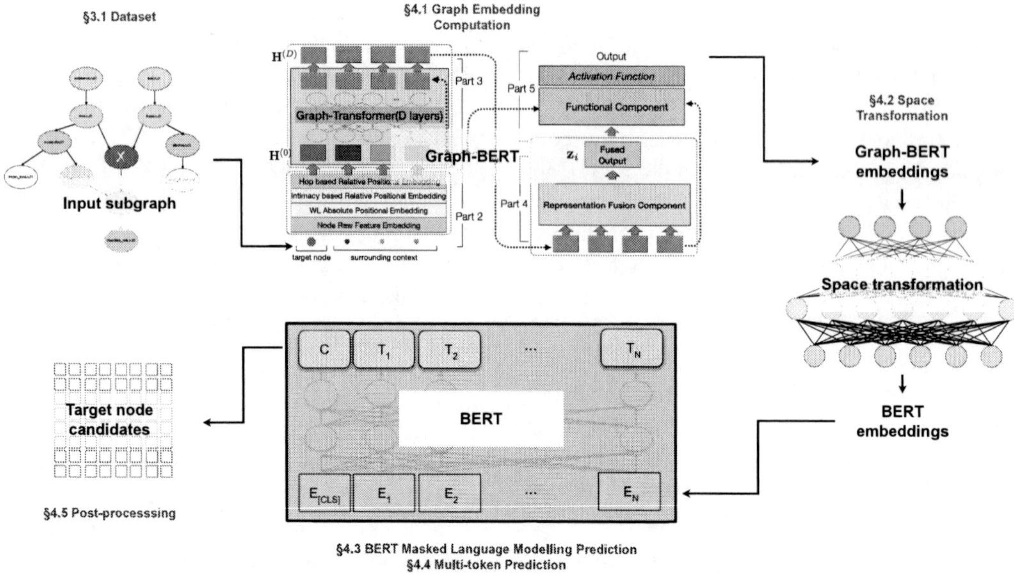

Figure 2: Cross-modal Contextualized Hidden State Projection Method (CHSP): graph-based BERT architecture that makes use of both node and text embeddings. Graph-BERT illustration source: (Zhang et al., 2020), BERT illustration source (Devlin et al., 2019). The input data is described in §3.1. §4.1 describes the choice of graph embedding algorithm. §4.2 explains the projection of embeddings from graph space to BERT space. § explains how BERT was used to predict candidates from the projected embeddings. §4.4 explains of the multi-token candidate generation algorithm. Finally §4.5 lists post-processing filters applied on the list of generated candidates.

Table 1: Graph embeddings comparison on the tree representation task.

	Embeddings	P@1	P@2	P@5	P@10	R@1	R@2	R@5	R@10
Inductive	Graph-BERT directed (node reconstruction)	0.127	0.099	0.064	0.041	0.127	0.113	0.150	0.182
	GraphBERT directed (graph recovery)	**0.190**	**0.163**	**0.115**	**0.073**	**0.190**	**0.182**	**0.260**	0.314
	Graph-BERT undirected (node reconstruction)	0.166	0.142	0.107	0.070	0.160	0.166	0.273	0.349
	Graph-BERT undirected (graph recovery)	0.164	0.140	0.100	0.062	0.164	0.153	0.227	0.268
	GCN	0.021	0.024	0.028	0.030	0.021	0.033	0.073	0.137
	GAT	0.018	0.016	0.014	0.011	0.008	0.021	0.068	0.099
Non-inductive	Node2vec directed root2leaf	0.227	0.217	0.212	0.181	0.227	0.241	0.368	0.509
	Node2vec directed leaf2root	0.451	0.359	0.244	0.173	0.451	0.470	0.563	0.674
	Node2vec undirected	**0.988**	**0.807**	**0.515**	**0.321**	**0.988**	**0.987**	**0.988**	**0.990**
	Poincare directed	0.769	0.671	0.464	0.297	0.769	0.818	0.882	0.910
	Poincare undirected	0.716	0.618	0.434	0.283	0.716	0.727	0.804	0.862
	TADW	0.006	0.005	0.005	0.004	0.006	0.006	0.008	0.010

learns low-dimensional representations for nodes in a graph through the use of random walks. However, as we will further see, good coverage of hyponyms in the nearest neighbour list does not guarantee high performance on hyponym prediction.

4.2 Space Transformation

In order to project graph embeddings into BERT embedding space, we use a simple multilayer perceptron (MLP). The architecture and training process are described in Appendix A.2.

BERT embeddings are contextualized. Therefore, for learning projection from graph space into BERT, the target words cannot be simply embedded as is because their representation will differ in various contexts. In order to generate contextualized embeddings we use a SemCor dataset (Langone et al., 2004). It consists of 352 texts from Brown Corpus (Kucera and Francis, 1967), which is an electronic collection of text samples in English language. SemCor contains manually annotated sentences where words are matched with according synsets. We adopt SemCor 3.0, which was automatically created from SemCor 1.6 by mapping senses from WordNet 1.6 to WordNet 3.0. We extract embeddings of annotated words and use as contextualized target synset embeddings for learning projection.

4.3 BERT Masked Language Modelling Prediction

We use *bert_base_uncased* pre-trained configuration of BERT to embed a structure "[MASK] is a {parent}" where "{parent}" is a lemma of a hypernym whose hyponyms are to be predicted. In the following parts we will refer to this structure as input context. The choice of the structure was not random. To begin with, we have evaluated three different context constructions suggested in (Hanna and Mareček, 2021): 1. "[MASK] is a/an {parent}"; 2. "My favourite {parent} is a [MASK]"; 3. "{parent} such as a [MASK]". The scores for the amount of true hyponyms in a list of predicted candidates are presented in the first three lines of Table 2 and Table 3, accordingly. The Precision@10 scores indicate that the best results were produced by the first prompt, which proved to be the most stable among the three, and it was used in all CHSP configurations. These experiments are also repurposed as three baselines.

Furthermore, we create three settings with different approaches to incorporation of graph embedding into the language model prediction:

- *pure-BERT* prediction: embedding of "[MASK]" token is left as is;
- *replaced* prediction: embedding of "[MASK]" token is replaced by projected graph embedding;
- *mixed* (or contextualized) prediction: embedding of "[MASK]" token is averaged with projected graph embedding.

The replacement can happen at three different stages: after first layer of BERT encoder, after sixth (middle) or after twelfth (last). In the first two cases space transformation learns to project graph embeddings into intermediate hidden states and after replacement the hidden states are passed through remaining encoder layers. The replacement strategies are illustrated in Fig. 3. Thus, by performing this process, we combine textual and graph modalities in order to improve candidate prediction at the certain place of the taxonomy.

4.4 Multi-token Prediction

For the experiments with single- and multi-token prediction we adopt a condBERT (Dementieva et al., 2021) multi-token generation mechanism. In addition to "[MASK] is a {parent}", "[MASK][MASK] is a {parent}" or "[MASK][MASK][MASK] is a {parent}" sentences are used. The tokens are generated progressively using beam search while each multi-token sequence is scored by the harmonic mean of the probabilities of its tokens. The beam search process is illustrated in Fig. 4. The algorithm generates 1-, 2- and 3-token predictions, which are merged into a final candidates list sorted according to their scores. The detailed description of the multi-token candidate generation algorithm is given in the Appendix A.3.

4.5 Post-processing

In order to eliminate noise from the predictions generated by the BERT language model, we apply several filters on the generated set of new words. First, we remove all predictions containing non-alphabetical symbols as well as stop-words from Stopwords Corpus (Porter, 1980) in NLTK library[1]. The multi-token generation case requires further post-processing: merging word-pieces and discarding candidates where all tokens start with "##".

Furthermore, we check merged candidates for containing permutations of same sets of words and eliminate the repeating ones with lower scores. For example, if there are two multi-token candidates "apple pie" and "pie apple", the one less-probable one is going to be discarded. Finally, the whole list of merged candidates is checked for duplicates and sorted by their scores.

5 Baselines

In our experiments we are using three baselines: 1. fastText (nearest neighbours); 2. BERT (parent embeddings on inference); 3. three patterns from (Hanna and Mareček, 2021; Schick and Schütze, 2019).

5.1 fastText (nearest neighbours)

The first baseline uses 300-dimensional fastText (Bojanowski et al., 2017) English embeddings pre-trained on Common Crawl and Wikipedia. Hypernym embeddings are computed as an average of all lemmas embeddings. Furthermore, nearest

[1] https://www.nltk.org/

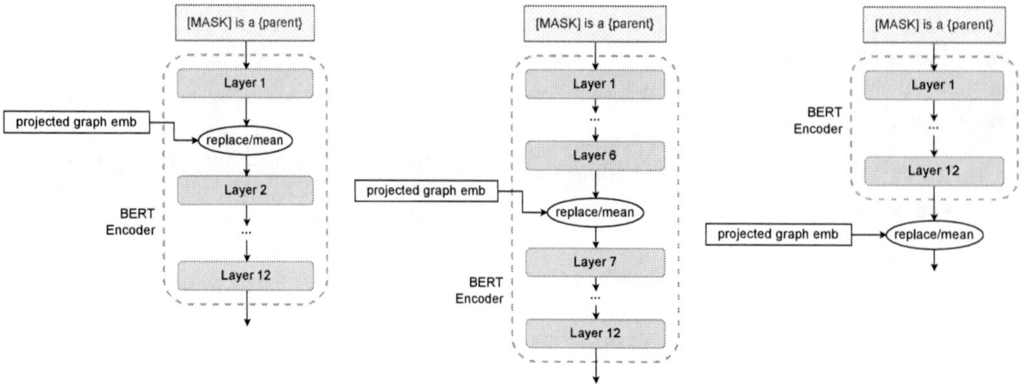

Figure 3: Illustration of replacement approaches. The projected graph embedding is inserted after (a) 1st BERT encoder layer, (b) 6th BERT encoder layer, (c) 12th BERT encoder layer. The "replace/mean" denote the replacement strategy: the projected embedding either replaces according hidden representation of "[MASK]" token, or averaged with it.

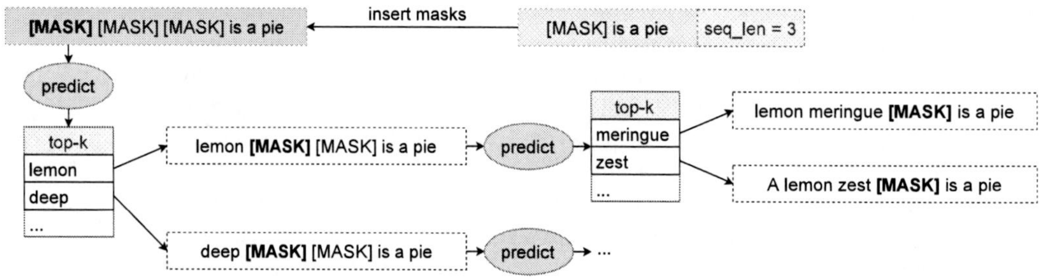

Figure 4: Beam search for multi-token generation. In this figure 3-token case is illustrated. In our research we also use 2-token case which is generated in a similar manner.

neighbours of the resulting vectors are retrieved and scored as hyponym predictions. Our approach can be seen as a reverse of the method from (Nikishina et al., 2020a). In a single-token evaluation case multi-token hyponyms are dropped from the list of gold hyponyms (see Section 3.2).

5.2 BERT (parent embeddings on inference)

The second baseline uses BERT to encode each hypernym lemma and decode it back in a single- or multi-token setting. Predictions for each parent lemma are aggregated and evaluated. This method is loosely motivated by the idea of lexical substitution (Anwar et al., 2020), which goal is to find meaning-preserving alternatives to a particular target word in its context. However, with this baseline we wanted to evaluate BERT's ability to predict hyponyms in a contextless setting.

5.3 Pattern Comparison

The last baseline is based on the approach described in these two publications: (Hanna and Mareček, 2021; Schick and Schütze, 2019). They propose a variety of constructions for prompting BERT in order to identify its linguistic capabilities and test its ability to capture semantic properties of words. Both works use the similar set of constructions, however, only (Hanna and Mareček, 2021) compare them against each other in order to identify the most efficient ones. According to their evaluations we have selected three best patterns: "[MASK] is a/an {parent}", "My favourite {parent} is a [MASK]", "{parent} such as a [MASK]". The constructions were encoded with BERT and then decoded in single- and multi-token settings with "[MASK]" predictions treated as new candidate hyponyms.

Table 2: Prediction scores for single-token hyponyms generation for different source graph embeddings and replacement strategies (x100).

Method	Context	Replaced	MRR@5	MRR@10	MRR@20	P@1	P@5	P@10
Pattern comparison (Hanna and Mareček, 2021)								
"[MASK] is a {parent}"	Yes	No	2.461	2.704	3.091	1.546	1.289	1.057
"My favourite {parent} is a [MASK]"	Yes	No	0.554	0.863	1.001	0.000	0.464	0.490
"A {parent} such as a [MASK]"	Yes	No	0.168	0.193	0.235	0.000	0.155	0.103
BERT (parent embedding on inference)	No	No	1.003	1.083	1.203	0.940	0.251	0.188
fastText (nearest neighbours)	No	No	2.400	3.500	4.000	0.130	1.839	2.100
CHSP (Graph-BERT)	Yes	Mix	**7.229**	**8.037**	**8.624**	**3.608**	**3.247**	**2.474**

Table 3: Prediction scores for multi-token hyponyms generation for different source graph embeddings and replacement strategies (x100).

Method	Context	Replaced	MRR@5	MRR@10	MRR@20	P@1	P@5	P@10
Pattern comparison (Hanna and Mareček, 2021)								
"[MASK] is a {parent}"	Yes	No	0.930	1.027	1.177	0.600	0.460	0.370
"My favourite {parent} is a [MASK]"	Yes	No	0.425	0.693	0.844	0.000	0.361	0.438
"A {parent} such as a [MASK]"	Yes	No	0.051	0.137	0.137	0.000	0.052	0.077
BERT (parent embedding on inference)	No	No	0.320	0.345	0.390	0.300	0.080	0.060
fastText (nearest neighbours)	No	-	1.860	**2.673**	**3.069**	0.100	**1.420**	**1.620**
CHSP (Graph-BERT)	Yes	Yes	**2.150**	2.281	2.378	**1.600**	0.740	0.530

6 Experiments

Our experiments can be categorised by following features: source graph embeddings, usage of context structure, replacement layer and replacement strategy. This section is divided into two parts. The first subsection compares various combinations of CHSP configurations. The second subsection analyzes performance of the best CHSP configurations against the baselines.

6.1 Graph Embeddings Comparison

Tables 5 and 6 compare single-token and multi-token hyponym predictions for methods with different source embeddings, replacement strategies and replacement layers. We observe that in single-token case for both node2vec and Graph-BERT the best replacement point is after the last (12th) BERT encoder layer with first and sixth being close seconds. We hypothesise that the reason is that, when injecting the projected graph embedding at earlier stages, remaining encoder layers dilute information incorporated in the embedding, thus deflecting from the right answers. In the case of single-token generation, Graph-BERT with the replacement point is after the last layer is a clear winning strategy among all the combinations. On the contrary, for multi-token generation significantly better scores were obtained by replacement after 6th layer. We suggest that this replacement strategy helped to diversify generated subwords and produce more meaningful results.

In general, "mixing" replacement strategy produces better results for the last-layer replacement strategy, because it allows incorporation of a context information encoded in a final hidden state of "[MASK]" token. However, there are some cases when the context actually diverts the method from the real answer (see Section 7). The complete replacement showed better scores in 1st and 6th layer replacement, because this strategy already incorporates a lot of context in the "[MASK]" embedding while passing it through remaining layers of the encoder, and "mixing" replacement reduces the influence of projected embedding too much. To sum up, both replacement strategies are important and none can be deemed winning as there is a clear pattern of where to apply each of them.

We can observe that node2vec did not perform as well as was expected judging from the graph embedding comparison. In many cases of single-token generation, words synonymous to the hypernym were predicted, instead of hyponyms. The reason for the low scores on node2vec embeddings might be explained by the fact that the Graph-BERT embeddings are easier to transform to the BERT vector space. Another hypothesis is that the performance on hyponym prediction does not guarantee high scores on predicting hyponyms for the taxonomy enrichment.

6.2 Overall Comparison

Tables 2 and 3 contain the overall scores for different hyponym prediction methods. We can see that our approach significantly outperforms other methods on single token setup, however, it fails on predicting multi-token candidates. We observe that the patterns from (Hanna and Mareček, 2021; Schick and Schütze, 2019) show results are mostly far from the top ones. This happened because the context encapsulated in the patterns in general contains little information. We also see that our method outperforms the BERT (parent embedding on inference) baseline (which is a simple prediction of encoded parent synset) and a simple approach on fastText nearest neighbours candidates. Even though the results for multi-token predictions are better for the fastText baseline, we still consider our method to be the most effective, as fastText is also not capable to predict multi-token candidates and yields to our method in the single token setup.

For all setups, the multi-token generation did not result in improvement of the scores. This can be explained by the flawed nature of our multi-token sampler and suggests major stream of future work.

7 Error Analysis

We can categorise common errors into several groups: failing to differentiate the real meaning of the hypernym, prediction of synonymical/same domain words instead of hyponyms, weakness of multi-token generator.

The first type of errors is related to incorrect recognition of a rare meaning of a synset and mistaking of it for a more common one. For example, for hypernym "depression.n.10" (pushing down) the correct prediction would be "click". However, almost all results are medical related predictions, e.g., headache, coma, schizophrenia.

An example of the second type of errors might be predictions of multi-token pipeline with Graph-BERT embeddings for "jazz_musician.n.01" hypernym. While the correct answer is "syncopator", top produced predictions are "singer", "dj", which obviously come from the same music-related domain.

For multi-token Node2vec we observed a lot of cases where one strong word was produced and further multi-token hypothesis would retain this first word and simply permute other different words.

Table 4: Example on Graph-BERT embeddings for the node "beverage.n.01" (single-token generation).

	beverage.n.01		
	Gold hyponyms: alcoholic drink, oenomel, fruit crush, cooler, alcoholic beverage, hot chocolate, fizz, ade, milk, inebriant, cocoa, drinking chocolate, drinking water, tea, java, mixer, refresher, tea-like drink, alcohol, coffee, fruit drink, ginger beer, wish-wash, potion, soft drink, near beer, smoothie, chocolate, cyder, intoxicant, fruit juice, cider, mate, hydromel		
	pure BERT	replaced	mixed
1	beer	**milk**	**coffee**
2	**coffee**	drink	**milk**
3	**alcohol**	**coffee**	drink
4	water	butter	**tea**
5	cola	pot	chocolate
6	**tea**	whisky	butter
7	wine	**tea**	beer
8	**milk**	turkey	whisky
9	chocolate	chocolate	brandy
10	rum	brandy	water

Example output for test hypernym "suburb.n.01": suburb, suburb suburbs, suburbs, suburb suburban, suburb suburbs suburban, etc.

Because of the weak multi-token decoding mechanism, many predictions failed. For example, none of the setups managed to produce adequate hyponyms for "berry.n.01", because all correct answers are multi-token in BERT vocabulary.

All in all, the results are diverse an controversial. For instance, Table 9 demonstrates that graph information from node2vec is confusing for the model. According to Tables 4 and 7, Graph-BERT improves the ranking of the results. However, none of the models handles multi-token prediction: the only case where the model manages to predict the correct answer is presented in Table 8.

For instance, the model can generate candidates that are correct but they are not yet included to the taxonomy. In this case, the evaluation system will still mark them as incorrect. Therefore, as future work we plan not only improve current methods but also perform human evaluation of the results.

Another reason for the absolute low scores is the way the test set was generated. While in (Cho et al., 2020) the data is selected from the well-known domains like "pets", "food", "sport", our test set is generated randomly and thus comprises rare terms, which may be harder to process. At the same time, simple examples like "beverage" or "meal" gain better scores. As future work we want to tackle the problem of rare terms.

8 Conclusion

In this work, we presented a novel candidate-free task formulation for taxonomy enrichment. The contribution is three-fold: task proposal, according dataset and test of multi-modal approach. We performed a computational study of various methods using knowledge from BERT. We compared different graph-based embeddings on the task and projected them to the BERT vector space. Then we identified the best position for the projected graph embedding to be injected to the BERT model. The results demonstrate that incorporation of graph embedding is beneficial in the task of hyponym prediction using BERT. Nevertheless, the BERT architecture does not allow us to easily operate with multi-token words and the pipeline accumulates errors in each component. This may be room for improvement for generative models like GPT or T5 and their prompt-tuning.

All in all, the proposed task is proven to be very challenging paving the way for future research.

Acknowledgments

The first author was partially supported by the DFG through the project "ACQuA 2: Answering Comparative Questions with Arguments" (grants BI 1544/7-2 and HA 5851/2-2) as part of the priority program "RATIO:Robust Argumentation Machines" (SPP 1999). The work of Alexander Panchenko and Alsu Vakhitova was conducted in the framework of joint MTS-Skoltech laboratory. The work of Elena Tutubalina was supported by a grant from the President of the Russian Federation for young scientists-candidates of science (MK-3193.2021.1.6).

References

Saba Anwar, Artem Shelmanov, Alexander Panchenko, and Chris Biemann. 2020. Generating lexical representations of frames using lexical substitution. In *Proceedings of the Probability and Meaning Conference (PaM 2020)*, pages 95–103, Gothenburg. Association for Computational Linguistics.

Nikolay Arefyev, Maksim Fedoseev, Andrew Kabanov, and Vadim Zizov. 2020. Word2vec not dead: Predicting hypernyms of co-hyponyms is better than reading definitions. In *Computational Linguistics and Intellectual Technologies*, pages 13–32.

Piotr Bojanowski, Edouard Grave, Armand Joulin, and Tomás Mikolov. 2017. Enriching word vectors with subword information. *Trans. Assoc. Comput. Linguistics*, 5:135–146.

Tom Brown, Benjamin Mann, Nick Ryder, Melanie Subbiah, Jared D Kaplan, Prafulla Dhariwal, Arvind Neelakantan, Pranav Shyam, Girish Sastry, Amanda Askell, Sandhini Agarwal, Ariel Herbert-Voss, Gretchen Krueger, Tom Henighan, Rewon Child, Aditya Ramesh, Daniel Ziegler, Jeffrey Wu, Clemens Winter, Chris Hesse, Mark Chen, Eric Sigler, Mateusz Litwin, Scott Gray, Benjamin Chess, Jack Clark, Christopher Berner, Sam McCandlish, Alec Radford, Ilya Sutskever, and Dario Amodei. 2020. Language models are few-shot learners. In *Advances in Neural Information Processing Systems*, volume 33, pages 1877–1901. Curran Associates, Inc.

Jose Camacho-Collados, Claudio Delli Bovi, Luis Espinosa-Anke, Sergio Oramas, Tommaso Pasini, Enrico Santus, Vered Shwartz, Roberto Navigli, and Horacio Saggion. 2018. SemEval-2018 task 9: Hypernym discovery. In *Proceedings of The 12th International Workshop on Semantic Evaluation*, pages 712–724, New Orleans, Louisiana. Association for Computational Linguistics.

Yejin Cho, Juan Diego Rodriguez, Yifan Gao, and Katrin Erk. 2020. Leveraging WordNet paths for neural hypernym prediction. In *Proceedings of the 28th International Conference on Computational Linguistics*, pages 3007–3018, Barcelona, Spain (Online). International Committee on Computational Linguistics.

David Dale. 2020. A simple solution for the taxonomy enrichment task: Discovering hypernyms using nearest neighbor search. In *Computational Linguistics and Intellectual Technologies*, pages 177–186.

Daryna Dementieva, Daniil Moskovskiy, Varvara Logacheva, David Dale, Olga Kozlova, Nikita Semenov, and Alexander Panchenko. 2021. Methods for detoxification of texts for the russian language. *CoRR*, abs/2105.09052.

Jacob Devlin, Ming-Wei Chang, Kenton Lee, and Kristina Toutanova. 2019. BERT: Pre-training of deep bidirectional transformers for language understanding. In *Proceedings of the 2019 Conference of the North American Chapter of the Association for Computational Linguistics: Human Language Technologies, Volume 1 (Long and Short Papers)*, pages 4171–4186, Minneapolis, Minnesota. Association for Computational Linguistics.

Allyson Ettinger. 2020. What BERT is not: Lessons from a new suite of psycholinguistic diagnostics for language models. *Transactions of the Association for Computational Linguistics*, 8:34–48.

Aditya Grover and Jure Leskovec. 2016. node2vec: Scalable feature learning for networks. In *Proceedings of the 22nd ACM SIGKDD International Conference on Knowledge Discovery and Data Mining*,

San Francisco, CA, USA, August 13-17, 2016, pages 855–864. ACM.

Michael Hanna and David Mareček. 2021. Analyzing BERT's knowledge of hypernymy via prompting. In *Proceedings of the Fourth BlackboxNLP Workshop on Analyzing and Interpreting Neural Networks for NLP*, pages 275–282, Punta Cana, Dominican Republic. Association for Computational Linguistics.

Marti A. Hearst. 1992. Automatic acquisition of hyponyms from large text corpora. In *COLING 1992 Volume 2: The 14th International Conference on Computational Linguistics*.

Jesús Herrera, Anselmo Peñas, and Felisa Verdejo. 2005. Textual entailment recognition based on dependency analysis and *WordNet*. In *Machine Learning Challenges, Evaluating Predictive Uncertainty, Visual Object Classification and Recognizing Textual Entailment, First PASCAL Machine Learning Challenges Workshop, MLCW 2005, Southampton, UK, April 11-13, 2005, Revised Selected Papers*, volume 3944 of *Lecture Notes in Computer Science*, pages 231–239. Springer.

Ganesh Jawahar, Benoît Sagot, and Djamé Seddah. 2019. What does BERT learn about the structure of language? In *Proceedings of the 57th Annual Meeting of the Association for Computational Linguistics*, pages 3651–3657, Florence, Italy. Association for Computational Linguistics.

Wei Jin, Tyler Derr, Yiqi Wang, Yao Ma, Zitao Liu, and Jiliang Tang. 2021. Node similarity preserving graph convolutional networks. In *WSDM '21, The Fourteenth ACM International Conference on Web Search and Data Mining, Virtual Event, Israel, March 8-12, 2021*, pages 148–156. ACM.

David Jurgens and Mohammad Taher Pilehvar. 2016. SemEval-2016 task 14: Semantic taxonomy enrichment. In *Proceedings of the 10th International Workshop on Semantic Evaluation (SemEval-2016)*, pages 1092–1102, San Diego, California. Association for Computational Linguistics.

Thomas N. Kipf and Max Welling. 2016. Semi-supervised classification with graph convolutional networks. *CoRR*, abs/1609.02907.

Henry Kucera and Winthrop Nelson Francis. 1967. *Computational analysis of present-day American English*. Brown University Press, Providence, RI.

Helen Langone, Benjamin R. Haskell, and George A. Miller. 2004. Annotating WordNet. In *Proceedings of the Workshop Frontiers in Corpus Annotation at HLT-NAACL 2004*, pages 63–69, Boston, Massachusetts, USA. Association for Computational Linguistics.

Ilya Loshchilov and Frank Hutter. 2017. Fixing weight decay regularization in adam. *CoRR*, abs/1711.05101.

George A. Miller. 1995. Wordnet: A lexical database for english. *Commun. ACM*, 38(11):39–41.

Andrea Moro and Roberto Navigli. 2015. SemEval-2015 task 13: Multilingual all-words sense disambiguation and entity linking. In *Proceedings of the 9th International Workshop on Semantic Evaluation (SemEval 2015)*, pages 288–297, Denver, Colorado. Association for Computational Linguistics.

Maximilian Nickel and Douwe Kiela. 2017. Poincaré embeddings for learning hierarchical representations. In *Advances in Neural Information Processing Systems 30: Annual Conference on Neural Information Processing Systems 2017, December 4-9, 2017, Long Beach, CA, USA*, pages 6338–6347.

Irina Nikishina, Varvara Logacheva, Alexander Panchenko, and Natalia V. Loukachevitch. 2020a. Russe'2020: Findings of the first taxonomy enrichment task for the russian language. In *Computational Linguistics and Intellectual Technologies*.

Irina Nikishina, Varvara Logacheva, Alexander Panchenko, and Natalia V. Loukachevitch. 2020b. Studying taxonomy enrichment on diachronic wordnet versions. In *Proceedings of the 28th International Conference on Computational Linguistics, COLING 2020, Barcelona, Spain (Online), December 8-13, 2020*, pages 3095–3106. International Committee on Computational Linguistics.

Irina Nikishina, Mikhail Tikhomirov, Varvara Logacheva, Yuriy Nazarov, Alexander Panchenko, and Natalia V. Loukachevitch. 2022. Taxonomy enrichment with text and graph vector representations. *Semantic Web*, 13(3):441–475.

Patrick Pantel and Marco Pennacchiotti. 2006. Espresso: Leveraging generic patterns for automatically harvesting semantic relations. In *Proceedings of the 21st International Conference on Computational Linguistics and 44th Annual Meeting of the Association for Computational Linguistics*, pages 113–120, Sydney, Australia. Association for Computational Linguistics.

Matthew E. Peters, Mark Neumann, Mohit Iyyer, Matt Gardner, Christopher Clark, Kenton Lee, and Luke Zettlemoyer. 2018. Deep contextualized word representations. In *Proceedings of the 2018 Conference of the North American Chapter of the Association for Computational Linguistics: Human Language Technologies, Volume 1 (Long Papers)*, pages 2227–2237, New Orleans, Louisiana. Association for Computational Linguistics.

Martin F. Porter. 1980. An algorithm for suffix stripping. *Program*, 14(3):130–137.

Abhilasha Ravichander, Eduard Hovy, Kaheer Suleman, Adam Trischler, and Jackie Chi Kit Cheung. 2020. On the systematicity of probing contextualized word representations: The case of hypernymy in BERT. In *Proceedings of the Ninth Joint Conference on Lexical and Computational Semantics*, pages 88–102,

Barcelona, Spain (Online). Association for Computational Linguistics.

Anna Rogers, Olga Kovaleva, and Anna Rumshisky. 2020. A primer in BERTology: What we know about how BERT works. *Transactions of the Association for Computational Linguistics*, 8:842–866.

Timo Schick and Hinrich Schütze. 2019. Rare words: A major problem for contextualized embeddings and how to fix it by attentive mimicking. *CoRR*, abs/1904.06707.

Michael Schlichtkrull and Héctor Martínez Alonso. 2016. MSejrKu at SemEval-2016 task 14: Taxonomy enrichment by evidence ranking. In *Proceedings of the 10th International Workshop on Semantic Evaluation (SemEval-2016)*, pages 1337–1341, San Diego, California. Association for Computational Linguistics.

Özge Sevgili, Artem Shelmanov, Mikhail Y. Arkhipov, Alexander Panchenko, and Chris Biemann. 2022. Neural entity linking: A survey of models based on deep learning. *Semantic Web*, 13(3):527–570.

Rion Snow, Daniel Jurafsky, and Andrew Y. Ng. 2006. Semantic taxonomy induction from heterogenous evidence. In *Proceedings of the 21st International Conference on Computational Linguistics and 44th Annual Meeting of the Association for Computational Linguistics*, pages 801–808, Sydney, Australia. Association for Computational Linguistics.

Petar Velickovic, Guillem Cucurull, Arantxa Casanova, Adriana Romero, Pietro Liò, and Yoshua Bengio. 2018. Graph attention networks. In *6th International Conference on Learning Representations, ICLR 2018, Vancouver, BC, Canada, April 30 - May 3, 2018, Conference Track Proceedings*. OpenReview.net.

Cheng Yang, Zhiyuan Liu, Deli Zhao, Maosong Sun, and Edward Y. Chang. 2015. Network representation learning with rich text information. In *Proceedings of the Twenty-Fourth International Joint Conference on Artificial Intelligence, IJCAI 2015, Buenos Aires, Argentina, July 25-31, 2015*, pages 2111–2117. AAAI Press.

Jiawei Zhang, Haopeng Zhang, Congying Xia, and Li Sun. 2020. Graph-bert: Only attention is needed for learning graph representations. *CoRR*, abs/2001.05140.

A Appendix

A.1 Hyperparameters for training graph embedding models

In this subsection we are listing the hyperparameters for training of graph embedding models. Unlisted parameters were set to default values.

Graph-BERT was initialized with fastText raw textual features (each node – average of according synset's lemmas). It was trained for 200 epochs on the node attribute reconstruction task, and the process continued for 200 more epochs on on the graph structure recovery task. The learning rate was set to 1e-3 and subgraph size to 5, and the resulting vectors were 300-dimensional.

Node2vec was trained to generate embeddings of same dimensionality, with 30 nodes in each random walk and 200 walks per node.

A.2 Space transformation MLP details

The MLP consists of three hidden layers (*source_embs* × 1024, 1024 × 512, 512 × *target_embs*) with exponential linear unit (ELU) activation. During training we used AdamW (Loshchilov and Hutter, 2017) optimizerFor the objective function we used a sum of cosine embedding loss between a model output and a target and a negated cosine similarity between a model output and a random negative example (any entity from the dataset that is not a target).

$$\begin{aligned} \mathcal{L} &= \mathcal{L}_+ - \mathcal{L}_- \\ \mathcal{L}_+ &= 1 - \cos(y, \hat{y}) \\ \mathcal{L}_- &= \max(0, \cos(y_{neg}, \hat{y})), \end{aligned} \tag{1}$$

where y – target embedding, $\hat{y}$ – predicted embedding, y_{neg} – negative example. The projection layer was trained for 500 epochs with batch size 64 and 1e-4 learning rate.

A.3 Multi-token generation algorithm details

The pseudocode for multi-token prediction is given in Algorithm 1. It is split into two functions: multi_tok_generate() and predict_candidates(). We are going to provide line-by-line explanation for each of them.

The multi_tok_generate() function takes as input the name of a parent synset, projected graph embedding, layer of replacement for the incorporation of the embedding and the replacement strategy. Line 2 generates tokens for the context construction "[MASK] is a {parent}", and line 3 encodes them with incorporation of projected embedding according to the scheme. Furthermore, the tokens and the hidden states are passed to the predict_candidates() function. It also takes the position of "[MASK]" token, which in this context prompt is 0. Finally, predict_candidates() returns a sorted list of tuples $(candidate, score)$, where each $candidate$ – predicted hyponym, and $score$ harmonic mean of scores for each token in the multi-token sequence.

The predict_candidates() function starts with saving the embedding of the "[MASK]" token that incorporates graph information (line 2). Furthermore, in the line 3 of the Algorithm 1 the single-token candidates are predicted. Function extract_mask_preds() (line 3) separates the predictions of hyponyms from the generated sentences. For example, sentence "[MASK] is a claim" was predicted into "dibs is a claim". Then extract_mask_preds() extracts the predicted hyponym "dibs" and returns it as a candidate paired with its score. Next, multi-token candidates of lengths 2 and 3 are generated (line 6). It is done with a beam search (line 7), which is illustrated schematically in Fig. 4. The beam_search() takes as input the tokenized sentence, position of a mask, saved embedding of a mask and a maximum length of the multi-token sequence. The beam search starts with insertion of one or two (according to the maximum length) additional mask tokens in the token sequence. Furthermore, the masks are predicted iteratively while maintaining best sequences as in a classical beam search algorithm.

The beam search generation ends when the maximum sequence length of the multi-token prediction is reached. The top hypotheses sentences as well as their scores are returned. Next, in the line 8 candidate hyponyms are extracted with extract_mask_preds() and together with scores are saved. Finally, multi- and single- token predictions are merged together and sorted by scores (line 10).

Algorithm 1 Algorithm of multi-token generation with BERT.
Inputs: name of parent synset *parent*, graph embedding of according masked child node projected into BERT space *proj_emb*, layer of replacement *l_num*, replacement strategy *repl_strategy*
Outputs: sorted list *final_res* that consists of tuples (*candidate, score*).

```
function MULTI_TOK_GENERATE(parent, proj_emb, l_num, repl_strategy)
    tokens ← tokenize("[MASK] is a {parent}")
    hidden_states ← BERT.encode(tokens, proj_emb, repl_strategy, l_num)
    final_res ← predict_candidates(hidden_states, tokens, mask_pos = 0)
    return final_res
end function
________________________________________________________________
function PREDICT_CANDIDATES(hidden_states, tokens, mask_pos)
    mask_hidden_state ← hidden_states[mask_pos]
    single_tokens, single_scores ← pred_single_mask(BERT, hidden_states, mask_pos)
    f_preds, f_scores ← extract_mask_preds(single_tokens, single_scores)
    multi_preds, multi_scores ← [], []
    for seq_len ∈ [2, 3] do
        new_tokens, new_scores ←
            ← beam_search(tokens, mask_pos, mask_hidden_state, seq_len)
        m_p, m_s ← extract_mask_preds(new_tokens, new_scores)
        multi_preds.append(m_p)
        multi_scores.append(m_s)
    end for
    final_res ← merge_sort_results(f_preds, f_scores, multi_preds, multi_scores)
    return final_res
end function
```

Table 5: CHSP prediction scores for single-token hyponyms generation for different source graph embeddings, replacement strategies and substitution layer (x100).

Graph embeddings	Context	Replaced	Layer	MRR@5	MRR@10	MRR@20	P@1	P@5	P@10
Node2vec	Yes	Yes	1st	0.975	1.831	2.252	0.000	0.670	1.186
		Mix	1st	2.328	2.685	2.903	1.546	1.186	1.005
		Yes	6th	3.316	3.799	4.070	1.031	1.804	1.340
		Mix	6th	2.414	3.079	3.391	1.289	1.289	1.469
		Yes	12th	2.436	3.185	3.486	1.289	1.082	1.160
		Mix	12th	3.329	4.073	4.597	1.031	1.649	1.675
Graph-BERT	Yes	Yes	1st	4.502	4.995	5.371	3.093	1.598	1.340
		Mix	1st	1.448	1.813	2.033	0.773	0.876	0.979
		Yes	6th	5.503	6.216	6.453	3.093	2.371	2.010
		Mix	6th	2.981	3.500	3.836	1.546	1.649	1.495
		Yes	12th	5.215	5.674	6.027	3.093	2.113	1.598
		Mix	12th	**7.229**	**8.037**	**8.624**	**3.608**	**3.247**	**2.474**

Table 6: CHSP prediction scores for multi-token hyponyms generation for different source graph embeddings, replacement strategies and substitution layer (x100).

Graph embeddings	Context	Replaced	Layer	MRR@5	MRR@10	MRR@20	P@1	P@5	P@10
Node2vec	Yes	Yes	1st	0.945	1.231	1.395	0.515	0.515	0.515
		Mix	1st	0.287	0.374	0.492	0.000	0.206	0.180
		Yes	6th	0.587	0.674	0.732	0.200	0.300	0.210
		Mix	6th	1.924	2.073	2.193	1.200	0.740	0.550
		Yes	12th	0.520	0.534	0.586	0.500	0.120	0.070
		Mix	12th	0.453	0.534	0.610	0.400	0.120	0.110
Graph-BERT	Yes	Yes	1st	1.908	2.054	2.149	1.400	0.680	0.500
		Mix	1st	1.350	1.522	1.625	0.800	0.600	0.500
		Yes	6th	**2.150**	**2.281**	**2.378**	**1.600**	**0.740**	0.530
		Mix	6th	1.468	1.694	1.806	0.700	0.700	**0.560**
		Yes	12th	1.278	1.312	1.368	1.200	0.340	0.190
		Mix	12th	1.767	1.899	2.071	1.400	0.540	0.390

Table 7: Example on Graph-BERT embeddings for the node "meal.n.01" (multi-token generation)

	meal.n.01 *Gold hyponyms: nosh-up, tea, snack, breakfast, supper, brunch, tiffin, lunch, refection, mess, ploughman's lunch, dejeuner, feast, spread, afternoon tea, picnic, dinner, square meal, luncheon, teatime, banquet, bite, buffet, potluck, collation*		
	pure BERT	replaced	mixed
1	life	**breakfast**	**breakfast**
2	food	breakfast lunch	breakfast lunch
3	**dinner**	**lunch**	**lunch**
4	**lunch**	breakfast dinner	breakfast dinner
5	**breakfast**	breakfast lunch dinner	breakfast lunch dinner
6	everything	lunch dinner	lunch dinner
7	love	breakfast dining	**dinner**
8	tomorrow	breakfast meals	breakfast meal
9	today	breakfast meal	breakfast lunch meal
10	nothing	breakfast lunch dining	breakfast meals

Table 8: Example on node2vec embeddings for the node "stock.n.01" (multi-token generation).

	stock.n.01 *Gold hyponyms: capital stock, treasury stock, quarter stock, preference shares, growth stock, preferred stock, no-par-value stock, voting stock, common shares, authorized shares, hot stock, ordinary shares, authorized stock, float, reacquired stock, common stock, no-par stock, common stock equivalent, treasury shares, preferred shares, hot issue, control stock, watered stock*		
	pure BERT	replaced	mixed
1	stock	capital	capital
2	one	capital cash	capital cash
3	c	capital investment	capital investment
4	b	capital financing	capital money
5	today	capital funds	capital financial
6	x	capital financial	capital equity
7	gold	capital income	**capital stock**
8	everything	capital funding	capital financing
9	life	capital revenue	capital funds
10	r	capital crop	capital leverage

Table 9: Example on node2vec embeddings for the node "citrus.n.01" (single-token generation)

	citrus.n.01 *Gold hyponyms: citrange, citron, grapefruit, kumquat, lemon, lime, mandarin, orange, pomelo*		
	pure BERT	replaced	mixed
1	fruit	date	date
2	one	year	tree
3	rose	horse	year
4	another	turkey	snow
5	**citrus**	dates	horse
6	cherry	tree	turkey
7	**orange**	snow	dates
8	tomato	calendar	winner
9	mine	winner	grass
10	wood	loser	trees

Sharing Parameter by Conjugation for Knowledge Graph Embeddings in Complex Space

Xincan Feng[†‡], Zhi Qu[†], Yuchang Cheng[‡], Taro Watanabe[†], Nobuhiro Yugami[‡]
[†]Natural Language Processing Laboratory, Nara Institute of Science and Technology
[‡]Multilingual Knowledge Computing Laboratory, Fujitsu Ltd.
{feng.xincan.fy2, qu.zhi.pv5, taro}@is.naist.jp
{cheng.yuchang, yugami}@fujitsu.com

Abstract

A Knowledge Graph (KG) is the directed graphical representation of entities and relations in the real world. KG can be applied in diverse Natural Language Processing (NLP) tasks where knowledge is required. The need to scale up and complete KG automatically yields Knowledge Graph Embedding (KGE), a shallow machine learning model that is suffering from memory and training time consumption issues. To mitigate the computational load, we propose a parameter-sharing method, i.e., using conjugate parameters for complex numbers employed in KGE models. Our method improves memory efficiency by 2x in relation embedding while achieving comparable performance to the state-of-the-art non-conjugate models, with faster, or at least comparable, training time. We demonstrated the generalizability of our method on two best-performing KGE models 5★E (Nayyeri et al., 2021) and ComplEx (Trouillon et al., 2016) on five benchmark datasets.

1 Introduction

A Knowledge Graph (KG) is a representation of confident information in the real world and employed in diverse Natural Language Processing (NLP) applications, e.g., recommender system, question answering, and text generation. A triple in the form of $(head, relation, tail)$ is widely used as the representation of elements in the KG instead of raw text for scalability. Cite $(clinician, synset\_domain\_topic\_of, psychology)$ as an example, $clinician$ and $psychology$ is the head and tail entity respectively, and $synset\_domain\_topic\_of$ is the relation of the head entity pointing to the tail entity.

Knowledge Graph Embedding (KGE) models are designed for automatic link prediction. Relations in KG have multiple categories, e.g., symmetry, antisymmetry, inversion, and hierarchical. Missing links indicate incomplete ties between entities and are a common phenomenon as finding the missed connections is labor-intensive work.

The theoretical space complexity of KGE models are often $\mathcal{O}(n_e d_e + n_r d_r)$, which is proportional to the number of KG elements, i.e. entities n_e and relations n_r, and embedding dimension d_e, d_r respectively. Scaling a KG is problematic as n_e, n_r can go up to millions; also because KGE models are often shallow machine learning models composed of simple operations, e.g., matrix multiplication. Caution that a shallow model needs a large dimension size d to depict the data feature, yielding the issue of the drastic increase of embedding parameters (Dettmers et al., 2018).

KGE models represented using complex numbers have state-of-the-art performance, while they demand high memory costs. E.g., if using one of the best models ComplEx (Trouillon et al., 2016) to create embedding for the benchmark dataset FB15K whose $n_e = 14,951, n_r = 1,345$, and the best-performing dimensionalities $d_e = 4000, d_r = 4000$, will result in the parameter size of $65,184,000$. Considering the data type 64-bit integer (signed), who has a size of 8 bytes in PyTorch, the memory cost will be $65,184,000 \times 8 \approx 497$ MB. A KG for real-world application could have a much larger size, e.g., IBM's KG contains entities > 100 million and relations > 5 billion, which is actively in use and continually growing (Noy et al., 2019), would need > 148 TB memory to do link prediction task.

Inspired by the improved performance of complex number representation and Non-Euclidean models where transformation parameters attempt to interact rather than be independent, we intuited the idea of sharing parameters for memory efficiency.

We demonstrate a parameter-sharing method for complex numbers employed in KGE models. Specifically, our method formulates conjugate parameters in appropriate dimensions of the transformation functions to reduce relation parameters. By

Proceedings of TextGraphs-16: Graph-based Methods for Natural Language Processing, pages 25–34
October 16, 2022.

using our method, models can reduce their space complexity to $\mathcal{O}(n_e d_e + n_r d_r/2)$, which means the relation embedding size is half the original model. In the second place, using conjugate parameters may help save training time, especially on the datasets who have more parameter patterns. Further, our method can be easily applied to various complex number represented models.

We verified our method on two best-performing KGE models, i.e., ComplEx (Trouillon et al., 2016) and 5★E (Nayyeri et al., 2021). The experiments were conducted on five benchmark datasets, i.e., FB15K-237, WN18RR, YAGO3-10, FB15K, and WN18, by which we empirically show that our method reserves the models' ability to achieve state-of-the-art results. We also see 31% training time saved on average for 5★E in addition to the memory. Our method is implemented in PyTorch[1] and the code with hyperparameter settings[2] are available online.

2 Related Works

We describe the categorizations of KGE models according to the representation method and the vector space that inspired our idea.

Representation Method Real and complex number representations are used to quantify entities and relations.

Translation approaches including TransE (Bordes et al., 2013) and its variants (Ji et al., 2015; Lin et al., 2015) describe embeddings using real number representation. Although these simple models cost fewer parameters, they can only encode two or three relation patterns, e.g., TransE cannot encode symmetric relations.

ComplEx (Trouillon et al., 2016) creates embedding with complex number representation, which can handle a wider variety of relations than using only real numbers, among them symmetric and antisymmetric relations (Trouillon et al., 2016). 5★E (Nayyeri et al., 2021) utilizes Möbius transformation, a projective geometric function that supports multiple simultaneous transformations in complex number representation and can embed entities in much lower ranks.

Vector Space Euclidean and Non-Euclidean spaces are practiced for the calculation of triple plausibility.

Factorization models such as RESCAL (Nickel et al., 2011) and DistMult (Yang et al., 2014) employ element-wise multiplication in Euclidean space. Correspondingly, the plausibility of a triple is measured according to the angle of transformed head and tail entities.

MuRP (Balazevic et al., 2019) minimizes hyperbolic distances other than Euclidean. It needs fewer parameters than its Euclidean analog. ATTH (Chami et al., 2020) leverages trainable hyperbolic curvatures for each relation to simultaneously capture logical patterns and hierarchies. Compared with Euclidean, the Hyperbolic models can save more structures using variational curvatures in different areas to depict hierarchical relations.

Relational Constrain on Parameters Replacing real number with complex number representation enables the imaginary part to have an effect on the real part parameters, the boosted performance of which indicates the **hidden relation** among parameter. Using hyperbolic space other than Euclidean enables the distances or angles at different positions to vary, the increased accuracy hints us to add **various constraints** on parameters. Learning from the work by Hayashi and Shimbo (2017), the potential of improving representations through conjugate symmetric constraint is revealed. Therefore, we hypothesize the efficiency of relational parameters and propose a parameter-sharing method using conjugate numbers.

3 Method

Complex number employed in current KGE models enforces **multiplicative constraint** on representations; our method further adds **conjugate constraint** within the parameters. Note that we don't reduce the dimensions of the parameters, instead, we share the dimensions.

We economize 50% of the memory in relation embedding by sharing half of the parameters in the conjugate form. Our approach is at least comparable in accuracy to the baselines. In addition, our method reduces calculation in the regularization process, e.g., for the $5^{\bigstar}\epsilon$ model, 31% of training time is saved on average for five benchmark datasets.

3.1 Preliminaries

Link prediction task inquires if a triple (h, r, t) constructed by existing head and tail entities $h, t \in \mathbb{V}^{d_e}$

[1] https://pytorch.org/

[2] github.com/xincanfeng/dimension

and relations $r \in \mathbb{V}^{d_r}$ ($\mathbb{V}^d$ is a d-dimensional vector space) is true or not. In KGE models, the relations are often represented as the transformation function ϑ that maps a head entity into a tail entity which are described as vectors in corresponding space, i.e., $\vartheta(h) = t$. Then, the score function $f : \mathbb{V}^{d_e} \times \mathbb{V}^{d_r} \times \mathbb{V}^{d_e} \to \mathbb{R}$ returns the plausibility p of constructing a true triple: $f(h, r, t) = p(\vartheta(h), t)$.

$a, b, c, d \in \mathbb{C}$ denote the parameters in the relation embedding matrices. $x \in \mathbb{C}$ is the parameter of the entity embedding matrices. a_i, x_i are the parameters of the submatrices of $[a]$ and $[x]$ respectively. $Re(z)$ is the real part of the complex number z, $\overline{z}$ is the complex conjugate of z.

ComplEx This is the first and one of the best-performing complex models in Euclidean space. Trouillon et al. (2016) demonstrated that complex number multiplication could capture antisymmetric relations while retaining the efficiency of the dot product, i.e., linearity in both space and time complexity. Balancing between model expressiveness and parameter size is also discussed as the keystone of KGE. However, targeting SOTA is still computational-expensive because Trouillon et al. (2016) didn't solve the performance deterioration problem when reducing parameters directly.

Performance deterioration can be severe whenever the KG needs to be expanded because the mispredicted links could lead to further misinformation. Hence we should always endeavour to adopt the best-performing embedding size in doing link prediction task, even though it could be hundreds of TB.

To obtain the best results, ComplEx needs embedding size of $rank = 2000$ on dataset FB15K-237, WN18RR, FB15K, WN18, and $rank = 1000$ on dataset YAGO3-10. $rank$ denotes the vector dimension of a single-functional parameter. Each entity and relation in this model needs $2 \times rank$ parameters, representing real and imaginary part, respectively.

In this model, relations are represented as the real part of low-rank matrix $\begin{bmatrix} a \end{bmatrix}$, which act as weights on each entity dimension x, followed by a projection onto the real subspace. The transformation of ComplEx is

$$x \to \begin{bmatrix} a \end{bmatrix} x \to ax. \tag{1}$$

5★E This is a novel model applying complex numbers in Non-Euclidean space. Nayyeri et al. (2021) tackled the problem of multiple subgraph structures in the neighborhood, e.g., combinations of path and loop structures. Unlike the ComplEx model, they replaced the dot product with the Möbius function which has several favorable theoretical properties. This model subsumes ComplEx in that it embeds entities in much lower ranks, i.e., about 25% or even smaller to achieve the state-of-the-art performance. However, 5★E is inferior to ComplEx in that it needs almost the same large size of relation parameters to do much more sophisticated calculation.

Following the hyperparameter search range of Nayyeri et al. (2021), the embedding sizes we tested for 5★E to obtain the best result are $rank = 500$ for all datasets. Each entity needs $2 \times rank$ parameters, and each relation needs $8 \times rank$ parameters that function differently.

In this model, relations are represented as $\begin{bmatrix} a & b \\ c & d \end{bmatrix}$. The transformation function ϑ of 5★E is

$$x \to \begin{bmatrix} x \\ 1 \end{bmatrix} \to \begin{bmatrix} a & b \\ c & d \end{bmatrix} \begin{bmatrix} x \\ 1 \end{bmatrix} \to \frac{ax + b}{cx + d}. \tag{2}$$

Möbius function ϑ is capable of representing various relations simultaneously because it combines five subsequent transformations: $\vartheta = \vartheta_4 \circ \vartheta_3 \circ \vartheta_2 \circ \vartheta_1$, where $\vartheta_1 = x + \frac{d}{c}$ is describing translation by $\frac{d}{c}$, $\vartheta_2 = \frac{1}{x}$ is describing inversion and reflection w.r.t. real axis, $\vartheta_3 = \frac{bc-ad}{c^2}x$ is describing homothety and rotation, and $\vartheta_4 = x + \frac{a}{c}$ is describing translation by $\frac{a}{c}$.

3.2 Method Formulation

Let $\begin{bmatrix} a_1 & a_2 \end{bmatrix}$ denotes the relation embedding matrix. Our method constrains half of the parameters a_2 using the complex conjugate of the other half $\overline{a_1}$, i.e., $a_2 = \overline{a_1}$; it is model-dependent to specify which parameters are suitable for conjugation. We formulated our method on above two baseline models.

Complϵx By using our method, the original model ComplEx is adapted to the parameter-sharing model Complϵx, where relations are represented as the real part of low-rank matrices with conjugate parameters. Specifically, we set the original square relation embedding matrices $\begin{bmatrix} a_1 & a_2 \end{bmatrix}$ to be half the normal parameters and the other half their conjugation, i.e., $\begin{bmatrix} a_1 & \overline{a_1} \end{bmatrix}$. In this model, since each parameter is functioning equally, the positions of the conjugate parameters can be set randomly.

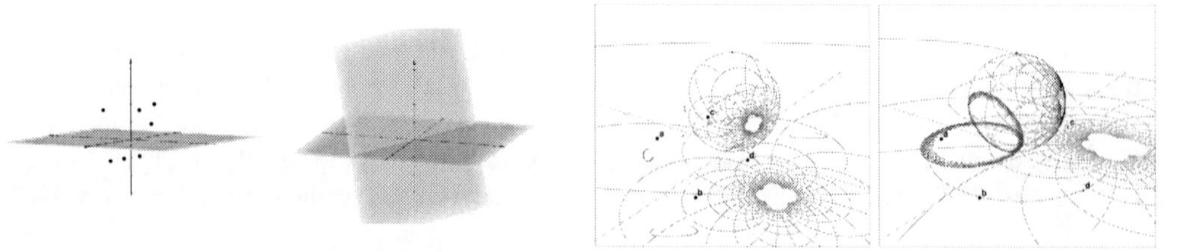

(a) Transformed entities by ComplEx (left) and Complϵx (right). In the left graph, a black point describes a transformed entity, and the vector values of a point are unrelated in each dimension. While in the right graph, half of the value $z_i, i \in [1, d/2]$ of a vector $z_1, z_2, ..., z_d$ that is describing a point are constrained as the other half $z_i, i \in [d/2+1, d]$ correspondingly. The linear constrain $z_i = a_i x_i + b_i y_i$ is illustrated in the right graph.

(b) Transformed entities by $5^{\bigstar}$E (left) and $5^{\bigstar}\epsilon_n$ (right). Note that we illustrate the negative conjugated model instead of the positive conjugated one for simplicity in plotting. Blue traces are the original entities and their projections in the Non-Euclidean space. Green traces are the multiple copies of the blue traces under iterations of the Möbius transformation. Red traces are the inverse of green traces. Apparently, the right graph has much neater geometric properties.

Figure 1: Transformed entities illustrated in 3D

$5^{\bigstar}\epsilon$ Our method transforms the original model $5^{\bigstar}$E into the parameter-sharing model $5^{\bigstar}\epsilon$, where relations are represented as the real part of low-rank matrices using conjugate parameters. Specifically, we set the original square relation embedding matrices $\begin{bmatrix} a & b \\ c & d \end{bmatrix}$ to be half the normal parameters and the other half their conjugate parameters, i.e., $\begin{bmatrix} a & b \\ \overline{b} & \overline{a} \end{bmatrix}$. In this model, parameters play distinct roles at different positions, and the best conjugation positions are the principal and secondary diagonal positions. Note that experiments showed that, the following negative conjugation method, i.e., $\begin{bmatrix} a & b \\ -\overline{b} & \overline{a} \end{bmatrix}$, achieves similar performance as above. Although the negative conjugation on this model is equivalent to restricting the original Möbius function to the unitary Möbius transformation, our approach is much more general to a variety of representations.

3.3 Transformation Analysis

Complϵx Let $a_2 = \overline{a_1}$, then the transformation of conjugate model Complϵx is

$$\begin{bmatrix} x_1 & x_2 \end{bmatrix} \rightarrow \begin{bmatrix} a_1 & \overline{a_1} \end{bmatrix} \begin{bmatrix} x_1 & x_2 \end{bmatrix} \rightarrow \begin{bmatrix} a_1 x_1 & \overline{a_1} x_2 \end{bmatrix}. \tag{3}$$

We can see that the resulted relation embedding is constrained to $\begin{bmatrix} a_1 & \overline{a_1} \end{bmatrix}$ other than $\begin{bmatrix} a_1 & a_2 \end{bmatrix}$; the predicted tail entity is constrained to $\begin{bmatrix} a_1 x_1 & \overline{a_1} x_2 \end{bmatrix}$ instead of $\begin{bmatrix} a_1 x_1 & a_2 x_2 \end{bmatrix}$ in original model, which does not narrow the rang of relation or tail embedding since the a_1, x_2 can be any value. Further, since tail entities also act as head entities, we can say that the range of both the entities and relations are not constrained.

$5^{\bigstar}\epsilon$ Let $c = \overline{b}, d = \overline{a}$, then the transformation of conjugate model $5^{\bigstar}\epsilon$ is

$$x \rightarrow \begin{bmatrix} x \\ 1 \end{bmatrix} \rightarrow \begin{bmatrix} a & b \\ \overline{b} & \overline{a} \end{bmatrix} \begin{bmatrix} x \\ 1 \end{bmatrix} \rightarrow \frac{ax + b}{\overline{b}x + \overline{a}}. \tag{4}$$

The five subsequent transformations turn into: $\vartheta_1 = x + \frac{\overline{a}}{\overline{b}}$ which depicts translation by $\frac{\overline{a}}{\overline{b}}$, $\vartheta_2 = \frac{1}{x}$ which depicts inversion and reflection w.r.t. real axis, $\vartheta_3 = \frac{b\overline{b} - a\overline{a}}{\overline{b}^2} x$ which depicts homothety and rotation, and $\vartheta_4 = x + \frac{a}{b}$ which depicts translation by $\frac{a}{b}$. We can see that, although the relation parameters are constrained comparing to the original model, the five sub-transformations are reserved in this conjugate model.

Characteristics For this reason, we consider our conjugate models retain expressiveness in function level for various relation patterns compared to their original counterparts. The difference between original models and our conjugate models is that, the latter ones have more linear constrain in its value of each embedding parameter, as illustrated in Figure 1.

3.4 Reduced Calculation

Sharing half of the parameters also reduces the computation for the regularization terms into half, where each parameter of relation is squared to the sum. For example, the original calculation $r_1^2 + r_2^2$ is turned into $r_1^2 \times 2$ in both baseline models, where r_1, r_2 denote the real or imaginary part of a complex number, and in which r_1 represents the shared

Dataset	#Training	#Validation	#Test	Ent	Rel	Exa
FB15K-237	272,115	17,535	20,466	14,541	237	544,230
WN18RR	86,835	3,034	3,134	40,943	11	173,670
YAGO3-10	1,079,040	5,000	5,000	123,188	37	2,158,080
FB15K	483,142	50,000	59,071	14,951	1,345	966,284
WN18	141,442	5,000	5,000	40,943	18	282,884

Table 1: Datasets statistics. #: Split in terms of number of triples; Ent: Entities; Rel: Relations; Exa: Examples.

parameter. However, the final time consumption depends on multiple aspects, such as formulation and coding, thus is not necessarily reduced.

4 Experiments

4.1 Experimental Setup

Metrics We followed the standard evaluation protocal for KGE models. T: the rank set of truth, r_i: the rank position r of the first true entity for the i-th query. We computed two rank-based metrics: (i) Mean Reciprocal Rank (MRR), which computes the arithmetic mean of reciprocal ranks of all true entities from the ranked list of answers to queries T, and (ii) Hits@N (N = 1, 3, 10), which counts the true entities $\mathbb{I}$ and calculate their proportion in the truth T in top N sorted predicted answers list.

$$\mathrm{MRR} = \frac{1}{T}\sum_{i=1}^{T}\frac{1}{r_i} \tag{5}$$

$$\mathrm{Hits@}N = \frac{1}{T}\sum_{r\in T, r\leq N}\mathbb{I} \tag{6}$$

We also use additional metric Time (seconds/epoch) to measure how many seconds each training epoch costs to demonstrate the time saved by our method. To do this, we conducted all experiments using the same GPUs. GeForce GTX 1080 Ti is used for all datasets except for the largest dataset YAGO3-10 who needs a larger GPU and we used Tesla V100S-PCIE-32GB for it.

Datasets We evaluated our method on five widely used benchmark datasets (See Table 1). FB15K (Bordes et al., 2013) is a subset of Freebase, the contents of which are general facts. WN18 (Bordes et al., 2013) is a subset of Wordnet, a database that features lexical relations between words. YAGO3-10 (Dettmers et al., 2018) is the largest common dataset, which mostly describes attributes of persons, and contains entities associated with at least ten different relations.

As was first noted by Toutanova and Chen (2015), FB15K and WN18 suffer from test leakage through inverse relations, e.g., the test set frequently contains triples such as $(s, hyponym, o)$ while the training set contains its inverse $(o, hypernym, s)$. To create a dataset without this property, they introduced FB15K-237, a subset of FB15K where inverse relations are removed. WN18RR was created for the same reason by Dettmers et al. (2018).

We adopted all of the five datasets for comprehensive comparison of models.

Hyperparameter Settings We explored the influence of hyperparameter settings to our method. To do this, we used the best hyperparameter settings for the original models (marked as ∇ or no mark), and applied the same settings on our conjugate models and ablation models. We adopted the best hyperparameter settings for ComplEx provided by Nayyeri et al. (2021), and fine-tuned the best hyperparameters ourselves for $5^{\bigstar}$E since there was no published best hyperparameter settings for this model at the time we did the experiments. We also fine-tuned the best hyperparameters for one of our conjugate model $5^{\bigstar}\epsilon$ (noted as $\diamondsuit$) to explore the upper bound.

We selected the hyperparameters based on the MRR on the validation set. Our grid search range refered to but was larger than Nayyeri et al. (2021). The optional optimizers are {Adagrad, Adam, SGD}. The range of embedding dimensions are {100, 500} with learning rates range in {1E-02, 5E-02, 1E-01}. The batch sizes attempted range in {100, 500, 1000, 2000}. Regularization coefficients are tested among {2.5E-03, 5E-03, 1E-02, 5E-02, 1E-01, 5E-01}.

5 Results

5.1 Main Results and Analysis

The main experimental results are shown in Table 2 and Table 3. The numbers with boldface indicate

Model	Time	MRR	H@1	H@3	H@10
ComplEx	42±8	**0.366±4e-4**	**0.271**	**0.402**	**0.558**
Complϵx	46±11	0.363±5e-4	0.268	0.400	0.555
$5^\bigstar$E	18±3	0.350±8e-4	0.257	0.386	0.538
$5^\bigstar\epsilon_\nabla$	**14±4**	0.353±7e-4	0.259	0.390	0.541
$5^\bigstar\epsilon_\diamondsuit$	**17±9**	0.354±8e-4	0.259	0.391	0.544

(a) FB15K-237

Model	Time	MRR	H@1	H@3	H@10
ComplEx	139±21	0.488±1e-3	0.442	0.503	0.579
Complϵx	146±45	0.475±9e-4	0.433	0.488	0.558
$5^\bigstar$E	16±1	0.490±5e-4	**0.444**	0.506	0.587
$5^\bigstar\epsilon_\nabla$	**11±1**	**0.493±8e-4**	0.442	**0.512**	0.588
$5^\bigstar\epsilon_\diamondsuit$	-	-	-	-	-

(b) WN18RR

Model	Time	MRR	H@1	H@3	H@10
ComplEx	370±2	**0.577±1e-3**	0.502	**0.622**	**0.712**
Complϵx	371±2	0.574±2e-3	0.500	0.618	0.707
$5^\bigstar$E	415±2	0.574±2e-3	0.502	0.617	0.701
$5^\bigstar\epsilon_\nabla$	**297±1**	0.576±2e-3	**0.505**	0.619	0.702
$5^\bigstar\epsilon_\diamondsuit$	-	-	-	-	-

(c) YAGO3-10

Table 2: Link prediction results on FB15K-237, WN18RR, YAGO3-10 datasets. Time, MRR and H@n are presented as mean (± standard deviation).

Model	Time	MRR	H@1	H@3	H@10
ComplEx	346±124	**0.855±1e-3**	0.823	**0.874**	**0.910**
Complϵx	293±16	**0.855±1e-3**	**0.827**	0.871	0.907
$5^\bigstar$E	42±9	0.812±1e-3	0.767	0.840	0.889
$5^\bigstar\epsilon_\nabla$	**26±0**	0.794±2e-3	0.743	0.827	0.882
$5^\bigstar\epsilon_\diamondsuit$	29±5	0.813±2e-3	0.766	0.844	0.894

(a) FB15K

Model	Time	MRR	H@1	H@3	H@10
ComplEx	57±3	0.951±3e-4	0.944	0.954	0.961
Complϵx	58±5	0.950±3e-4	0.945	0.953	0.960
$5^\bigstar$E	43±6	**0.952±5e-4**	0.946	**0.955**	**0.962**
$5^\bigstar\epsilon_\nabla$	**29±6**	0.949±6e-4	0.944	0.953	0.959
$5^\bigstar\epsilon_\diamondsuit$	**26±2**	**0.952±3e-4**	**0.947**	**0.955**	**0.962**

(b) WN18

Table 3: Link prediction results on FB15K and WN18 datasets. Instructions for this table are the same as those in Table 2.

the best results among all the models.

We mainly tested whether the conjugate models perform consistent with their original counterparts, especially whether they can achieve the same state-of-the-art results. We conducted one set of experiments using the best hyperparameters of the original models (marked as ∇ or no mark), and the other set of experiments tuning the hyperparameters for one of our conjugate model (marked as $\diamondsuit$).

The results show that both Complϵx and $5^\bigstar\epsilon$ consistently achieve results comparable to their original models on the datasets without test set leakage, including the largest dataset, i.e., YAGO3-10; and obtain the same optimal accuracies as the original models on all datasets with possibly-required fine-tuning. From the perspective of training time, we see $5^\bigstar\epsilon$ spends 31% less time on average for all datasets; and both conjugate models perform substantially best in training time on datasets FB15K, who have the most relations.

Complϵx Under the best hyperparameter settings of the original model, the performance of Complϵx are consistently comparable with ComplEx on all five datasets. We speculate the reason for the consistent but tiny performance drop might come from the computation precision, but we will leave it as our future studies.

Although our method reduces the computation, applying the method on this model requires splitting and concatenating matrices to keep the shape of outputs which incurs additional time-consuming operations. Consequently, the total time cost is not reduced much. However, training time on dataset FB15K, who has the most relations, becomes very stable.

Overall results imply our conjugate model Complϵx is at least comparative with its baseline model ComplEx.

$5^\bigstar\epsilon$ Under the best hyperparameter settings of the original $5^\bigstar$E, the conjugate $5^\bigstar\epsilon_\nabla$ consistently achieve competitive results on the datasets FB15K-237, WN18RR and YAGO3-10. The tiny but consistent accuracy enhancement on these three datasets is probably caused by similar programming artifacts as observed in ComplEx.

We hypothesize that the accuracy fluctuation of $5^\bigstar\epsilon_\nabla$ on FB15K and WN18 is caused by the test leakage issue which makes the model sensitive to its hyperparameter setting. Because the only difference of these two datasets comparing to their subsets FB15K-237 and WN18RR is the 81% and 94% inverse relations (Toutanova and Chen, 2015), i.e., $(s, hyponym, o)$ and $(o, hypernym, s)$ in the training set and the test set respectively, which is known as test leakage. Note that the accuracy fluctuation was simply solved by fine-tuning the hyperparameters (See results marked as $5^\bigstar\epsilon_\diamondsuit$).

Notice that in Table 2, we didn't report the fine-tuned results of $5^\bigstar\epsilon_\diamondsuit$ on datasets WN18RR and YAGO3-10, because the results abtained with the original settings ∇ is already the best.

Model	Time	MRR	H@1	H@3	H@10
$5^\bigstar\epsilon_\nabla$	**14±4**	0.353±7e-4	0.259	0.390	0.541
$5^\bigstar\epsilon_n$	**13±2**	0.353±8e-4	0.259	0.389	0.541
$5^\bigstar\mathrm{E_r}$	16±0	0.326±1e-3	0.238	0.357	0.505
$5^\bigstar\epsilon_v$	13±1	0.264±4e-4	0.192	0.288	0.404
$5^\bigstar\epsilon_h$	12±0	0.301±4e-4	0.221	0.329	0.458

(a) FB15K-237

Model	Time	MRR	H@1	H@3	H@10
$5^\bigstar\epsilon_\nabla$	**11±1**	**0.493±8e-4**	0.442	**0.512**	0.588
$5^\bigstar\epsilon_n$	14±3	0.485±1e-3	0.432	0.506	**0.589**
$5^\bigstar\mathrm{E_r}$	16±0	0.410±3e-3	0.391	0.417	0.447
$5^\bigstar\epsilon_v$	12±5	0.026±2e-4	0.015	0.025	0.045
$5^\bigstar\epsilon_h$	14±3	0.026±3e-4	0.016	0.025	0.046

(b) WN18RR

Model	Time	MRR	H@1	H@3	H@10
$5^\bigstar\epsilon_\nabla$	**297±1**	0.576±2e-3	**0.505**	0.619	0.702
$5^\bigstar\epsilon_n$	**298±1**	0.574±1e-3	0.502	0.618	0.701
$5^\bigstar\mathrm{E_r}$	416±2	0.569±2e-3	0.499	0.611	0.695
$5^\bigstar\epsilon_v$	297±1	0.562±8e-4	0.488	0.607	0.695
$5^\bigstar\epsilon_h$	298±1	0.546±1e-3	0.471	0.592	0.680

(c) YAGO3-10

Table 4: Ablation studies on FB15K-237, WN18RR, YAGO3-10 datasets. Instructions for this table are the same as those in Table 2.

Model	Time	MRR	H@1	H@3	H@10
$5^\bigstar\epsilon_\nabla$	**26±0**	0.794±2e-3	0.743	0.827	0.882
$5^\bigstar\epsilon_n$	**31±12**	0.799±2e-3	0.750	0.831	0.883
$5^\bigstar\mathrm{E_r}$	37±1	0.807±3e-3	0.760	0.838	0.888
$5^\bigstar\epsilon_v$	31±7	0.801±8e-4	0.753	0.833	0.885
$5^\bigstar\epsilon_h$	28±2	0.787±2e-3	0.735	0.822	0.877

(a) FB15K

Model	Time	MRR	H@1	H@3	H@10
$5^\bigstar\epsilon_\nabla$	**29±6**	0.949±6e-4	0.944	0.953	0.959
$5^\bigstar\epsilon_n$	**26±0**	**0.952±3e-4**	0.946	**0.955**	**0.962**
$5^\bigstar\mathrm{E_r}$	40±0	0.943±9e-4	0.935	0.950	0.954
$5^\bigstar\epsilon_v$	31±11	0.892±2e-3	0.836	0.944	0.958
$5^\bigstar\epsilon_h$	26±0	0.822±2e-3	0.719	0.920	0.949

(b) WN18

Table 5: Ablation studies on FB15K and WN18 datasets. Instructions for this table are the same as those in Table 2.

Training time in this model was reduced by 22%, 31%, 28%, 38% and 33% on each dataset respectively, and 31% on average. $5^\bigstar$E has eight parameter matrices in the coding. By using our method, the parameter matrices are directly reduced to four with no additional coding operations, which makes the significant saved training time.

Above results mean our conjugate model $5^\bigstar\epsilon$ exceeds the baseline model $5^\bigstar$E in all respect of accuracy, memory-efficiency and time footprint.

5.2 Ablation Studies

We did two kinds of ablation studies. The results are shown in Table 4 and Table 5. We know the reduced calculation is mainly in the regularization process because we only use half of the parameters. Thus we experimented where the regularization term is only half of the parameters on the original model (See results for $5^\bigstar\mathrm{E_r}$) to explore whether the effect of our method is similar to the reduced parameters regularization.

Then we experimented with conjugations in different positions to explore how the models perform differently. We set negative conjugation $c = -\overline{b}, d = \overline{a}$ in model $5^\bigstar\epsilon_n$, where half of the conjugate parameters are using negative conjugation instead of positive conjugation; we set vertical conjugation $c = \overline{a}, d = \overline{b}$ in model $5^\bigstar\epsilon_v$, where parameters are conjugated in their vertical direction instead of the diagonal direction; and we let $b = \overline{a}, d = \overline{c}$ in model $5^\bigstar\epsilon_h$, the horizontal conjugation, where parameters are conjugated in their horizontal direction.

The studies show that, first, by comparing the accuracy of $5^\bigstar\epsilon$ and $5^\bigstar E_r$, we know that reducing parameters in the regularization process hurts the accuracy significantly, which indicates our conjugation method indeedly reserves model's ability even when the parameters are reduced. Second, the negative conjugate model $5^\bigstar\epsilon_n$ performs as well as $5^\bigstar\epsilon$. Last but not least, conjugate method should choose suitable positions, e.g., $5^\bigstar\epsilon_v$ and $5^\bigstar\epsilon_h$ do not perform as well.

5.3 Statistical Methods

To clarify the difference between original models and their conjugate models, we took the highest mean as the best result, with the standard deviation as a secondary judgement, and ultimately two-sample t-tests (See Table 6 in Appendix) are conducted to decide whether two similar results can be considered statistically equivalent and which is the best.

The two-sample t-test estimates if two population means are equal. Here we use the t-test to judge if the Time or MRR means of two models are equal. We set significance level $\alpha = 0.05$, and the null hypothesis assumed that the two data samples are from normal distributions with unknown and unequal variances. (h, p) means the result h and p-value of the hypothesis test. $h = 1, 0$. $h = 1$

means rejection to the null hypothesis at the significance level α. $h = 0$ indicates the failure to reject the null hypothesis at the significance level α. $p \in [0, 1]$ is a probability of observing a test statistic as extreme as, or more extreme than, the observed value under the null hypothesis. A small p value suggests suspicion on the validity of the null hypothesis.

To prepare data for the t-tests, experiments on ComplEx, Complϵx, $5^\bigstar$E, $5^\bigstar\epsilon_\nabla$, $5^\bigstar\epsilon_\diamond$ and $5^\bigstar\epsilon_n$ are conducted 17 times each. Apart from that, the $5^\bigstar\mathrm{E}_r$, $5^\bigstar\epsilon_v$, $5^\bigstar\epsilon_h$ apparently perform worse than the former six models, thus the t-tests are not needed and their experiments are conducted 5 times each.

Most of our t-tests were done among the original model and its conjugate models as the distribution differs significantly if the base model is different. However, since the accuracies among different models are similar on the YAGO3-10 and WN18 datasets, we did several supplementary t-tests (indicated in *italics*). The supplementary t-tests showed that the distributions are different indeed when based on different original models even though they appear to be similar. On the contrary, there exist similar distributions among the results distribution of the original model and its conjugate model.

5.4 Advantages of Parameter Sharing

Approching for the best accuracy in link prediction task has the trade off of misinformation effect or inevitable high memory and time costs. Our parameter-sharing method by using half conjugate parameters is very easy to apply and can help control these costs, and potentially no trade off.

The original ComplEx and $5^\bigstar$E each has their own strength in the perspective of accuracy on different datasets; while ComplEx costs much more memory and time than $5^\bigstar$E when compared under similar accuracy.

Our conjugate models consume less memory and time, and not inferior to the original models in accuracy, which shows that our parameter-sharing method makes a complex number represented KGE model superior to itself.

6 Conclusions

We propose using shared conjugate parameters for transformations, which suffices to accurately represent the structures of the KG.

Our method can help scaling up KG with less carbon footprints easily: first, it reduces parameter size and consumes less or at least comparable training time while achieving consistent accuracy as the non-conjugate model, including reaching state-of-the-art results; second, it is easily generalizable across various complex number represented models.

7 Future Work

We would like to deal with the interpretation of the linear constrain of our method. For example, to explore the effect of this method on different relation patterns. Moreover, many KG applications like the work done by Hongwimol et al. (2021) regard visual appeal as important, where appropriate visuals can better convey the points of the data and facilitate user interaction. We can see that the vector representations of transformed entities using this method have more substantial geometric constrains (See transformed entities illustrated in Figure 1). We want to explore if our method can obtain better KG visualization.

Acknowledgements

This work was supported by JSPS KAKENHI Grant Numbers 21H05054.

References

Ivana Balazevic, Carl Allen, and Timothy Hospedales. 2019. Multi-relational poincaré graph embeddings. In *Advances in Neural Information Processing Systems*, volume 32. Curran Associates, Inc.

Antoine Bordes, Nicolas Usunier, Alberto Garcia-Duran, Jason Weston, and Oksana Yakhnenko. 2013. Translating embeddings for modeling multi-relational data. In *Advances in Neural Information Processing Systems*, volume 26. Curran Associates, Inc.

Ines Chami, Adva Wolf, Da-Cheng Juan, Frederic Sala, Sujith Ravi, and Christopher Ré. 2020. Low-dimensional hyperbolic knowledge graph embeddings. In *Proceedings of the 58th Annual Meeting of the Association for Computational Linguistics*, pages 6901–6914, Online. Association for Computational Linguistics.

Tim Dettmers, Pasquale Minervini, Pontus Stenetorp, and Sebastian Riedel. 2018. Convolutional 2d knowledge graph embeddings. In *AAAI*.

Katsuhiko Hayashi and Masashi Shimbo. 2017. On the equivalence of holographic and complex embeddings for link prediction. In *Proceedings of the 55th Annual Meeting of the Association for Computational Linguistics (Volume 2: Short Papers)*, pages 554–559, Vancouver, Canada. Association for Computational Linguistics.

Pollawat Hongwimol, Peeranuth Kehasukcharoen, Pasit Laohawarutchai, Piyawat Lertvittayakumjorn, Aik Beng Ng, Zhangsheng Lai, Timothy Liu, and Peerapon Vateekul. 2021. ESRA: Explainable scientific research assistant. In *Proceedings of the 59th Annual Meeting of the Association for Computational Linguistics and the 11th International Joint Conference on Natural Language Processing: System Demonstrations*, pages 114–121, Online. Association for Computational Linguistics.

Guoliang Ji, Shizhu He, Liheng Xu, Kang Liu, and Jun Zhao. 2015. Knowledge graph embedding via dynamic mapping matrix. In *Proceedings of the 53rd Annual Meeting of the Association for Computational Linguistics and the 7th International Joint Conference on Natural Language Processing (Volume 1: Long Papers)*, pages 687–696, Beijing, China. Association for Computational Linguistics.

Yankai Lin, Zhiyuan Liu, Maosong Sun, Yang Liu, and Xuan Zhu. 2015. Learning entity and relation embeddings for knowledge graph completion. *Proceedings of the AAAI Conference on Artificial Intelligence*, 29(1).

Mojtaba Nayyeri, Sahar Vahdati, Can Aykul, and Jens Lehmann. 2021. 5* knowledge graph embeddings with projective transformations. *Proceedings of the AAAI Conference on Artificial Intelligence*, 35(10):9064–9072.

Maximilian Nickel, Volker Tresp, and Hans-Peter Kriegel. 2011. A three-way model for collective learning on multi-relational data. In *ICML*.

Natasha Noy, Yuqing Gao, Anshu Jain, Anant Narayanan, Alan Patterson, and Jamie Taylor. 2019. Industry-scale knowledge graphs: Lessons and challenges. *Communications of the ACM*, 62 (8):36–43.

Kristina Toutanova and Danqi Chen. 2015. Observed versus latent features for knowledge base and text inference. In *Proceedings of the 3rd Workshop on Continuous Vector Space Models and their Compositionality*, pages 57–66, Beijing, China. Association for Computational Linguistics.

Théo Trouillon, Johannes Welbl, Sebastian Riedel, Éric Gaussier, and Guillaume Bouchard. 2016. Complex embeddings for simple link prediction. *CoRR*, abs/1606.06357.

Bishan Yang, Wen-tau Yih, Xiaodong He, Jianfeng Gao, and Li Deng. 2014. Embedding entities and relations for learning and inference in knowledge bases.

A Two-sample t-test

	Time t-test (h, p)						MRR t-test (h, p)					
	ComplEx	Complϵx	$5^\star$E	$5^\star\epsilon_\nabla$	$5^\star\epsilon_\diamond$	$5^\star\epsilon_n$	ComplEx	Complϵx	$5^\star$E	$5^\star\epsilon_\nabla$	$5^\star\epsilon_\diamond$	$5^\star\epsilon_n$
ComplEx	-	(0, 2e-1)	-	-	-	-	-	(1, 8e-17)	-	-	-	-
Complϵx	-	-	-	-	-	-	-	-	-	-	-	-
$5^\star$E	-	-	-	(1, 8e-3)	(0, 6e-1)	(1, 4e-5)	-	-	-	(1, 1e-12)	(1, 1e-14)	(1, 1e-10)
$5^\star\epsilon_\nabla$	-	-	-	-	(0, 4e-1)	(0, 4e-1)	-	-	-	-	(1, 6e-3)	(1, 1e-2)
$5^\star\epsilon_\diamond$	-	-	-	-	-	(0, 2e-1)	-	-	-	-	-	(1, 7e-6)
$5^\star\epsilon_n$	-	-	-	-	-	-	-	-	-	-	-	-

(a) FB15K-237

	Time t-test (h, p)						MRR t-test (h, p)					
	ComplEx	Complϵx	$5^\star$E	$5^\star\epsilon_\nabla$	$5^\star\epsilon_\diamond$	$5^\star\epsilon_n$	ComplEx	Complϵx	$5^\star$E	$5^\star\epsilon_\nabla$	$5^\star\epsilon_\diamond$	$5^\star\epsilon_n$
ComplEx	-	(0, 6e-1)	-	-	-	-	-	(1, 3e-28)	-	-	-	-
Complϵx	-	-	-	-	-	-	-	-	-	-	-	-
$5^\star$E	-	-	-	(1, 4e-11)	-	(1, 6e-3)	-	-	-	(1, 9e-11)	-	(1, 2e-15)
$5^\star\epsilon_\nabla$	-	-	-	-	-	(1, 2e-2)	-	-	-	-	-	(1, 4e-21)
$5^\star\epsilon_\diamond$	-	-	-	-	-	-	-	-	-	-	-	-
$5^\star\epsilon_n$	-	-	-	-	-	-	-	-	-	-	-	-

(b) WN18RR

	Time t-test (h, p)						MRR t-test (h, p)					
	ComplEx	Complϵx	$5^\star$E	$5^\star\epsilon_\nabla$	$5^\star\epsilon_\diamond$	$5^\star\epsilon_n$	ComplEx	Complϵx	$5^\star$E	$5^\star\epsilon_\nabla$	$5^\star\epsilon_\diamond$	$5^\star\epsilon_n$
ComplEx	-	(0, 4e-1)	-	-	-	-	-	(1, 3e-6)	*(1, 2e-7)*	*(1, 7e-3)*	-	*(1, 3e-8)*
Complϵx	-	-	-	-	-	-	-	-	-	-	-	-
$5^\star$E	-	-	-	(1, 5e-47)	-	(1, 1e-46)	-	-		(1, 5e-4)	-	(0, 6e-1)
$5^\star\epsilon_\nabla$	-	-	-	-	-	(0, 7e-1)	-	-	-	-	-	(1, 3e-4)
$5^\star\epsilon_\diamond$	-	-	-	-	-	-	-	-	-	-	-	-
$5^\star\epsilon_n$	-	-	-	-	-	-	-	-	-	-	-	-

(c) YAGO3-10

	Time t-test (h, p)						MRR t-test (h, p)					
	ComplEx	Complϵx	$5^\star$E	$5^\star\epsilon_\nabla$	$5^\star\epsilon_\diamond$	$5^\star\epsilon_n$	ComplEx	Complϵx	$5^\star$E	$5^\star\epsilon_\nabla$	$5^\star\epsilon_\diamond$	$5^\star\epsilon_n$
ComplEx	-	(0, 1e-1)	-	-	-	-	-	(0, 8e-2)	-	-	-	-
Complϵx	-	-	-	-	-	-	-	-	-	-	-	-
$5^\star$E	-	-	-	(1, 2e-6)	(1, 3e-5)	(1, 8e-3)	-	-	-	(1, 2e-21)	(1, 2e-2)	(1, 6e-21)
$5^\star\epsilon_\nabla$	-	-	-	-	(1, 3e-2)	(0, 1e-1)	-	-	-	-	(1, 1e-23)	(1, 3e-9)
$5^\star\epsilon_\diamond$	-	-	-	-	-	(0, 5e-1)	-	-	-	-	-	(1, 3e-22)
$5^\star\epsilon_n$	-	-	-	-	-	-	-	-	-	-	-	-

(d) FB15K

	Time t-test (h, p)						MRR t-test (h, p)					
	ComplEx	Complϵx	$5^\star$E	$5^\star\epsilon_\nabla$	$5^\star\epsilon_\diamond$	$5^\star\epsilon_n$	ComplEx	Complϵx	$5^\star$E	$5^\star\epsilon_\nabla$	$5^\star\epsilon_\diamond$	$5^\star\epsilon_n$
ComplEx	-	(0, 5e-1)	-	-	-	-	-	(0, 8e-2)	-	-	*(1, 1e-17)*	*(1, 1e-13)*
Complϵx	-	-	-	-	-	-	-	-	-	-	*(1, 5e-21)*	*(1, 2e-16)*
$5^\star$E	-	-	-	(1, 1e-7)	(1, 4e-9)	(1, 6e-9)	-	-		(1, 3e-14)	(1, 5e-5)	(0, 2e-1)
$5^\star\epsilon_\nabla$	-	-	-	-	(0, 2e-1)	(0, 8e-2)	-	-	-	-	(1, 4e-15)	(1, 5e-14)
$5^\star\epsilon_\diamond$	-	-	-	-	-	(0, 1e-1)	-	-	-	-	-	(1, 3e-5)
$5^\star\epsilon_n$	-	-	-	-	-	-	-	-	-	-	-	-

(e) WN18

Table 6: t-test (h, p) of Time and MRR on FB15K-237, WN18RR, YAGO3-10, FB15K and WN18 datasets.

A Clique-based Graphical Approach to Detect Interpretable Adjectival Senses in Hungarian

Enikő Héja and **Noémi Ligeti-Nagy**
Hungarian Research Centre for Linguistics
Institute of Language Technology and Applies Sciences
Language Technology Research Group
[heja.eniko,ligeti-nagy.noemi]@nytud.hu

Abstract

The present paper introduces an ongoing research which aims to detect interpretable adjectival senses from monolingual corpora applying an unsupervised WSI approach. According to our expectations the findings of our investigation are going to contribute to the work of lexicographers, linguists and also facilitate the creation of benchmarks with semantic information for the NLP community. For doing so, we set up four criteria to distinguish between senses. We experiment with a graphical approach to model our criteria and then perform a detailed, linguistically motivated manual evaluation of the results.

1 Introduction

The objective of this ongoing research is to model human intuition regarding meaning distinctions, and anchor it to observable data. Its importance is given by the fact that according to several authors (eg. Véronis, 2003; Kuti et al., 2010) human intuition on sense distinctions varies greatly among individuals, which in turn has a serious effect on lexicography, lexical semantics and NLP, as well. It goes without saying in the lexicographic community that in spite of scrupulous corpus-based investigations, monolingual dictionaries greatly vary with regard to their macro- and microstructure (Adamska-Sałaciak, 2006). The same problem arises in the field of NLP: the sense inventories or knowledge-bases exhibit a great variance regarding how fine-grained meaning distinctions they apply. Although lexical semantics in linguistics and word sense induction in NLP are widely studied fields (cf. Geeraerts, 2015; Amrami and Goldberg, 2019; Wiedemann et al., 2019), to our knowledge there is still no agreement on how the meaning space of a word should be partitioned to obtain well-motivated senses. For instance, Pustejovsky (1995, p. 32) introduces a very fine-grained meaning distinction asserting that "adjectives such as *good* have multiple meanings depending on what they are modifying: *good car, good meal, good knife*". However, he also adds that *good* may be conceived of merely "as a positive evaluation of the nominal head it is modifying." Accordingly, the present experiment has two main objectives: first, we aim to come up with a definition that is able to provide necessary criteria to distinguish between senses. This definition should enable us to anchor meaning distinctions to not only a set of contexts, but conceptual categories as well. Secondly, we aim to model this definition via an unsupervised approach that is able to grasp this definition to minimize the role of human introspection in meaning distinction. We think that our approach is quite promising as one of the main drawbacks of unsupervised models is their poor interpretability, as pointed out by Camacho-Collados and Pilehvar (2018). On top of that, in their survey they tied graphical models to knowledge-based semantic representations, which implies that unsupervised graph-based WSI is underrepresented in the field.

The usual conception of meaning starts from meaning identity: the definition of synonymy (two expressions are synonymous iff they are interchangeable in every context preserving the original meaning) has a long tradition going back at least to Frege (1892), and all the senses that are not synonyms are considered to be different senses. The subsequent research tends to accept this chain of thoughts. However, in the present discussion we put it in the other way: as opposed to Frege and his followers, we do not give a definition for synonymy, but give one to distinguish between meanings. This choice is motivated by the fact that the notion of synonymy is intimately tied to truth-conditions, which are notoriously missing from pure distributional semantics. That is why it is so hard to detect true synonyms solely on distributional grounds. And indeed, automatically detected synonym-classes tend to cover also tight seman-

Proceedings of TextGraphs-16: Graph-based Methods for Natural Language Processing, pages 35–43
October 16, 2022.

tic classes, such as names of nations, colors, even antonyms exhibiting very similar distributional behavior. Starting from the presupposition that attributive adjectives can be characterized in a rather simple feature space – constituted only by the following nouns – in the present research we confine ourselves to the investigation of the semantic properties of attributive adjectives. The paper is structured as follows: in section 2 our hypotheses are presented, section 3 describes our methodology, in section 4 we present our validation techniques, while section 5 focuses on the evaluation of our results. We conclude with a summary in section 6.

2 Criteria for meaning distinction

In what follows, we describe the applied criteria, which were implemented in the next phase. Contrary to the usual procedure of definition, instead of searching an identity criteria to "give the necessary and sufficient conditions for a to be identical to b when a and b are Ks" (cf. Carrara and Giaretta, 2004), we search for necessary and sufficient conditions to discriminate between a and b. That is, instead of modeling synonymy, we strive to grasp when the target word surely conveys different meanings on distributional grounds. For doing so, we introduce the notion of near-synonymy (cf. Ploux and Victorri, 1998) – a relaxed version of synonymy: two words are *near-synonyms* if they are interchangeable in a restricted set of contexts so that they preserve the meaning of the original sentence.[1] Moreover, in accordance with our original purpose (i.e. meaning distinction), we also consider the members of tight semantic classes to be near-synonyms, inasmuch various tight semantic classes denote different senses of a word, even though they do not preserve the truth value.[2]

According to our hypothesis two senses have to be differentiated iff:

1. There is (at least) one near-synonym for each sense of the adjective.
2. There is a set of context-nouns which form grammatical constructions with both the original adjective and with the near-synonym.
3. The two sets of context-nouns characterizing the different senses are non-overlapping sets.
4. The non-overlapping set of nouns form a semantic category "reflecting the sub-selectional properties of adjectives" (Pustejovsky, 1995).

Example 1 is intended to further illustrate the above criteria, using the automatically extracted two senses of the adjective *napfényes* ('sunny'). As can be seen, there is a near-synonym for both senses: *napsütéses* ('sunshiny') for the first one and *napsütötte* ('sunlit') for the second one. The nouns listed below the adjectives are the ones that form grammatical constructions with the near-synonyms: *napfényes/napsütéses vasárnap* ('sunny/sunshiny Sunday'), *napfényes/napsütéses nap* ('sunny/sunshiny day'), etc., and *napfényes/napsütötte terület* ('sunny/sunlit area'), *napfényes/napsütötte terasz* ('sunny/sunlit terrace'), etc. However, the two sets of nouns do not overlap: there is no *napsütéses terasz* ('sunshiny terrace') or *napsütötte nap* ('sunlit day'), and the same goes for all adjective-noun pairs where the noun comes from the context noun set of the other sense. Finally, the nouns that match the above criteria form a semantic category: time periods with the first sense, and areas, places with the second.

(1) Sense 1: *napfényes* 'sunny', *napsütéses* 'sunshiny'
Nouns of sense 1: *vasárnap* 'Sunday', *nap* 'day'

Sense 2: *napfényes* 'sunny', *napsütötte* 'sunlit'
Nouns of sense 2: *terület* 'area', *sziget* 'island', *oldal* 'side', *terasz* 'terrace'

We wish to examine to what extent the above conditions are necessary and sufficient to differentiate between meanings. For doing so, in Section 3 an unsupervised word sense induction experiment on Hungarian monolingual data will be described using cliques of target words and their contexts to retrieve senses. The workflow conceptually comprises two main stages: i) the detection of near-synonymy classes for a given adjective, ii) discriminating between the various meanings of the given adjective by the extraction of the relevant context nouns.

3 Method

Our methodology is based on Ah-Pine and Jacquet (2009), as far as meaning distinctions are mod-

[1] For instance, *finom* ('fine') and *lágy* ('soft') are synonyms before nouns related to music, such as the Hungarian counterparts of 'music', 'rhythm', 'melody', etc.

[2] For example, *fekete* ('black') may belong to two different near-synonymy sets: one containing surnames and the other containing names of colors.

eled via cliques. However, there are two main differences: first, instead of named entities we focused on adjectival meanings. As overproduction of cliques is much less pronounced in this case, clustering becomes an unnecessary step. However, the resulting cliques need to be validated in terms of the following nouns, possibly along with the subcategorization patterns of the adjectives. Secondly, adjectives are represented with static dense embeddings instead of frequency based sparse vectors.

3.1 Input data

The adjectives of our interest were selected on the basis of the 180 million word Hungarian National Corpus (Váradi, 2002). Although the frequency list contains adjectives with various case suffixes, we took only nominative adjectives into consideration, presuming that the adjective is always in nominative in the Adj + Noun constructions.

3.2 Representations

3.2.1 Representation of adjectives

As opposed to Ah-Pine and Jacquet (2009), instead of count vectors we decided to use static word embeddings to represent adjectives. Our choice was motivated by Baroni et al. (2014), who presented a systematic comparison of traditional "context-counting" vectors (eg. Turney and Pantel, 2010; Clark, 2015) and the more recent "context-predicting" ones (eg. Bengio et al., 2003; Mikolov et al., 2013a) on a set of various standard lexical semantic benchmarks. Their findings show that the predictive models achieve an impressive overall performance, beating count vectors in all tasks. Therefore, a word2vec language model (Mikolov et al., 2013a,b) was trained on the first 999 file (21GB raw texts) of a Hungarian language corpus, the Webcorpus 2.0 (Nemeskey, 2020) containing the normalized version of the original texts, cc. 170M sentences[3]. 300-dimension vectors were trained using the Gensim Python package (Rehurek and Sojka, 2011) to perform CBoW training with a $6k$ window size and a minimum frequency of 3. Since Hungarian is a highly inflective language and we trained embeddings on raw texts, this is not a pure bag-of-words model, as the abbreviation CBoW would imply. Our choice of input data was based on the presupposition that morphosyntactic information may contribute to the characterization of adjectival meanings. This hypothesis is in accordance with the findings of Novák and Novák (2018), who investigated the performance of various Hungarian static word embeddings in a word similarity task. Their experiment concludes that adjectival senses are best represented via embeddings trained on surface forms of words. Roughly 8,5M word forms were assigned embeddings as the result of our training. The trained LMs are available on GitHub: `https://github.com/nytud/w2v_models`.

3.2.2 Representation of semantic similarity

In our graph-based representation of adjectives, vertex-labeled undirected graphs were generated. Vertices and their labels represent the adjectives, while the edges (or their lack) denote whether there is a semantic similarity relation between two adjectives (or not). This structure encodes some basic intuitions about meaning similarity:

(1) 'Undirectedness' guarantees the symmetric nature of meaning similarity: if a meaning M is similar to meaning M', then the reverse is also true.

(2) Since every adjective is similar to itself, there is a self-loop at every node of the graph.

3.2.3 Representing near-synonyms as cliques

Meaning is grasped through the notion of near-synonymy. Following Ah-Pine and Jacquet (2009), near-synonyms which exhibit "very similar" distributional behavior, are grasped by cliques in the graph: that is, we search for those maximally connected subgraphs. Now the nodes in the clique represent a set of adjectives with "very similar" distributional behavior.

3.2.4 Representing meaning-discrimination as shared cliques

This approach, on the one hand, makes possible the detection of multiple near-synonymy classes comprising a common adjectival lexeme, where the corresponding cliques represent differing sense candidates. In addition, ideally, it also enables meaning discrimination based on explicit surface data, inasmuch all the resulting cliques are anchored to the contexts in which each element of the adjectival clique may occur.

Therefore, according to our hypothesis, an adjective has multiple meanings if it belongs to multiple

[3] As the evaluation of the model trained on the whole Webcorpus 2.0 (cc. 591.4M sentences) yielded only a slight improvement on the Hungarian translation of the Google Analogy Test Set (Makrai, 2015), this smaller model was used in our experiment.

cliques, and the cliques are characterized by non-overlapping sets of context nouns.

3.3 Extraction of cliques

First a similarity matrix was created (A_{sim}) containing adjectives as rows and columns. For doing so, a suitable similarity measure was applied to fill in the cells of A_{sim}. That is, $A_{sim}(i,j) = sim(a_i, a_j)$, where a_i and a_j denote the word2vec representations of adjectives from the selected vocabulary. The usual cosine similarity was calculated. That is:

$$sim_{cos}(v_1, v_2) = \frac{\mathbf{v_1} \cdot \mathbf{v_2}}{||v_1||||v_2||} \quad (1)$$

In the second step A_{sim} similarity matrix was converted into an adjacency matrix A_a based on suitable cutting heuristics indicating whether the corresponding adjectives are semantically similar or not. Here a K cut-off parameter was set.

As a result, in this step A'_a symmetric square matrix is generated containing boolean values. A'_a adjacency matrix can be conceived of as a graph representation of the adjectives. Note that the use of cosine similarity guarantees that A'_a matrix is symmetric. Due to the reflexive nature of 'similarity' all the diagonal values of A'_a equal to 1.

In the last phase cliques were retrieved from the graph represented by the adjacency matrix to grasp adjectival near-synonymy classes.

3.4 Retrieving context nouns

In this phase adjectival cliques are validated by retrieving the set of nouns they may co-occur with. According to our expectation, different senses of an adjective are characterized by the different sets of nouns they co-occur with. These non-overlapping sets provide explicit information on the context of meaning discrimination. A characteristic set of nouns is found as follows:

1. We collect all the nouns an adjective co-occurs with; we do this for all adjectives in a clique. This step was performed on the basis of a 91.4 million-token subcorpus of the Hungarian Gigaword Corpus (Oravecz et al., 2014) compiled specifically for the present experiment. During the compilation process we aimed at preserving the original proportion of the genres, thus, every domain of HGC was included in the new corpus: newspapers, literature, scientific, official, personal and spoken language. Accordingly, our corpus was made up of 30.5m, 6.5 m, 11.6m, 8.8m, 28m and 6.6m tokens, respectively.

2. We compute the intersection of the above sets: those are the nouns that co-occur with each adjective of a clique. If at least one such noun exist for a clique, then we consider the given clique as a potential meaning candidate.

3. We repeat step 1 and step 2 for each clique a given adjective belongs to. This results in a set of nouns for each clique.

4. Finally, we take these sets and omit the intersections: we keep only the nouns for a clique which are exclusive to the given clique; they do not appear in the sets of the other cliques. Example (2) shows the cliques of the adjective *cinikus* 'cynical'. The nouns listed below the cliques are those shared by all members of the clique. Nouns in bold are the ones specific to the clique. These are the nouns indicating the specific meanings, therefore, we kept them for further evaluation.

(2) *cinikus* 'cynical'
Clique 1: *ostoba* 'silly', *cinikus* 'cynical', *demagóg* 'demagogic'
Nouns: *dolog* 'thing', *kérdés* 'question', *lépés* 'move', *mód* 'way', ***szöveg*** 'text'

Clique 2: *ostoba* 'silly', *cinikus* 'cynical', *arcátlan* 'impudent'
Nouns: *dolog* 'thing', ***ember*** 'person', *kérdés* 'question', *lépés* 'move', *mód* 'way'

Our presumption is that the resulting sets of nouns are the ones specific to the given cliques: they capture the given sense of the adjective that is shared among the other adjectives of the clique.

3.5 Evaluation

Finally, the results were evaluated according to different parameter settings. Since, to our knowledge, there is no similar database available for Hungarian, a qualitative evaluation was performed.

The main objective of the evaluation phase was twofold. On the one hand we aimed to verify our basic hypothesis, according to which the proposed techniques are able to provide a solid methodological background to discriminate between meanings. On the other hand, we also had the intention to catalogue the automatically retrieved adjectival senses with their salient context nouns and their perceived semantic categories, if possible. For doing so, first a coarse-grained evaluation was performed focusing on the main semantic properties of the automatically retrieved adjectival cliques. This was followed by a fine-grained evaluation phase where we concentrated on the context nouns.

3.6 Parameter setting

Three parameters were identified as having a serious impact on the results.

(i) The frequency of adjectives in the Hungarian National Corpus

(ii) The K cut-off parameter

(iii) The minimum frequency count of the nouns in the clique-validation step

The frequency of the adjectives
This parameter had to be taken into account to ensure that the word2vec representations were trained on sufficient amount of data.
The impact of K cut-off value
Interestingly, we found that the value of the K cut-off parameter has a serious impact not only on the number of the resulting cliques but also on the semantic field to which they belong to. For instance, in the case of adjectives occurring at least 200 times, $K = 0.9$ yielded only a handful of results: only 8 adjectives were assigned to more than one clique and only two cliques were validated by nouns. The retrieved cliques refer to numbers, months and days exclusively, therefore, they are not very interesting from a sense discrimination perspective. On the other hand, with the same parameter settings, but with a lower similarity cut-off value ($K = 0.7$)[4] we had 187 different adjectives belonging to multiple cliques, where all cliques are validated and discriminated by at least one following noun. Setting K to 0.7 resulted in 3847 single nodes and 1085 node pairs with one edge leaving only 1110 adjectives to possibly belong to multiple cliques. The high proportion of single nodes clearly implies that the K cut-off value should be set to a lower value.
The effect of the frequency count of the following noun
The minimum frequency count of the validating nouns ($Freq_n$) also had to be taken into consideration. Two settings were tested ($Freq_{ADJ} = 200, K = 0.7$). In the first setting a clique was considered valid if there was at least 1 noun occurring at least 5 times with every element of the clique ($Freq_n \geq 5$). Validating only a handful of cliques, this threshold value was deemed to be too high. To keep the coverage as high as possible, the value of $Freq_n$ was set to 2. This change clearly improved the coverage, yielding 446 adjectives belonging to multiple cliques – out of the 6042 adjectives occurring at least 200 times in our input corpus with a word2vec representation.

In the rest of this section the results of the qualitative evaluation of these cliques will be presented ($Freq_{ADJ} = 200, K = 0.7, Freq_n = 2$).

4 Relevant senses

In the present section we introduce some linguistic consideration that had to be taken into account during the evaluation phase to detect distinct classes of attributive modification.

4.1 Productivity

Distinct meanings may come from different sources. It is common to differentiate between collocational and more productive uses of an expression. In the course of the present research productivity is interpreted as a scale. On the one end of this scale there are collocations where both the adjective and the noun are fixed. In this case the meaning of the construction is yielded in a fully non-compositional way: neither component can be substituted with a near-synonym preserving the original meaning of the expression (eg. *fehér zaj* 'white noise' or *fekete doboz* 'black box').

Albeit collocations are possible sources of additional meanings, we are more interested in 'semi-compositional' constructions in the present WSI task, where compositionality operates on a restricted set of adjectives or nouns. For example, *fehér/szürke/fekete gazdaság* (literally 'white/gray/black economy')[5] are not considered collocations in the strict sense, since the restricted set of colors denotes a new dimension of meaning in the context of the noun *gazdaság* ('economy') (i.e. the extent to which a sector of economy is monitored and taxed). That is, one step further from collocations on the 'productivity scale' more interesting instances emerge, for example, *ékes* ('ornate') means *tipikus* ('typical') before a restricted

[4]Our findings meet with the results of Veremyev et al. (2019). They constructed semantic networks based on word2vec representations of words with various thresholds and found that the threshold 0.7 resulted in the smallest, most compact cliques (largest clique size equaled to 245 and to 14, for the threshold 0.5 and 0.7, respectively).

[5]Here, as opposed to the meaning of the English expression ('health related goods and services'), the Hungarian counterpart of 'white economy' refers to the monitored and taxed sectors of economy.

set of nouns (*példa* 'example' and *képviselő* 'representative').

4.2 Subcategorization

And indeed, the most interesting cases are those where the nouns form one or more semantic classes allowing the adjectives in the cliques to be synonyms in those semantically restricted contexts. In these cases the adjective subcategorizes the subsequent nouns (cf. Pustejovsky, 1995). For example, the different meanings of *könnyű* ('easy'), *komoly* ('serious'), *szép* ('nice'), *éles* ('sharp'), *finom* ('fine, delicate'), all can be discriminated on the basis of a set of synonym adjectives along with their semantically constrained nominal contexts. For example *könnyű* ('easy') has different meanings in the context of nouns referring to physical objects ('a lightweight bag'), nouns referring to clothes ('a light clothing'), foods ('a light lunch'), and before nouns like 'answer', 'task', 'solution' ('an easy answer/task/solution').

The size of the semantically constrained nominal sets may vary: on the other end of the scale there are really productive uses of adjectives that are still important for our purposes. For instance, the retrieved cliques imply that *vidám* 'merry' and *szomorú* 'sad' have different meanings when modifying nouns denoting humans and when modifying nouns referring to time periods. According to the cliques, we can say both *szomorú [időszak, év, nap]* ('sad [period, year, day]') and *gyászos [időszak, év, nap]* ('mournful [period, year, day]') but there is neither *bánatos [időszak, év, nap]* ('sorrowful [period, year, day]'), nor *gyászos [lány, ember]* ('mournful [girl, human]').

(3) Clique 1: *szomorú* 'sad', *gyászos* 'mournful'
Nouns: *időszak* 'period', *year* 'év', *nap* 'day'

Clique 2: *szomorú* 'sad', *bánatos* 'sorrowful'
Nouns: *lány* 'girl', *ember* 'human'

The adjective *vidám* 'merry' exhibits rather similar behavior to *szomorú* 'sad' from this perspective.

(4) Clique 1: *vidám* 'merry', *derűs* 'bright'
Nouns: *perc* 'minute', *nap* 'day', *hétvége* 'weekend'

Clique 2: *vidám* 'merry', *jókedvű* 'cheerful'
Nouns: *fiú* 'boy', *delfin* 'dolphin'

As opposed to humans (and dolphins), periods of time cannot be *jókedvű*, and in tandem with this, *derűs fiú* and *derűs delfin* are not well-formed constructions in Hungarian[6].

5 Evaluation

5.1 Coarse-grained classification of adjectival cliques

Tight semantic classes

One problem we had to face during the evaluation phase is that not all adjectives were equally relevant from a meaning discrimination perspective. For example, dates and measures did not exhibit any interesting properties in most cases, even if they were assigned to multiple cliques. Instead, adjectives from these tight semantic classes tended to belong to multiple cliques with the very same meaning. According to our hypothesis, due to their varying sizes and varying distances between the elements, the adjectives belonging to tight semantic classes cannot be grouped into one clique in a coherent way, no matter what the parameter setting is. Another reason to disregard adjectives from tight semantic classes is that their lexical meaning seems to be rather straightforward not allowing for polysemy, except for a handful of more complex ones (eg. *fekete* 'black', *fehér* 'white', *szürke* 'gray'). For instance, *hétfői* ('of.Monday') was grouped under two different cliques:

(5) Clique 1: *hétfői* 'of.Monday', *pénteki* 'of.Friday', *szombati* 'of.Saturday',*vasárnapi* 'of.Sunday'

Clique 2: *hétfői* 'of.Monday', *tegnapi* 'of.yesterday', *keddi* 'of.Tuesday', *csütörtöki* 'of.Thursday', *szerdai* 'of.Wednesday', *szombati* 'of.Saturday', *pénteki* 'of.Friday'

In the case of numerals, dates, names of colors, units of measurements and various national currencies the nouns did not supply enough evidence to accept the meaning discrimination indicated by the cliques.

Named entities

Another class of adjectives was made up of named entities, primarily countries, cities and surnames. In spite of the rather striking results, they were not considered in the present investigation, since our main focus is on lexical meaning here, while the clique-membership of NEs tend to reflect factual knowledge rather than lexical meaning. For instance, *egri* (related to the city of Eger) was assigned to two cliques *[egri, soproni, veszprémi]* (related to the cities of Eger, Sopron and Veszprém,

[6]Interestingly, this is a well-known example in the lexical semantic research concerning English. As Pustejovsky (1995, p. 48) notes "[...] *sad* and *happy* are able to predicate of both individuals [...] as well as event denoting nouns".

respectively) indicating viticultural areas, whereas the other clique [*egri*, *esztergomi*] (related to the cities of Eger and Esztergom, respectively) are referring to archdioceses.

One interesting finding of the manual evaluation was that the $6k$ window size word2vec representation was rather efficient in the detection of tight semantic classes and cliques of named entities: out of the 446 adjectives 99 belonged to some types of named entities, 28 adjectives were terms of measurements, while 11 adjectives assigned to at least two cliques referred to numerals.

Emotive intensifiers

We found that emotive intensifiers tend to group in cliques not conveying separate meanings. For example:

(6) Clique 1: *borzalmas* 'terrible', *iszonyatos* 'terrific', *rettenetes* 'awful'
Nouns: *szenvedés* 'suffering', *kép* 'picture', *körülmény* 'circumstance'

Clique 2: *borzalmas* 'terrible', *félelmetes* 'dreadful', *rettenetes* 'awful', *szörnyű* 'horrible'
Nouns: *látvány* 'spectacle', *nap* 'day', *érzés* 'feeling'

Clique 3: *borzalmas* 'terrible', *borzasztó* 'terrifying', *rettenetes* 'awful', *szörnyű* 'horrible', *rémes* 'fearful'
Nouns: *emlék* 'memory', *élmény* 'experience'

While the cliques imply that negative emotive intensifiers form a coherent semantic class among adjectives, neither the cliques nor the following nouns do not supply enough evidence to discriminate between the meaning of cliques.

nagy 'great'

The adjective *nagy* ('great') and related notions, such as *óriási* ('huge'), *hatalmas* ('large'), etc, are posing another problem: here the abstraction step is quite easy to make along the various dimensions, therefore, in this case, lumping the sub-meanings indicated by the cliques may be a motivated choice. For example, *óriási* belongs to two different cliques characterized by plenty of nouns:

(7) Clique 1: *óriasi* 'huge', *nagy* 'great', *hatalmas* 'large'
Nouns: *mosoly* 'smile', *oroszlán* 'lion', *roham* 'attack', *piramis* 'piramid', etc.

Clique 2: *óriási* 'huge', *komoly* 'serious'
Nouns: *kaland* 'adventure', *konkurencia* 'concurrence', *kérdés* 'question', *lemaradás* 'lag', *marketing* 'marketing', *infláció* 'inflation', etc.

However, although *komoly* ('serious') cannot be used as a synonym of 'huge' before the elements of the first clique (eg. *komoly mosoly* 'a serious smile' $\neq$ *óriási mosoly* 'a huge smile' and *komoly oroszlán* 'a serious lion' $\neq$ *óriási oroszlán* 'a giant lion'), someone may claim that – in certain contexts at least – *óriási* and *komoly* conveys the same meaning at a certain level of abstraction. We confine ourselves only to make a notice on this phenomenon in the present paper and do not want to take a definite stance on this question.

5.2 Fine-grained evaluation of cliques

After excluding the irrelevant cases (cc. 240 adjectives altogether), a detailed evaluation took place aiming to create an adjectival database, where each sense is well-motivated and is characterized by the set of the context nouns. We also investigated whether these nouns can help humans to form concepts. For doing so, we went through on the resulting cliques manually. Maximum five context nouns were included into our database and we strove to select the salient context nouns for the given sense. We followed the procedure below:

1. The word2vec representations of the context nouns were used. They were generated as described in subsection 3.1.

2. The noun vectors were clustered using a hierarchic agglomerative algorithm to find subcategorization patterns.

For instance, we had *mindennapi* ('common') assigned to two cliques: dendograms in Figure 1 and Figure 2 depict the clusters of the context nouns. On the one hand, the respective near-synonyms are rather enlightening with regards to the two senses of the adjective, one of them being 'normal' or 'ordinary' while the other referring to regular, everyday activities. Based on the figures we can conclude that for example language-related things, such as *szóhasználat* ('word usage'), *nyelvhasználat* ('language use') are rather common or ordinary things than periodical ones; while *gyakorlás* ('practice') or *testmozgás* ('exercise') are regular, everyday activities and not necessarily common or ordinary ones. Therefore, the branches

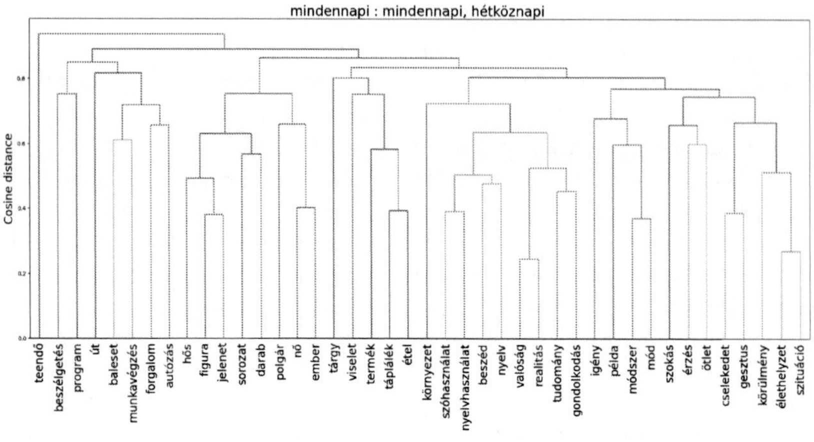

Figure 1: The clusters of the context nouns of the adjectival clique [*mindennapi* 'common', *hétköznapi* 'normal']

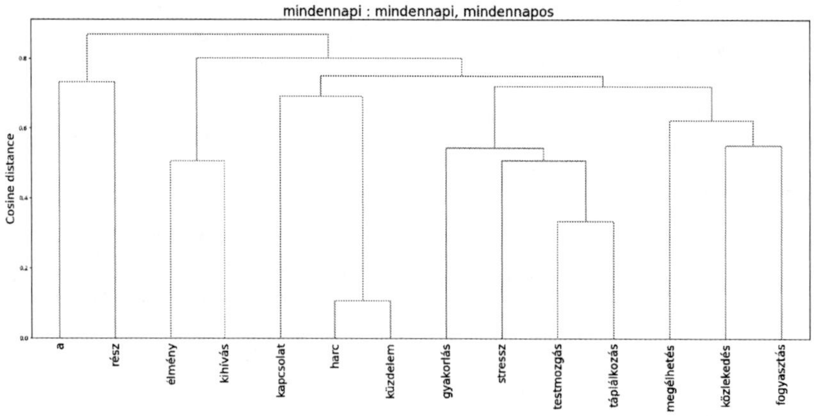

Figure 2: The clusters of the context nouns of the adjectival clique [*mindennapi* 'common', *mindennapos* 'everyday']

of the dendogram indicate the semantic classes of nouns the adjectival senses subcategorize.

As a result, out of the 446 adjectives with the given parameter setting, 53 adjectives were assigned to multiple cliques: to 118 cliques altogether. The list is available on GitHub: `https://github.com/nytud/HuWiC`. The qualitative evaluation yielded surprisingly insightful results in many cases, which may be not accessed with an introspective or even with a corpus-based methodology. Therefore, in spite of the low coverage we think that the research discussed here definitively worth pursuing in the future.

6 Conclusion and future work

The present paper describes an ongoing research, which intends to apply an unsupervised WSI approach to detect interpretable senses from monolingual corpora to contribute to the work of lexicographers, linguists and facilitate the creation of related benchmarks for the NLP community. For doing so, we came up with 4 necessary criteria to distinguish between senses, which were implemented in the next step. Finally, a detailed evaluation of the sense distinctions was performed yielding the conclusion that although the coverage definitively needs to be improved, in many cases the attained senses were surprisingly insightful supplying interpretable and intuitively not obvious sense distinction. However, during the evaluation it turned out that belonging to multiple near-synonymy classes is only a necessary but not sufficient condition for meaning discrimination, as adjectives may have collocate nouns or subcategorizate multiple sets of nouns in a single clique (see the case of *könnyű* 'easy' in subsection 4.2). Since this method does not rely on any external knowledge base, it should be suitable for any low- or medium-resourced language.

References

Arleta Adamska-Sałaciak. 2006. *Meaning and the Bilingual Dictionary. The Case of English and Polish. (Polish Studies in English Language and Literature 18)*. Peter Lang, Frankfurt am Main.

Julien Ah-Pine and Guillaume Jacquet. 2009. Clique-Based Clustering for Improving Named Entity Recognition Systems. In *Proceedings of the 12th Conference of the European Chapter of the ACL (EACL 2009)*, pages 51–59, Athens, Greece. Association for Computational Linguistics.

Asaf Amrami and Yoav Goldberg. 2019. Towards better substitution-based word sense induction. *ArXiv*, abs/1905.12598.

Marco Baroni, Georgiana Dinu, and Germán Kruszewski. 2014. Don't count, predict! a systematic comparison of context-counting vs. context-predicting semantic vectors. In *Proceedings of the 52nd Annual Meeting of the Association for Computational Linguistics (Volume 1: Long Papers)*, pages 238–247, Baltimore, Maryland. Association for Computational Linguistics.

Yoshua Bengio, Réjean Ducharme, Pascal Vincent, and Christian Janvin. 2003. A neural probabilistic language model. *J. Mach. Learn. Res.*, 3:1137–1155.

Jose Camacho-Collados and Mohammad Taher Pilehvar. 2018. From word to sense embeddings: A survey on vector representations of meaning.

Massimiliano Carrara and Pierdaniele Giaretta. 2004. The many facets of identity criteria. *Dialectica*, 58(2):221–232.

Stephen Clark. 2015. Vector space models of lexical meaning. In *The Handbook of Contemporary Semantic Theory*, chapter 16, pages 493–522. John Wiley & Sons, Ltd.

G. Frege. 1892. Uber Sinn und Bedeutung. In Mark Textor, editor, *Funktion - Begriff - Bedeutung*, volume 4 of *Sammlung Philosophie*. Vandenhoeck & Ruprecht, Göttingen.

Dirk Geeraerts. 2015. Lexical semantics. *International Encyclopedia of the Social & Behavioral Sciences*, pages 273–295.

Judit Kuti, Enikő Héja, and Bálint Sass. 2010. Sense disambiguation - 'Ambiguous sensation'? In *Proceedings of the Seventh Conference on International Language Resources and Evaluation (LREC 2010)*, page 23–30, la Valetta, Malta.

Márton Makrai. 2015. Comparison of distributed language models on medium-resourced languages. In *XI. Magyar Számítógépes Nyelvészeti Konferencia (MSZNY 2015)*.

Tomas Mikolov, Kai Chen, Greg Corrado, and Jeffrey Dean. 2013a. Efficient Estimation of Word Representations in Vector Space.

Tomas Mikolov, Ilya Sutskever, Kai Chen, G.s Corrado, and Jeffrey Dean. 2013b. Distributed Representations of Words and Phrases and their Compositionality. *Advances in Neural Information Processing Systems*, 26.

Dávid Márk Nemeskey. 2020. *Natural Language Processing Methods for Language Modeling*. Ph.D. thesis, Eötvös Loránd University.

Attila Novák and Borbála Novák. 2018. Pos, ana and lem: Word embeddings built from annotated corpora perform better. In *Computational Linguistics and Intelligent Text Processing: 17th International Conference, (CICLing 2018)*, Hanoi, Vietnam. Springer International Publishing, Cham.

Csaba Oravecz, Tamás Váradi, and Bálint Sass. 2014. The Hungarian Gigaword Corpus. In *Proceedings of the Ninth International Conference on Language Resources and Evaluation (LREC'14)*, pages 1719–1723, Reykjavik, Iceland. European Language Resources Association (ELRA).

Sabine Ploux and Bernard Victorri. 1998. Construction d'espaces sémantiques a l'aide de dictionnaires de synonymes. *Traitement automatique des langues*, 1(39):146–162.

James Pustejovsky. 1995. *The Generative Lexicon*. MIT Press, Cambridge, MA.

Radim Rehurek and Petr Sojka. 2011. Gensim–python framework for vector space modelling. *NLP Centre, Faculty of Informatics, Masaryk University, Brno, Czech Republic*, 3(2).

Peter D. Turney and Patrick Pantel. 2010. From frequency to meaning: Vector space models of semantics. *J. Artif. Int. Res.*, 37(1):141–188.

Alexander Veremyev, Alexander Semenov, Eduardo L. Pasiliao, and Vladimir Boginski. 2019. Graph-based exploration and clustering analysis of semantic spaces. *Applied Network Science*, 4:1–26.

Tamás Váradi. 2002. The Hungarian National Corpus. In *Proceedings of the Second International Conference on Language Resources and Evaluation, Las Palmas*, pages 385–389.

Jean Véronis. 2003. Sense tagging: does it make sense? In *Corpus Linguistics by the Lune: a festschrift for Geoffrey Leech*, Frankfurt. Peter Lang.

Gregor Wiedemann, Steffen Remus, Avi Chawla, and Chris Biemann. 2019. Does BERT make any sense? interpretable word sense disambiguation with contextualized embeddings. *CoRR*, abs/1909.10430.

GUSUM: Graph-Based Unsupervised Summarization using Sentence Features Scoring and Sentence-BERT

Tuba Gokhan, Phillip Smith and **Mark Lee**
School of Computer Science
University of Birmingham, United Kingdom
{txg857|smithpm|m.g.lee}@cs.bham.ac.uk

Abstract

Unsupervised extractive document summarization aims to extract salient sentences from a document without requiring a labelled corpus. In existing graph-based methods, vertex and edge weights are usually created by calculating sentence similarities. In this paper, we develop a Graph-Based Unsupervised Summarization(GUSUM) method for extractive text summarization based on the principle of including the most important sentences while excluding sentences with similar meanings in the summary. We modify traditional graph ranking algorithms with recent sentence embedding models and sentence features and modify how sentence centrality is computed. We first define the sentence feature scores represented at the vertices, indicating the importance of each sentence in the document. After this stage, we use Sentence-BERT for obtaining sentence embeddings to better capture the sentence meaning. In this way, we define the edges of a graph where semantic similarities are represented. Next we create an undirected graph that includes sentence significance and similarities between sentences. In the last stage, we determine the most important sentences in the document with the ranking method we suggested on the graph created. Experiments on CNN/Daily Mail, New York Times, arXiv, and PubMed datasets show our approach achieves high performance on unsupervised graph-based summarization when evaluated both automatically and by humans.

1 Introduction

Text summarization is the process of compressing a long text into a shorter version while preserving key information and significance of the content. Researchers have examined two summarization models as *extractive* and *abstractive* summarization (Nenkova et al., 2011). Extractive summarization creates summaries by extracting text from source documents, whereas abstractive summarization rewrites documents by paraphrasing or deleting some words or phrases.

Modern text summarization approaches focus on supervised neural networks, which adapt sequence-to-sequence translation, reinforcement learning and large-scale pre-training techniques. These approaches have accomplished favourable results thanks to the availability of large-scale datasets (Nallapati et al., 2016; Cheng and Lapata, 2016; Gehrmann et al., 2018; Liu and Lapata, 2019; Wang et al., 2020). Nevertheless, a major limitation of those supervised methods is that their success is strongly reliant on the availability of large training corpora with human-generated high-quality summaries which are both expensive to produce and difficult to obtain. We focus on unsupervised summarization in this study, where we simply need unlabeled documents.

The fundamental issue with unsupervised summarizing is determining which sentences in a document are important. Graph-based algorithms, in which each vertex is a sentence and the weights of the edges are measured by sentence similarity, are the most prevalent approaches among these studies. The relevance of each sentence is then estimated using a graph ranking approach. A vertex's *centrality* is often measured using graph-based ranking algorithms such as PageRank (Brin and Page, 1998) to decide which sentence to include in the summary.

We observe that the importance of the sentences in the document should be emphasized in addition to the semantic similarity of the sentences in the summary. Accordingly, we suggest in this study that the centrality measure can be enhanced in two significant ways. First, we define an initial score that specifies the importance of the sentence that each vertex represents. Second, we use Sentence-BERT (Reimers and Gurevych, 2019) which is a modification of the pre-trained BERT network (Devlin et al., 2019) that uses Siamese and triplet network structures to derive semantically meaningful sentence embeddings to better capture the sentence

Proceedings of TextGraphs-16: Graph-based Methods for Natural Language Processing, pages 44–53
October 16, 2022.

meaning and calculate sentence similarity.

In this paper, we propose a novel approach, GUSUM (as shorthand for **G**raph-Based **U**nsupervised **Sum**marization) which is a simple and powerful approach to improving graph-based unsupervised extractive text summarization. We evaluate the GUSUM on the CNN/Daily Mail and New York Times short document summarization datasets and arXiv and PubMed long document summarization datasets. For graph-based summarization tasks, pre-trained embeddings are generally used only for measuring sentence similarities in graph-based summarization systems. However, this situation causes the importance of the sentences in the document to be ignored. In our approach, we applied a ranking method that combines sentence similarities and sentence features to calculate sentence centrality. Our experiments show that better results are obtained by creating weighted graphs in which the main features of the sentence are represented in the ordering stage based on sentence centrality. Our code is available at `https://github.com/tubagokhan/GUSUM`

2 Related Work

The proposed method is based on graph-based, unsupervised extractive text summarization techniques. In this section, we introduce work on graph-based summarization, unsupervised summarization and pre-training.

2.1 Graph-Based Unsupervised Summarization

The majority of summarization methods rely on labeled datasets containing documents that match pre-prepared summaries. Compared to supervised models, unsupervised models only need unlabeled documents during training. Most unsupervised extractive models are graph-based (Carbonell and Goldstein, 1998; Erkan and Radev, 2004; Mihalcea and Tarau, 2004; Zheng and Lapata, 2019; Xu et al., 2020; Liang et al., 2021; Liu et al., 2021). Among the representative examples of early work in inferential summarization, the study by Carbonell and Goldstein (1998) includes the Maximum-Marginal Relevance (MMR) principle of selecting sentences based on both the relevance and diversity of the selected sentences and the PageRank (Brin and Page, 1998) scores of the sentences in sentence similarity graphs. TEXTRANK (Mihalcea and Tarau, 2004) interprets sentences in a document as nodes in an undirected graph, with edge weights based on sentence occurrence similarity. The final ranking scores for sentences are then determined using graph-based ranking algorithms such as PageRank. Similarly, Erkan and Radev (2004) provided extractive summaries by scoring sentences with the LEXRANK approach, they calculated the importance of sentences in representative graphs based on the measurement of eigenvector centrality.

Recently, researchers have continued to develop graph-based methods. Zheng and Lapata (2019) created a directed graph using BERT (Devlin et al., 2019) to calculate sentence similarities. The importance score of a sentence is the weighted sum of all its outer edges, where weights for edges between the current sentence and preceding sentences are negative. In the directed graph that Zheng and Lapata (2019) created, the edges represent the relative position of the sentences in the document. In our study, we represented sentence similarities at the edges from a completely different point of view. We also showed vertexes by blending the features of the sentences such as the position of the sentence. Thus, we created graphs that provide greater semantic integrity. Xu et al. (2020) design two summarization tasks related to pre-training tasks to improve sentence representation. Then they proposed a rank method that combines attention weight with reconstruction loss to measure the centrality of sentences. Liang et al. (2021) proposed a facet-sensitive centrality-based model. It aims to measure the relationship between the summary and the document by calculating a similarity score between the summary sentences and the document for each candidate summary. Liu et al. (2021) published a graph-based single-document unsupervised extractive method that constructs a Distance-Augmented Sentence Graph from a document that enables the model to perform more fine-grained modeling of sentences and better characterize the original document structures.

2.2 Pre-trained Language Models

Pre-trained language models have been shown to make significant progress in a variety of NLP tasks. These models are based on the concept of word embeddings (Pennington et al., 2014), but they go even further by pre-training a sentence encoder on a large unlabeled corpus. Bidirectional Encoder Representations from Transformers (BERT) (Devlin et al., 2019), one of the state-of-art language

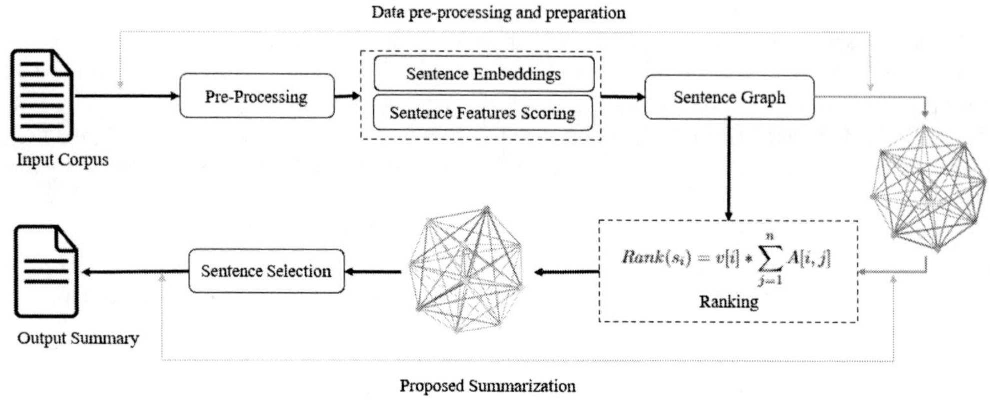

Figure 1: The complete pipeline of the proposed method.

models, is trained with a masked language model and a next-sentence-predicting task. Pre-trained language models have recently become popular for improving performance in language comprehension tasks. Recent research (Liu and Lapata, 2019; Bae et al., 2019) has shown that using pre-trained language models to extractive summarization models, such as BERT, is quite advantageous. As for the extractive summarization task, it provides the powerful sentence embeddings and the contextualized information among sentences (Zhong et al., 2019), which have been proven to be critical to extractive summarization.

3 Methodology

In this section, we describe our unsupervised summarization method GUSUM. The system is composed of four main steps: first, we calculate sentence features for defining vertex weight; second, we produce sentence embeddings by Sentence-BERT to measure sentence similarities; next, we create a graph by comparing all the pairs of sentence embeddings obtained; finally, we rank the sentences by their degree centrality in this graph. Figure 1 gives an overview of the whole proposed method.

3.1 Computing Sentence Features

In traditional embedding-based systems, sentence features are transformed into dense vector representation. These features are attributes that attempt to represent the data used for their task (Suanmali et al., 2009).

Unlike traditional methods, GUSUM uses sentence features to determine the initial rank of the vertex in the generated graphs rather than vectorizing them. GUSUM focuses on four features for each sentence based on Shirwandhar and Kulkarni (2018). After the scores for each sentence were determined, the sum of the scores was assigned by taking the weight of the vertex representing the sentence.

Sentence length: This feature is useful for filtering out short phrases commonly found in news articles, such as dates and author names. Short sentences do not contain much information and are not expected to belong to the summary. To find the important sentence based on its length, the feature score is calculated using 1:

$$Score_{f1}(S_i) = \frac{No.\,Word\,in\,S_i}{No.Word\,in\,Longest\,Sentence} \quad (1)$$

Sentence position: On the basis of sentence position, its relevance is known. The first and the last sentence of a document are typically important and involve maximum information. Position feature is calculated using 2:

$$Score_{f2}(S_i) = \begin{cases} 1 & if\,the\,first\,or\,last\,sentence \\ \frac{N-P}{N} & if\,others \end{cases} \quad (2)$$

where, N is the total number of sentences and P is the position of the sentence.

Proper nouns: Usually, the sentence that contains more proper nouns is an important one and it is most probably included in the document summary. The score for this feature is calculated as the ratio of the number of proper nouns in a sentence over the sentence length using a POS tagger as in 3.

$$Score_{f3}(S_i) = \frac{No.\,Proper\,Noun\,in\,S_i}{Length\,S_i} \quad (3)$$

Numerical token: The number of numerical tokens that present in the sentence is another feature that shows the importance of the sentence in the document and is calculated with 4:

$$Score_{f4}(S_i) = \frac{num\_numeric_i}{Length\ S_i} \quad (4)$$

where, $num\_numeric_i$ is the total number of numerical tokens in sentence i.

3.2 Computing Sentence Embeddings

The first step in our pipeline is to generate a list of sentences from the compilation text. After extracting the sentences, the next step is to produce the sentence embedding of each sentence using Sentence-BERT (Reimers and Gurevych, 2019). Sentence-BERT is a modification of the pre-trained BERT (Devlin et al., 2019) network that uses Siamese and triplet network structures to derive semantically meaningful sentence embeddings that can be compared using vector similarity methods.

The proposed approach uses Sentence-BERT[1] embeddings to represent sentences as fixed-size vectors. Thus, all sentences and the source is mapped in the same semantic space and taken as inputs to the system.

3.3 Generation of the Sentence Graph

In our unsupervised graph-based extractive summarization approach, the document is represented as a graph, where each node represents a sentence in the input document.

Given a document D, it contains a set of sentences $(s_1, s_2, ..., s_n)$. Graph-based algorithms treats D as a graph $G = (V; E)$. $V = (v_1, v_2, ..., v_n)$ is the vertex set where v_i is the representation of sentence s_i. E is the edge set, which is an $n \times n$ matrix. Each $= e_{i,j} \in E$ denotes the weight between vertex v_i and v_j.

In graph-based summarization methods, centrality is used to select the most salient sentence to construct summaries through ranking. Centrality of a node measures its importance within a graph. The key idea of graph-based ranking is to calculate the centrality score of each sentence (or vertex). Traditionally, this score is measured by ranking algorithms (Mihalcea and Tarau, 2004; Erkan and Radev, 2004) based on PageRank (Brin and Page, 1998). The sentences with the top score are extracted as a summary. The undirected graph algorithm computes the sentence centrality score as follows:

$$Centrality(s_i) = \sum_{j=1}^{N} e_{ji} \quad (5)$$

After obtaining the centrality score for each sentence, sentences are sorted in reverse order and the top ranked are included in the summary. GUSUM includes the vertex weights of the sentence graph in the calculation of the centrality. Thus, as a first step, the initial rank values of the sentence graph are determined.

The second step to build the sentence graph is to generate the edges that represent semantic sentence similarities. Cosine similarity can be used as a measure to find similarity between sentences of the graph. In this step, all the pairwise Cosine similarities are gathered in a matrix. Cosine similarity is defined as:

$$Cosine\ Similarity = \frac{\sum_{i=1}^{N} A_i B_i}{\sqrt{\sum_{i=1}^{N} \mathrm{A}_i^2}\sqrt{\sum_{i=1}^{N} \mathrm{B}_i^2}} \quad (6)$$

(where A_i and B_i are the components of vector A and B respectively)

Let $D = (s_1; s_2; ...; s_n)$ be a document. We produced using sentence feature scores, $V = (v_1, v_2, ..., v_n)$ is the vertex set where v_i is the representation of sentence s_i. $(e_1; e_2; ...; e_n)$ is a set of vectors , where e_i is the sentence embedding of s_i. Its edges are weighted according to the cosine similarities of the corresponding sentence embeddings. Next, we compute the matrix A with 7:

$$A[i, j] = Cosine\ Similarity(e_i; e_j) \quad (7)$$

Thus, matrix A can be interpreted as the adjacency matrix of an undirected weighted complete graph.

3.4 Ranking and Summary Selection

We propose a variation of weighted undirected graph-based ranking in this section. Based on the idea that the most important sentence in a document is the sentence most similar to all other sentences according to the similarity metric, we modify Equation 5 to include the vertex weights. As a consequence, we define the importance rank for each sentence as follows:

$$Rank(s_i) = v[i] * \sum_{j=1}^{n} A[i, j] \quad (8)$$

where v is the corresponding feature score for s_i, e_i and e_j are the corresponding Sentence-BERT sentence embedding for s_i and s_j .

[1] https://www.sbert.net/

We finally rank and select sentences with Equation 9. The number of sentences in the summary is represented by the k value.

$$summary = topK(\{Rank_{(si)})\}_{i=1,\dots,n} \quad (9)$$

where the top-ranked k sentences will be extracted as summary.

Datasets	#docs	avg. doc. length (word)	avg. doc. length (sent.)	avg. sum. length (word)	avg. sum. length (sent.)
CNN/DM	11490	773.22	33.36	57.75	3.79
NYT	6508	1109.10	32.17	96.31	1.18
PubMed	6658	3142.92	101.60	208.02	7.58
arXiv	6440	6446.10	250.36	166.72	6.22

Table 1: Statistic of our CNN/DM , NYT, PubMed and arXiv datasets

4 Experimental Setup

In this section we assess the performance of GUSUM on the document summarization task. We first introduce the datasets that we used, then give our pre-processing and implementation details.

4.1 Summarization Datasets

CNN/DM dataset contains 93k articles from CNN, and 220k articles from Daily Mail newspapers, which uses their associated highlights as reference summaries (Hermann et al., 2015). We use the test set which includes 11490 documents provided by hugging face version 3.0.0[2] (See et al., 2017).

NYT dataset contains over 1.8 million articles written and published by the New York Times between January 1, 1987 and June 19, 2007 and summaries are written by library scientists. Different from CNN/DM, salient sentences are distributed evenly in each article. We use The New York Times Annotated Corpus provided by the Linguistic Data Consortium[3] (Sandhaus, 2008). We filter out documents whose summaries are between January 1, 2007 and June 19, 2007 and documents whose length of summaries are shorter than 50 tokens and finally retain 6508 documents (Zheng and Lapata, 2019) .

PubMed & arXiv datasets are two long documents datasets of scientific papers. The datasets are obtained from arXiv and PubMed OpenAccess repositories. The summaries are created from the documents. PubMed contains 215k and arXiv contains 113k documents. We use test sets which includes 6658 documents for PubMed and 6440 documents for arXiv provided by hugging face[4].

4.2 Implementation Details

In GUSUM, during the pre-processing stage, NLTK (Natural Language Toolkit)(Bird and Loper, 2004) was used to collect corpus statistics and process documents using methods such as sentence segmentation, word tokenization, Part of Speech (POS) tagging and using regular expressions to remove parenthesis and some characters.

In the process of creating the graph, we first applied Equations 1, 2, 3 and 4 to calculate sentence feature scores and defined the sums of the obtained values as vertex weights. Next, we calculated the edge weights representing the sentence similarities. For each dataset, we used the publicly released Sentence-BERT model *roberta-base-nli-stsb-mean-tokens* [5] to initialize our sentence embeddings. The *bert-base-nli-mean-tokens*[6] model was also tested in our experiments. However, the *roberta-base-nli-stsb-mean-tokens* showed slightly higher performance (see Table 6). Alternative models that can be applied in our method are listed on Github[7]. In this manner, the model maps sentences and paragraphs to a 768-dimensional dense vector space.

In our experiments, Cosine distance and Euclidean distance were tested to measure the distances between sentence embedding vectors. However, it was observed that higher performance was obtained with the Cosine similarity (see Equation 6) method of Sentence-BERT (see Table 6). The scores obtained as a result of similarity measure were assigned as the edge weight of the graph.

In the last stage, we ranked the sentences using Equation 5 and determined the three most important sentences that should be included in the summary. Table 2 presents a sample golden reference summary and the summary created by GUSUM.

[2] https://huggingface.co/datasets/cnn_dailymail

[3] https://catalog.ldc.upenn.edu/LDC2008T19

[4] https://www.tensorflow.org/datasets/catalog/scientific_papers

[5] https://huggingface.co/sentence-transformers/roberta-base-nli-stsb-mean-tokens

[6] https://huggingface.co/sentence-transformers/bert-base-nli-mean-tokens

[7] https://github.com/tubagokhan/GUSUM/blob/main/QAforHumanEvaluation.json

Gold-standard Reference
Food and Drug Administration has not found rat poison in pet food that has been killing cats and dogs, but it has found melamine, chemical commonly used to make plastic cutlery that is also used in fertilizer. Mationwide pet food recall , which has involved wet foods all manufactured by Menu Foods and sold under variety of brand names is expanded to include one brand of dry cat food made by Hills Pet Nutrition. brand was found to have been made with batch of wheat gluten shipped to US from China that FDA says was laced with melamine
GUSUM
The Food and Drug Administration said yesterday that it had not found rat poison in pet food that has been killing animals, but that it had found melamine, a chemical commonly used to make plastic cutlery that is also used in fertilizer. Scientists found melamine, which is used as a slow-release fertilizer in Asia, in the urine of cats sickened by the recalled pet foods made by Menu Foods, officials said at a news conference. The recalled pet food has been blamed for at least 16 deaths of pets. Additionally, F. D. A. officials said that they did not believe the contaminated wheat gluten had entered the human food supply, but that they were testing all wheat gluten imported from China for melamine.

Table 2: An example summary generated by GUSUM compared with gold-standard summary

5 Results

5.1 Automated evaluation

ROUGE (Lin and Hovy, 2003) was used to assess the quality of summaries from different models. We report the full length F1 based ROUGE-1, ROUGE-2, ROUGE-L on both CNN/DM, NYT, PubMed and arXiv datasets. The py-rouge package[8] is used to calculate these ROUGE scores.

Table 3 and Table 4 summarize our results on the CNN/DM and NYT short document dataset and arXiv and PubMed long document datasets respectively. The first blocks present the results of strong unsupervised baselines LEAD-3, TEXTRANK (Mihalcea and Tarau, 2004)), LEXRANK (Erkan and Radev, 2004) previous unsupervised graph-based methods. LEAD-3 simply selects the first three sentences as the summary for each document. TEXTRANK (Mihalcea and Tarau, 2004) displays a document as a graph with sentences as nodes and edge weights using sentence similarity and bases PageRank (Brin and Page, 1998) when selecting the best scores. LEXRANK (Erkan and Radev, 2004) also calculates the significance of sentences in representative graphs based on a measure of eigenvector centrality (based on node centrality). The second blocks shows recent supervised methods. For supervised extractive models, we compare with PTR-GEN (See et al., 2017), REFRESH (Narayan et al., 2018a), BertEx (Liu and Lapata, 2019) , Discourse-aware (Cohan et al., 2018), SummaRuNNer (Nallapati et al., 2017) and GlobalLocalCont (Xiao and Carenini, 2019). The third blocks includes recent state-of-the-art unsupervised graph-based methods for document summarization. PACSUM (Zheng and Lapata, 2019), FAR (Liang et al., 2021), STAS (Xu et al., 2020) and Liu et al. (2021) are detailed in Section 2. The last blocks in Table 3 and Table 4 reports results of our method, GUSUM.

As can be seen in Table 3, GUSUM achieves the highest ROUGE F1 score, compared to all other graph-based unsupervised methods on both CNN/DM and NYT datasets. From the results, we can see that our method outperforms all strong baselines in the first block. Furthermore, our method achieves better results than PACSUM and FAR on both datasets. When we compare our method with STAS, our method produces better results, except for the F-1 R-2 metric on CNN/DM. The success of GUSUM can be seen when the latest state-of-the-art unsupervised graph-based method by Liu et al. (2021) and GUSUM is compared. Moreover, it is seen in Table 4, GUSUM also performed very well on arXiv and PubMed long document datasets. Especially F1 R-L provides very high results compared to all other studies.

5.2 Human evaluation

In addition to the Rouge metric, we also evaluated the system output via human judgments. In the experiment, we evaluated the extent to which our approach retained important information in the document, following a question-answer (QA) paradigm used to evaluate the summary quality and text compression (Narayan et al., 2018b).

We created a set of questions based on the assumption that gold-standard summaries highlight the most important content of the document. Then, we examined whether participants could answer these questions simply by reading the system summaries without accessing the article. We created 71 questions from 20 randomly selected documents for the CNN/DM datasets and 59 questions from 18 randomly selected documents for the NYT dataset. We wrote multiple fact-based question-answer

[8] https://pypi.org/project/py-rouge/

Method	CNN/DM R-1	CNN/DM R-2	CNN/DM R-L	NYT R-1	NYT R-2	NYT R-L
LEAD-3	40.49	17.66	36.75	35.50	17.20	32.00
TEXTRANK (Mihalcea and Tarau, 2004)	33.85	13.61	30.14	33.24	14.74	29.92
LEXRANK (Erkan and Radev, 2004)	34.68	12.82	31.12	30.75	10.49	26.58
PTR-GEN (See et al., 2017)	39.50	17.30	36.40	42.70	**22.10**	38.00
REFRESH (Narayan et al., 2018a)	41.30	18.40	35.70	41.30	22.00	37.80
BertExt (Liu and Lapata, 2019)	43.25	**20.24**	39.63	-	-	-
PACSUM (Zheng and Lapata, 2019)	40.70	17.80	36.90	41.40	21.70	37.50
FAR (Liang et al., 2021)	40.83	17.85	36.91	41.61	21.88	37.59
STAS (Xu et al., 2020)	40.90	18.02	37.21	41.46	21.80	37.57
Liu et al. (Liu et al., 2021)	41.60	18.50	37.80	42.20	21.80	**38.20**
GUSUM	**43.40**	17.02	**42.38**	**43.64**	22.01	37.90

Table 3: Test set results on the CNN/DM and NYT datasets using ROUGE F1. Results are taken from (Liang et al., 2021)

Method	arXiv R-1	arXiv R-2	arXiv R-L	PubMed R-1	PubMed R-2	PubMed R-L
LEAD-3	33.66	8.94	22.19	35.63	12.28	25.17
TEXTRANK (Mihalcea and Tarau, 2004)	24.38	10.57	22.18	38.66	15.87	34.53
LEXRANK (Erkan and Radev, 2004)	33.85	10.73	28.99	39.19	13.89	34.59
PTR-GEN (See et al., 2017)	32.06	9.04	25.16	35.86	10.22	29.69
Discourse-aware (Cohan et al., 2018)	35.80	11.05	31.80	38.93	15.37	35.21
SummaRuNNer (Nallapati et al., 2017)	42.81	16.52	28.23	43.89	18.78	30.36
GlobalLocalCont (Xiao and Carenini, 2019)	**43.62**	**17.36**	29.14	44.85	**19.70**	31.43
PACSUM (Zheng and Lapata, 2019)	39.33	12.19	34.18	39.79	14.00	36.09
FAR (Liang et al., 2021)	40.92	13.75	35.56	41.98	15.66	37.58
GUSUM	40.98	11.76	**39.49**	**44.98**	16.26	**43.98**

Table 4: Test set results on the arXiv and PubMed datasets using ROUGE F1.Results are taken from (Liang et al., 2021)

Method	CNN/DM Score	CNN/DM %	NYT Score	NYT %
LEAD-3	54.75	77.11	42.00	71.19
TEXTRANK	56.38	79.40	39.50	66.95
GUSUM	**57.00**	**80.28**	**46.25**	**78.39**

Table 5: Results of QA-based evaluation on CNN/DM, NYT. We compute a system's final score as the average of all question scores.

pairs for each gold summary. Our Question and Answer set is available at `https://github.com/tubagokhan/GUSUM/blob/main/QAforHumanEvaluation.json`.

We compared GUSUM against LEAD-3 and TEXTRANK on CNN/DM and NYT. We used the same scoring mechanism from Ziheng and Lapata (2019), a correct answer was marked with a score of one, partially correct answers with a score of 0.5, and zero otherwise. The final score for a system is the average of all its question scores. Four fluent English speakers answered the questions for each summary. The participants were chosen from university volunteers who gave their consent to contribute to the study.

The results of our QA evaluation are shown in Table 5. Based on summaries generated by LEAD-3 participants can answer 77.11% and 71.19% respectively CNN/DM and NYT of questions correctly. Summaries produced by TEXTRANK have 79.40% and 66.95% scores. When the scores of GUSUM are compared with the scores of the other two systems, the high performance of GUSUM is seen. The main reason for GUSUM's slightly higher performance in CNN/DM dataset compared to NYT is thought to be the use of human-generated gold summaries in NYT. Another possibility is that the summaries created from the CNN/DM dataset are shorter and users can focus more. It is thought that the participants have a leaning to become distracted with the longer summaries in the NYT dataset compared to CNN/DM.

5.3 Ablation Study

In order to access the contribution of three components of GUSUM, we remove or change each component of them and report ablation study results in Table 6. Since short and long documents have different structures, separate experiments are carried out. In Table 6, the results of the NYT dataset in the first block and the PubMed dataset in the second block are presented.

NYT			
	R-1	R-2	R-L
GUSUM	**43.64**	**22.01**	**37.90**
-Removed All Sentence Features	36.63	14.91	30.58
-bert-base-nli-mean-tokens	43.28	21.73	37.48
-Eucludian Distance	35.35	16.43	31.10
PubMed			
GUSUM	**44.98**	**16.26**	**43.98**
-Removed All Sentence Features	44.08	15.53	43.32
-bert-base-nli-mean-tokens	44.27	15.66	43.36
-Eucludian Distance	37.77	11.29	37.40

Table 6: Ablation study results on NYT and PubMed datasets using ROUGE F1.

We can observe that sentence feature scoring is critical to GUSUM's performance, mainly on NYT. When all sentence features are eliminated, the performance of GUSUM drops sharply. In another experiment, we replaced the *roberta-base-nli-stsb-mean-tokens* model with the *bert-base-nli-mean-tokens* model in both datasets and discovered just a minor difference in performance. In our last experiment, we changed the method of measuring the similarity of sentence embeddings to generate the graph. When we employ the Euclidean method, there is a dramatic decrease in the performance of GUSUM.

6 Discussion

There are two basic stages in document summarization: (1) Identification of the most salient sentences in the document, (2) Removal of similar sentences from the summary. Generally in graph-based approaches, graphs are created based on only sentence similarity, and then the most salient sentences are selected. On the contrary, in GUSUM we included these two basic steps in our approach. Along with the semantic similarity, we also embedded the attributes of the sentences in our graph. Furthermore, GUSUM advocates the idea that the most important sentence in a document is the sentence most similar to the others. For this reason, the total similarity value for each sentence is evaluated in the ranking stage. The experimental results of GUSUM, which is a simple and effective method based on these ideas, prove the validity of our ideas.

As seen in the experimental results, GUSUM showed high performance on all datasets. However, the limitation of GUSUM is that sentence features scoring does not have a significant impact on long documents as can be see in Table 6. The main reason for this situation is that the ranking algorithm we use in long documents produces results that are very close to each other. Therefore, we argue that for long documents, sentence feature scores should be enriched by including thematic word, sentence centrality, title similarity, the similarity to the first sentence, cue-phrases, term weight scores, etc. Moreover, adding section segmentation for long document summarization can significantly improve performance.

The most difficult part of this study is the evaluation stage. Evaluating the performance of summarization systems poses a problem for many researchers (Schluter, 2017). It is a known fact by researchers that human evaluation is the best summary performance evaluation method. For this reason, we included human evaluation as a performance evaluation method in our study. However, what we noticed in our study is that the questions used for human evaluation based on the QA paradigm in other studies published to date have not been shared by the researchers. As a result of this situation, researchers prepare their own questions and the results cannot be compared with the literature. As a solution to this problem, we publish the questions and answers that we prepared from the CNN/DM and NYT datasets based on the QA paradigm for use in future studies (See 5.2).

7 Conclusions and Future Works

In this paper, we have proposed a graph-based single-document unsupervised extractive summarization method. We revisited traditional graph-based ranking algorithms and refined how sentence centrality is computed. We defined values indicating the importance of the sentences in the document for the node weights in the graphs and we built graphs with undirected edges by employing Sentence-BERT to better capture sentence similarity. Experimental results on four summarization benchmark datasets demonstrated that our method outperforms other recently proposed extractive graph-based unsupervised methods and achieves performance comparable to many state-of-the-art supervised approaches which shows the effectiveness of our method.

In the future, we would like to remove the limitations that would increase the performance of GUSUM in long document summarization with the ideas introduced in this study and explore the performance of GUSUM in multi-document summarization.

References

Sanghwan Bae, Taeuk Kim, Jihoon Kim, and Sanggoo Lee. 2019. Summary level training of sentence rewriting for abstractive summarization. In *Proceedings of the 2nd Workshop on New Frontiers in Summarization*, pages 10–20, Hong Kong, China. Association for Computational Linguistics.

Steven Bird and Edward Loper. 2004. NLTK: The natural language toolkit. In *Proceedings of the ACL Interactive Poster and Demonstration Sessions*, pages 214–217, Barcelona, Spain. Association for Computational Linguistics.

Sergey Brin and Lawrence Page. 1998. The anatomy of a large-scale hypertextual web search engine. *Computer Networks and ISDN Systems*, 30(1):107–117. Proceedings of the Seventh International World Wide Web Conference.

Jaime Carbonell and Jade Goldstein. 1998. The use of mmr, diversity-based reranking for reordering documents and producing summaries. In *Proceedings of the 21st Annual International ACM SIGIR Conference on Research and Development in Information Retrieval*, SIGIR '98, page 335–336, New York, NY, USA. Association for Computing Machinery.

Jianpeng Cheng and Mirella Lapata. 2016. Neural summarization by extracting sentences and words. In *Proceedings of the 54th Annual Meeting of the Association for Computational Linguistics (Volume 1: Long Papers)*, pages 484–494, Berlin, Germany. Association for Computational Linguistics.

Arman Cohan, Franck Dernoncourt, Doo Soon Kim, Trung Bui, Seokhwan Kim, Walter Chang, and Nazli Goharian. 2018. A discourse-aware attention model for abstractive summarization of long documents. In *Proceedings of the 2018 Conference of the North American Chapter of the Association for Computational Linguistics: Human Language Technologies, Volume 2 (Short Papers)*, pages 615–621, New Orleans, Louisiana. Association for Computational Linguistics.

Jacob Devlin, Ming-Wei Chang, Kenton Lee, and Kristina Toutanova. 2019. BERT: Pre-training of deep bidirectional transformers for language understanding. In *Proceedings of the 2019 Conference of the North American Chapter of the Association for Computational Linguistics: Human Language Technologies, Volume 1 (Long and Short Papers)*, pages 4171–4186, Minneapolis, Minnesota. Association for Computational Linguistics.

Günes Erkan and Dragomir R. Radev. 2004. Lexrank: Graph-based lexical centrality as salience in text summarization. *Journal Of Artificial Intelligence Research*, 22(1):457–479.

Sebastian Gehrmann, Yuntian Deng, and Alexander Rush. 2018. Bottom-up abstractive summarization. In *Proceedings of the 2018 Conference on Empirical Methods in Natural Language Processing*, pages 4098–4109, Brussels, Belgium. Association for Computational Linguistics.

Karl Moritz Hermann, Tomáš Kočiský, Edward Grefenstette, Lasse Espeholt, Will Kay, Mustafa Suleyman, and Phil Blunsom. 2015. Teaching machines to read and comprehend. In *Proceedings of the 28th International Conference on Neural Information Processing Systems - Volume 1*, NIPS'15, page 1693–1701, Cambridge, MA, USA. MIT Press.

Xinnian Liang, Shuangzhi Wu, Mu Li, and Zhoujun Li. 2021. Improving unsupervised extractive summarization with facet-aware modeling. In *Findings of the Association for Computational Linguistics: ACL-IJCNLP 2021*, pages 1685–1697, Online. Association for Computational Linguistics.

Chin-Yew Lin and Eduard Hovy. 2003. Automatic evaluation of summaries using n-gram co-occurrence statistics. In *Proceedings of the 2003 Human Language Technology Conference of the North American Chapter of the Association for Computational Linguistics*, pages 150–157.

Jingzhou Liu, Dominic J. D. Hughes, and Yiming Yang. 2021. *Unsupervised Extractive Text Summarization with Distance-Augmented Sentence Graphs*, page 2313–2317. Association for Computing Machinery, New York, NY, USA.

Yang Liu and Mirella Lapata. 2019. Text summarization with pretrained encoders. In *Proceedings of the 2019 Conference on Empirical Methods in Natural Language Processing and the 9th International Joint Conference on Natural Language Processing (EMNLP-IJCNLP)*, pages 3730–3740, Hong Kong, China. Association for Computational Linguistics.

Rada Mihalcea and Paul Tarau. 2004. TextRank: Bringing order into text. In *Proceedings of the 2004 Conference on Empirical Methods in Natural Language Processing*, pages 404–411, Barcelona, Spain. Association for Computational Linguistics.

Ramesh Nallapati, Feifei Zhai, and Bowen Zhou. 2017. Summarunner: A recurrent neural network based sequence model for extractive summarization of documents. In *Proceedings of the Thirty-First AAAI Conference on Artificial Intelligence*, AAAI'17, page 3075–3081. AAAI Press.

Ramesh Nallapati, Bowen Zhou, Cicero dos Santos, Çağlar Gulçehre, and Bing Xiang. 2016. Abstractive text summarization using sequence-to-sequence RNNs and beyond. In *Proceedings of The 20th SIGNLL Conference on Computational Natural Language Learning*, pages 280–290, Berlin, Germany. Association for Computational Linguistics.

Shashi Narayan, Shay B. Cohen, and Mirella Lapata. 2018a. Ranking sentences for extractive summarization with reinforcement learning. In *Proceedings of the 2018 Conference of the North American Chapter of the Association for Computational Linguistics:*

Human Language Technologies, Volume 1 (Long Papers), pages 1747–1759, New Orleans, Louisiana. Association for Computational Linguistics.

Shashi Narayan, Shay B. Cohen, and Mirella Lapata. 2018b. Ranking sentences for extractive summarization with reinforcement learning. In *Proceedings of the 2018 Conference of the North American Chapter of the Association for Computational Linguistics: Human Language Technologies, Volume 1 (Long Papers)*, pages 1747–1759, New Orleans, Louisiana. Association for Computational Linguistics.

Ani Nenkova, Sameer Maskey, and Yang Liu. 2011. Automatic summarization. In *Proceedings of the 49th Annual Meeting of the Association for Computational Linguistics: Tutorial Abstracts*, page 3, Portland, Oregon. Association for Computational Linguistics.

Jeffrey Pennington, Richard Socher, and Christopher Manning. 2014. GloVe: Global vectors for word representation. In *Proceedings of the 2014 Conference on Empirical Methods in Natural Language Processing (EMNLP)*, pages 1532–1543, Doha, Qatar. Association for Computational Linguistics.

Nils Reimers and Iryna Gurevych. 2019. Sentence-BERT: Sentence embeddings using Siamese BERT-networks. In *Proceedings of the 2019 Conference on Empirical Methods in Natural Language Processing and the 9th International Joint Conference on Natural Language Processing (EMNLP-IJCNLP)*, pages 3982–3992, Hong Kong, China. Association for Computational Linguistics.

Evan Sandhaus. 2008. The New York times annotated corpus ldc2008t19. *Linguistic Data Consortium, Philadelphia*.

Natalie Schluter. 2017. The limits of automatic summarisation according to ROUGE. In *Proceedings of the 15th Conference of the European Chapter of the Association for Computational Linguistics: Volume 2, Short Papers*, pages 41–45, Valencia, Spain. Association for Computational Linguistics.

Abigail See, Peter J. Liu, and Christopher D. Manning. 2017. Get to the point: Summarization with pointer-generator networks. In *Proceedings of the 55th Annual Meeting of the Association for Computational Linguistics (Volume 1: Long Papers)*, pages 1073–1083, Vancouver, Canada. Association for Computational Linguistics.

Nikhil S. Shirwandkar and Samidha Kulkarni. 2018. Extractive text summarization using deep learning. In *2018 Fourth International Conference on Computing Communication Control and Automation (ICCUBEA)*, pages 1–5.

Ladda Suanmali, Mohammed Salem Binwahlan, and Naomie Salim. 2009. Sentence features fusion for text summarization using fuzzy logic. In *2009 Ninth International Conference on Hybrid Intelligent Systems*, volume 1, pages 142–146.

Danqing Wang, Pengfei Liu, Yining Zheng, Xipeng Qiu, and Xuanjing Huang. 2020. Heterogeneous graph neural networks for extractive document summarization. In *Proceedings of the 58th Annual Meeting of the Association for Computational Linguistics*, pages 6209–6219, Online. Association for Computational Linguistics.

Wen Xiao and Giuseppe Carenini. 2019. Extractive summarization of long documents by combining global and local context. In *Proceedings of the 2019 Conference on Empirical Methods in Natural Language Processing and the 9th International Joint Conference on Natural Language Processing (EMNLP-IJCNLP)*, pages 3011–3021, Hong Kong, China. Association for Computational Linguistics.

Shusheng Xu, Xingxing Zhang, Yi Wu, Furu Wei, and Ming Zhou. 2020. Unsupervised extractive summarization by pre-training hierarchical transformers. In *Findings of the Association for Computational Linguistics: EMNLP 2020*, pages 1784–1795, Online. Association for Computational Linguistics.

Hao Zheng and Mirella Lapata. 2019. Sentence centrality revisited for unsupervised summarization. In *Proceedings of the 57th Annual Meeting of the Association for Computational Linguistics*, pages 6236–6247, Florence, Italy. Association for Computational Linguistics.

Ming Zhong, Pengfei Liu, Danqing Wang, Xipeng Qiu, and Xuanjing Huang. 2019. Searching for effective neural extractive summarization: What works and what's next. In *Proceedings of the 57th Annual Meeting of the Association for Computational Linguistics*, pages 1049–1058, Florence, Italy. Association for Computational Linguistics.

The Effectiveness of Masked Language Modeling and Adapters for Factual Knowledge Injection

Sondre Wold
University of Oslo

Abstract

This paper studies the problem of injecting factual knowledge into large pre-trained language models. We train adapter modules on parts of the ConceptNet knowledge graph using the masked language modeling objective and evaluate the success of the method by a series of probing experiments on the LAMA probe. Mean P@K curves for different configurations indicate that the technique is effective, increasing the performance on subsets of the LAMA probe for large values of *k* by adding as little as 2.1% additional parameters to the original models.

1 Introduction

Large pre-trained language models (PLMs) are difficult to interpret due to their complexity and large parameter size. This can partly be explained by the nature of popular training regimens, such as the masked language modelling objective, which encodes distributional knowledge. Such regimens have proven effective for a range of downstream NLP tasks, but they also make it difficult to determine and validate the origin of whatever knowledge the models end up with.

Consequently, there have been multiple efforts to integrate structured information into PLMs (Peters et al., 2019; Yasunaga et al., 2021; Kaur et al., 2022). This has not only been motivated by the promise of better interpretability, but also the observation that there exist scenarios where we would want to stress information that might not be so easily encoded by modelling long range dependencies between fragments of text. This includes knowledge intensive tasks where employing the correct factual knowledge is crucial, for example within the medical domain (Zhang et al., 2021) and question answering (Zhang et al., 2022). At the same time, there exist multiple structured sources that attempt to capture factual knowledge. These sources range from domain specific knowledge graphs for medical information (Shi et al., 2017), commonsense graphs like Yago or ConceptNet (Suchanek et al., 2007; Speer et al., 2017), to lexico-semantic networks like WordNet (Miller, 1995).

In this paper, we attempt to inject the structured information found in the ConceptNet knowledge graph (Speer et al., 2017) into pre-trained language models. The injection is done by training relatively small neural networks, known as adapter modules (Houlsby et al., 2019; Pfeiffer et al., 2020), on subject—predicate—object triples. As in Lauscher et al. (2020), we extract the triples using a random walk procedure and then translate them into natural language so that we can use masked language modeling as the training objective. The resulting adapters are injected into all layers of two popular pre-trained language models: BERT base (Devlin et al., 2019) and RoBERTa base (Liu et al., 2019). Our code and data is made publicly available[1].

For the injection to be deemed effective, we argue that the adapter-injected models must be able to use the knowledge gained from the adapter training together with what the models learned during their initial pre-training. In order to quantitatively assess this, we evaluate our models in a zero-shot setting on the ConceptNet subset of the LAMA probe (Petroni et al., 2019). As ConceptNet is the source for both our training corpus and the LAMA probe, we can better measure how much of the factual knowledge seen during adapter training the models can be expected to recall.

2 Related work

Combining structured information with language models is a standing problem in NLP. One approach to overcome this has been to combine knowledge graphs with PLMs, augmenting the distributional knowledge encoded in the models with the structured information found in the graphs (Sun et al.,

[1] `https://github.com/SondreWold/adapters-mlm-injection`

Proceedings of TextGraphs-16: Graph-based Methods for Natural Language Processing, pages 54–59
October 16, 2022.

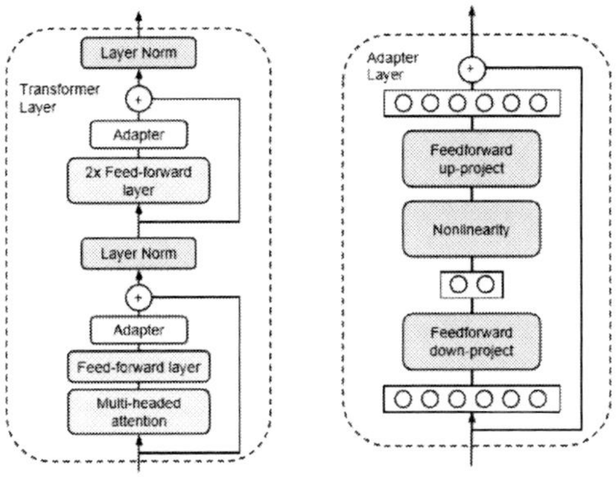

Figure 1: Left: how adapters are injected into each transformer layer. Right: the components of each adapter module. Figure from Houlsby et al. (2019).

2021; Liu et al., 2020; Wang et al., 2021). Within this approach, we find several uses of adapters. First introduced for NLP by Houlsby et al. (2019), and popularized by the AdapterHub framework Pfeiffer et al. (2020), adapters are small neural networks injected into larger, often pre-trained models. During training the original model weights are kept static, and only the set of newly introduced weights from the adapter are adjusted. Figure 1 illustrates the architecture proposed by Houlsby et al. (2019) and how it is injected into a transformer layer.

The methodology in this paper is inspired by Lauscher et al. (2020), who inject commonsense information and world knowledge into BERT by using such adapter modules. As in our work, the adapters train with the masked language modeling objective over subject—predicate—object triples from the ConceptNet graph, but they are evaluated on the GLUE benchmark (Wang et al., 2018). Although the result are inconclusive for most of the tasks in GLUE, the injected models perform better than their base model counterparts on the world knowledge and commonsense categories of the diagnostic set.

A similar approach is taken by Wang et al. (2021). Their K-DAPTER model has one adapter for factual knowledge, trained on aligned text triplets from Wikipedia and Wikidata, and one for linguistic knowledge, obtained via dependency parsing. Results on knowledge-driven tasks, including relation classification, entity typing, and question answering, show that this setup improves performance, and furthermore, that K-ADAPTER captures more versatile knowledge than ROBERTA.

In a more domain specific context, Meng et al. (2021) use adapter modules to infuse a large biomedical knowledge graph into an underlying BERT model. By partitioning the large graph into smaller sub-graphs, which are then fed into distinct adapter modules and fused using a mixture layer that combine the knowledge from all the adapters using an attention layer, they achieve a new state-of-the-art performance on five domain specific datasets.

3 Experiments

Following Lauscher et al. (2020), we use the same configuration for our adapter modules as in Houlsby et al. (2019). We set the size of the adapter modules to 64, which implies a reduction factor of 12 from the original transformer layer size of 768 in $\text{BERT}_{\text{BASE}}$. This increases the total amount of parameters by 2.1%. We use GELU (Hendrycks and Gimpel, 2020) as the activation function inside the adapters, and the Adam optimizer from (Kingma and Ba, 2017). We set the learning rate to *1e-4* with 10.000 warm-up steps and weight decay factor of 0.01. We allow the adapter to train for 100.000 optimization steps while freezing all the original transformer weights. The adapters are implemented using the `adapter-transformers` library (Pfeiffer et al., 2020). Throughout the remainder of this paper, the resulting configuration is referred to as $\text{CN}_{\text{HOULSBY 100K}}$ in figures and as the Houlsby configuration in text.

The adapters train on the same subset of ConceptNet as in Lauscher et al. (2020). As this study was named Retrograph, we refer to this particular set of predicate types as the Retrograph predicate set. The predicates in this set are: ANTONYMOF, SYNONYMOF, ISA and MANNEROF. Subject—predicate—object triplets with one of these predicates in their middle position are extracted through a random traversal procedure[2] and then subsequently chained so that we get blocks of text in natural language on the following format:

possible is a synonym of possibility.
possibility is a concept.
concept is a synonym of conception.
conception is a synonym of fertilization.
fertilization is a enrichment.
enrichment is a gift.

[2]Details on this traversal procedure can be found in Lauscher et al. (2020) or in appendix A.

The corpus is processed using masked language modeling (MLM), parsed line for line with a MLM probability of 0.15, as in the original BERT paper (Devlin et al., 2019). We also experiment by training on the corpus by a maximum sequence length instead of line by line training. However, this did not affect the performance of the models in any significant way.

3.1 Evaluation

We evaluate our injected models on the ConceptNet split of the LAMA (LAnguage Model Analysis) probe (Petroni et al., 2019), which allows for testing of the factual and commonsense knowledge of language models. Facts are presented as fill-in-the-blank cloze statements, e.g: "Ibsen was born in [MASK] in the year 1828", and models are ranked based on how highly it ranks the ground truth token. All models are evaluated in a zero-shot setting, using the same prediction head as in their pre-training.

As we train our adapter modules on ConceptNet and also evaluate on the ConceptNet split from LAMA, it is important to note that what we test here is not the model's ability to generalize on unseen data in the traditional sense, but whether or not they are able to reproduce the factual information extracted from the knowledge graph during adapter training. The phrasing of the cloze statements in LAMA is not the same as in the training corpus for the adapters, although fairly similar. For example, one sentence in LAMA derived from the source triple `communicating hasSubevent knowledge` is presented in the probe as *Communicating is for gaining [MASK]*, while the same triple would be phrased as *communication has subevent knowledge* in the training corpus for the adapters. This makes it possible to control the degree of overlap between instances of factual knowledge in the training corpus and the concepts at the object position in the statements from LAMA. The degree of overlap is numerically specified in the discussion of each result.

3.1.1 Evaluation metric

Following Petroni et al. (2019), we use mean precision at different values of k as the evaluation metric over the LAMA resource. Normally, as in information retrieval, we calculate the precision of a retrieved collection as the number of relevant documents proportionate to the total number of retrieved documents. Here, however, we only have one true positive for collections of all sizes. Thus, the mean precision at various values for k is equal to the whether or not the correct word is a member of the set of predictions of size k. If $k = 100$, we return a precision of 1 if the correct word is one of the top 100 predictions.

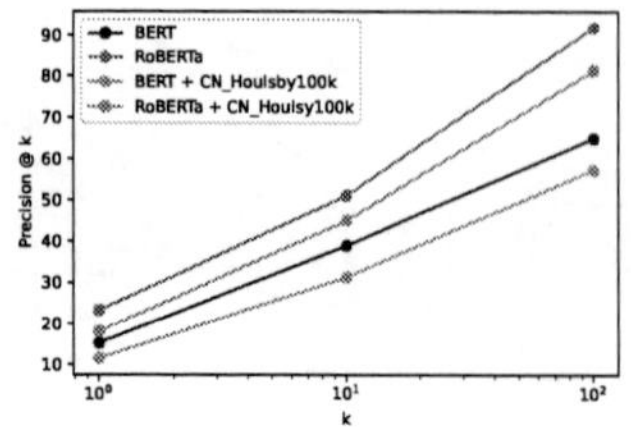

(a) ALL PREDICATES

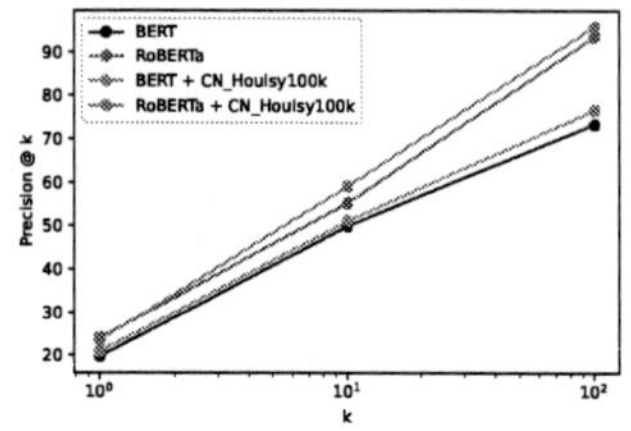

(b) THE ISA PREDICATE

Figure 2: Mean P@k curve for base models and the Houlsby adapter configuration. Base 10 log scale for the X axis. **a)** shows the result for all the predicates in the ConceptNet split of LAMA while **b)** shows results for the "ISA" predicate only

4 Results

Figure 2 shows the mean P@K curves for two language models, with and without an adapter. Part *(a)* of the figure shows the result over all the predicate types present in the ConceptNet split of LAMA ($N = 29774$). The injection of the adapter module decreases the performance of both BERT and ROBERTA for all values of k. However, the corpus with the Retrograph predicate set that adapters trained on only includes one of these types. Hence, there is little similarity between the two sets, and the reproduction of factual knowledge cannot be expected here. This also indicate that training on one set of predicate types does not improve the reproduction of facts on others.

Part *(b)* of figure 2, on the other hand, shows the same models and adapters, but with the probe restricted only to the ISA predicate type — which is then present both in the training corpus and in the

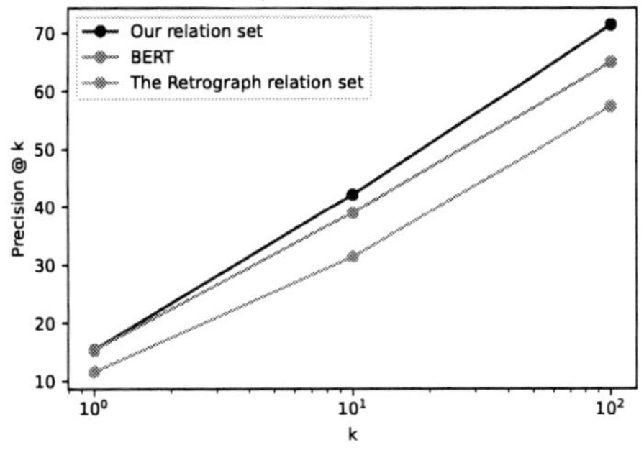

Figure 3: The result of different training configurations on the ConceptNet split of LAMA (Petroni et al., 2019). The two models, in dark blue and orange, use $\mathrm{BERT}_{\mathrm{BASE}}$ as the root model and the Houlsby configuration for their adapter, but are trained on different predicate sets of the ConceptNet graph. The gray line represents a BERT model without any adapter training.

probe. In the corpus from Lauscher et al. (2020), triples with this predicate type make up 23% of the total corpus ($N = 69843$).

Since both resources are extracted from ConceptNet, we check the overlap between the masked tokens in the object position in LAMA and the object position in the triplets in the training set for the adapters. The actual percentage will depend on the random walk procedure, but for the sets used in figure 2 there is a 5.7% overlap between concepts. That is, approximately five percent of the concepts from LAMA that the models are expected to predict are also in the training corpus in some form, either with the same predicate type as in the probe, IsA, or one of the others in the Retrograph set.

Despite this, the injected models perform consistently better. As this performance gain is achieved by adding only 2.1% additional parameters to the original model, and without adjusting the original weights at all, we interpret the results as an indication that this method of knowledge injection is effective.

5 Changing the predicate set

In order to further probe the effectiveness of the proposed method, we introduce a new corpus ($N =$ 99603 triples) — distilled with the same random walk procedure, but over a new set of predicate types, namely the same set of predicate types found in the ConceptNet split of LAMA. By intuition, if the method is effective, the injected models should score higher on average over all these predicate types than their non-injected counterparts. A list of these predicate types can be found in appendix A.

Figure 3 compares the result of the injected models trained over our predicate set with that of the Retrograph set and a plain BERT model for different values of k. As can be seen from the P@K curves, models trained over our predicate set improve the performance on the full ConceptNet split of the LAMA (N= 29774) probe by up to 6.39% for BERT at large values of k. For k=1, where the model must guess the correct masked object "at first try", we see little difference. Compared to the Retrograph set, which has fewer predicate types, the difference in performance indicate that predicate type specificity is important (e.g subgraph quality). For this comparison, the overlap between the training corpus for the adapters and the full ConceptNet split of LAMA is 36% on the object level, meaning that roughly one third of the concepts were seen during training in some form.

This provides some evidence for the success of the knowledge injection. Models are able to reproduce factual knowledge when queried over the LAMA probe, even though the phrasing of the questions in LAMA is different than the strict triplet-style of the training corpus.

6 Conclusion and Future Work

Combining structured information and large pre-trained language models is a standing problem in NLP research. In this work, we show that training adapter modules on triplets extracted from ConceptNet using masked language modeling can help language models reproduce factual knowledge. Experiments on the ConceptNet split of the LAMA probe show that our adapter-injected models perform better in a zero-shot setting than non-injected models, having seen only a third of the relevant factual knowledge during pre-training in some form, encoded into only 2.1% of the total parameters of the total model. Future work should investigate how this type of knowledge injection can augment language models on other types of tasks, such as language generation, multiple choice questions or natural language inference, which would require more fine-grained annotations of downstream tasks targeted at some form of knowledge.

References

Jacob Devlin, Ming-Wei Chang, Kenton Lee, and Kristina Toutanova. 2019. BERT: Pre-training of deep bidirectional transformers for language understanding. In *Proceedings of the 2019 Conference of the North American Chapter of the Association for Computational Linguistics: Human Language Technologies, Volume 1 (Long and Short Papers)*, pages 4171–4186, Minneapolis, Minnesota. Association for Computational Linguistics.

Aditya Grover and Jure Leskovec. 2016. node2vec: Scalable feature learning for networks.

Dan Hendrycks and Kevin Gimpel. 2020. Gaussian error linear units (gelus).

Neil Houlsby, Andrei Giurgiu, Stanislaw Jastrzebski, Bruna Morrone, Quentin De Laroussilhe, Andrea Gesmundo, Mona Attariyan, and Sylvain Gelly. 2019. Parameter-efficient transfer learning for NLP. In *Proceedings of the 36th International Conference on Machine Learning*, volume 97 of *Proceedings of Machine Learning Research*, pages 2790–2799. PMLR.

Jivat Kaur, Sumit Bhatia, Milan Aggarwal, Rachit Bansal, and Balaji Krishnamurthy. 2022. LM-CORE: Language models with contextually relevant external knowledge. In *Findings of the Association for Computational Linguistics: NAACL 2022*, pages 750–769, Seattle, United States. Association for Computational Linguistics.

Diederik P. Kingma and Jimmy Ba. 2017. Adam: A method for stochastic optimization.

Anne Lauscher, Olga Majewska, Leonardo F. R. Ribeiro, Iryna Gurevych, Nikolai Rozanov, and Goran Glavaš. 2020. Common sense or world knowledge? investigating adapter-based knowledge injection into pretrained transformers. In *Proceedings of Deep Learning Inside Out (DeeLIO): The First Workshop on Knowledge Extraction and Integration for Deep Learning Architectures*, pages 43–49, Online. Association for Computational Linguistics.

Weijie Liu, Peng Zhou, Zhe Zhao, Zhiruo Wang, Qi Ju, Haotang Deng, and Ping Wang. 2020. K-bert: Enabling language representation with knowledge graph. *Proceedings of the AAAI Conference on Artificial Intelligence*, 34(03):2901–2908.

Yinhan Liu, Myle Ott, Naman Goyal, Jingfei Du, Mandar Joshi, Danqi Chen, Omer Levy, Mike Lewis, Luke Zettlemoyer, and Veselin Stoyanov. 2019. Roberta: A robustly optimized bert pretraining approach. *arXiv preprint arXiv:1907.11692*.

Zaiqiao Meng, Fangyu Liu, Thomas Clark, Ehsan Shareghi, and Nigel Collier. 2021. Mixture-of-partitions: Infusing large biomedical knowledge graphs into BERT. In *Proceedings of the 2021 Conference on Empirical Methods in Natural Language Processing*, pages 4672–4681, Online and Punta Cana, Dominican Republic. Association for Computational Linguistics.

George A Miller. 1995. Wordnet: a lexical database for English. *Communications of the ACM*, 38(11):39–41.

Matthew E. Peters, Mark Neumann, Robert Logan, Roy Schwartz, Vidur Joshi, Sameer Singh, and Noah A. Smith. 2019. Knowledge enhanced contextual word representations. In *Proceedings of the 2019 Conference on Empirical Methods in Natural Language Processing and the 9th International Joint Conference on Natural Language Processing (EMNLP-IJCNLP)*, pages 43–54, Hong Kong, China. Association for Computational Linguistics.

Fabio Petroni, Tim Rocktäschel, Sebastian Riedel, Patrick Lewis, Anton Bakhtin, Yuxiang Wu, and Alexander Miller. 2019. Language models as knowledge bases? In *Proceedings of the 2019 Conference on Empirical Methods in Natural Language Processing and the 9th International Joint Conference on Natural Language Processing (EMNLP-IJCNLP)*, pages 2463–2473, Hong Kong, China. Association for Computational Linguistics.

Jonas Pfeiffer, Andreas Rücklé, Clifton Poth, Aishwarya Kamath, Ivan Vulić, Sebastian Ruder, Kyunghyun Cho, and Iryna Gurevych. 2020. AdapterHub: A framework for adapting transformers. In *Proceedings of the 2020 Conference on Empirical Methods in Natural Language Processing: System Demonstrations*, pages 46–54, Online. Association for Computational Linguistics.

Longxiang Shi, Shijian Li, Xiaoran Yang, Jiaheng Qi, Gang Pan, and Binbin Zhou. 2017. Semantic health knowledge graph: semantic integration of heterogeneous medical knowledge and services. *BioMed research international*, 2017.

Robyn Speer, Joshua Chin, and Catherine Havasi. 2017. Conceptnet 5.5: An open multilingual graph of general knowledge. In *Thirty-first AAAI conference on artificial intelligence*.

Fabian M Suchanek, Gjergji Kasneci, and Gerhard Weikum. 2007. Yago: a core of semantic knowledge. In *Proceedings of the 16th international conference on World Wide Web*, pages 697–706.

Yueqing Sun, Qi Shi, Le Qi, and Yu Zhang. 2021. Jointlk: Joint reasoning with language models and knowledge graphs for commonsense question answering.

Alex Wang, Amanpreet Singh, Julian Michael, Felix Hill, Omer Levy, and Samuel Bowman. 2018. GLUE: A multi-task benchmark and analysis platform for natural language understanding. In *Proceedings of the 2018 EMNLP Workshop BlackboxNLP: Analyzing and Interpreting Neural Networks for NLP*, pages 353–355, Brussels, Belgium. Association for Computational Linguistics.

Ruize Wang, Duyu Tang, Nan Duan, Zhongyu Wei, Xuanjing Huang, Jianshu Ji, Guihong Cao, Daxin Jiang, and Ming Zhou. 2021. K-Adapter: Infusing Knowledge into Pre-Trained Models with Adapters. In *Findings of the Association for Computational Linguistics: ACL-IJCNLP 2021*, pages 1405–1418, Online. Association for Computational Linguistics.

Michihiro Yasunaga, Hongyu Ren, Antoine Bosselut, Percy Liang, and Jure Leskovec. 2021. QA-GNN: Reasoning with language models and knowledge graphs for question answering. In *Proceedings of the 2021 Conference of the North American Chapter of the Association for Computational Linguistics: Human Language Technologies*, pages 535–546, Online. Association for Computational Linguistics.

Taolin Zhang, Zerui Cai, Chengyu Wang, Minghui Qiu, Bite Yang, and Xiaofeng He. 2021. SMedBERT: A knowledge-enhanced pre-trained language model with structured semantics for medical text mining. In *Proceedings of the 59th Annual Meeting of the Association for Computational Linguistics and the 11th International Joint Conference on Natural Language Processing (Volume 1: Long Papers)*, pages 5882–5893, Online. Association for Computational Linguistics.

Xikun Zhang, Antoine Bosselut, Michihiro Yasunaga, Hongyu Ren, Percy Liang, Christopher D Manning, and Jure Leskovec. 2022. GreaseLM: Graph REASoning enhanced language models. In *International Conference on Learning Representations*.

A Appendix

The ConceptNet split of the LAMA probe includes the following predicate types:

atLocation, capableOf, causes, causesDesire, desires, hasA, hasPrerequisite, hasProperty, hasSubevent, isA, locatedNear, madeOf, motivatedByGoal, partOf, receivesAction, usedFor.

A.1 Random walk procedure

Retrograph uses the weighted random walk algorithm from NODE2VEC (Grover and Leskovec, 2016) in order to extract the `subject--predicate--object` triples from ConceptNet. The pseudocode from the original publication on this algorithm is presented below. The alias method refers to a way of sampling from a discrete probability distribution.[3]

Algorithm 1 The random walk procedure from Lauscher et al. (2020)

procedure NODE2VECWALK(Graph G' = (V, E, π), Start node *u*, Length *l*)
  $Inititalizewalkto[u]$
  for `walk_iter = 1` **to** *l* **do**
    $curr = walk[-1]$
    $V_{curr} = GetNeighbors(curr, G')$
    $s = AliasSample(V_{curr}, \pi)$
    Appendstowalk
  return walk

[3] `https://lips.cs.princeton.edu/the-alias-method-efficient-sampling-with-many-discret`

Text-Aware Graph Embeddings for Donation Behavior Prediction

MeiXing Dong
University of Michigan
meixingd@umich.edu

Xueming Xu
University of Michigan
xueming@umich.edu

Rada Mihalcea
University of Michigan
mihalcea@umich.edu

Abstract

Predicting user behavior is essential for a large number of applications including recommender and dialog systems, and more broadly in domains such as healthcare, education, and economics. In this paper, we show that we can effectively predict donation behavior by using text-aware graph models, building upon graphs that connect user behaviors and their interests. Using a university donation dataset, we show that the graph representation significantly improves over learning from textual representations. Moreover, we show how incorporating implicit information inferred from text associated with the graph entities brings additional improvements. Our results demonstrate the role played by text-aware graph representations in predicting donation behavior.

1 Introduction

Understanding and predicting user behavior from their digital traces is important for many applications, such as recommender systems (Resnick and Varian, 1997), information filtering (Belkin and Croft, 1992), or dialogue agents (Mazare et al., 2018), as well as numerous behavioral interventions in healthcare, education, economics, and more. Prior research efforts have modeled user interests for predicting future behavior such as purchases (Pradel et al., 2011) or click-through likelihood (Qin et al., 2020), using signals like engagement with social media content or purchase history.

Traditional approaches to user behavior prediction use machine learning models that make use of input features in a linear fashion. These models, including the more advanced neural network architectures, assume that individual data samples are provided one at a time and independent of one another. Example user modeling approaches include using recurrent neural networks to encode the behavioral history of each user (Zhang et al., 2014) or linearly aggregating different parts of a user's background and behavior, such as their demographics and online posting patterns (Xu et al., 2020). Such approaches do not take full advantage of the relations between entities; for instance, two products in one's purchase history may be different but still be related to one another; or two users may have interests that are seemingly diverse, but which have some degree of similarity. Richer input representations that incorporate such relations can improve the performance of downstream machine learning models used to predict user behavior.

Graph models are a prominent way of representing relational information between entities. In particular, knowledge graphs have been used widely in the context of recommender systems. For example, one can construct a knowledge graph consisting of clothing brands and items and retrieve the most relevant or similar items to recommend to a user based on their most recent clothing purchase (Wang et al., 2019; Palumbo et al., 2018). Further, interactions between users and entities can also be included in the graph, such as clicks or purchases. Such a graph and its resulting node embeddings can better capture the relations between entities that arise from the aggregate behaviors of all the users.

However, these relations still only come from explicitly observed interactions like someone clicking on one entity and then also purchasing another entity, or multiple people co-clicking or co-purchasing the same entity. In many contexts, the resulting knowledge graph is sparse, as there is an absence of many co-occurring user-entity interactions due to factors such as a very large number of entities, or users having on average a very low number of interactions. As such, the learning models applied on these sparse graphs can be lacking.

In this paper, we explore user behavior prediction by using text-aware graph representations in the context of university alumni donations. We model alumni donation behavior through text and graph-based representations and evaluate our meth-

Proceedings of TextGraphs-16: Graph-based Methods for Natural Language Processing, pages 60–69
October 16, 2022.

ods by predicting how likely a potential alumnus will donate to specific charitable funds. We conduct our experiments using the history of donations and university engagement newsletters of a large Midwest public university.

We start by building a graph representation of alumni and associated entities, such as academic majors, university funds, and articles in engagement newsletters. Alumni actions, such as donating to a fund or clicking on an article in an engagement newsletter, are represented as edges connecting an alumnus node with a fund or article node. Node embedding representations derived from this graph are thus capturing how different funds or engagement articles are related with respect to the alumni who donated to or clicked on them. We then use this graph to predict the likelihood of an alumnus to donate to a given charitable fund.

Specifically, our paper makes the following two main research contributions. First, we propose a graph framework to represent and predict user behavior, and show that it improves significantly over a linear representation that does not incorporate relational information. Second, we show how this graph representation can be further enriched with implicit links drawn using semantic connections between the textual information associated with the graph entities, leading to additional performance improvements in user behavior prediction. Overall, through experiments on a large alumni donations dataset, we demonstrate the effectiveness of using graph representations enhanced with implicit information for the purpose of user behavior prediction.

2 Related Work

2.1 Combining Graphs and Text

Graph models and knowledge bases are commonly used in a wide range of tasks. However, given the nature of dealing with discrete entities and relations, they can suffer from incomplete coverage or difficulty reasoning over entity relationships.

Advancements in representation learning on graphs have proven helpful in predictive tasks, such as link prediction (Wang et al., 2014), node classification (Cai et al., 2018), and node retrieval or recommendation (Zhao et al., 2015; Li et al., 2016). Many methods build embedding representations of graph nodes (Goyal and Ferrara, 2018) derived from the graph's link structure, using adjacency matrix factorization methods (Tang et al., 2015) or random walks (Grover and Leskovec, 2016).

Work has also been done towards creating text-aware graph embedding models. Methods include representing an entity through a text embedding of the entity name (Socher et al., 2013) and jointly learning embeddings for entities and words (Toutanova et al., 2015; Xiao et al., 2017).

In our work, we leverage node embedding methods to build continuous vector representations of university alumni and charitable funds, and show that they improve over text-based representations.

2.2 Predicting User Behavior

Much research has focused on predicting future user behavior based on user characteristics or prior behavior. Types of predicted behavior span a wide spectrum, including what online content someone will consume (Yin et al., 2014), what types of everyday activities someone does (Wilson and Mihalcea, 2020), and whether someone will persistent in personal improvement (Dong et al., 2021).

In the space of charitable giving, much prior work has targeted identifying factors behind why people choose to make monetary contributions. These factors include socio-demographic and personality characteristics such as age, level of education, income, agreeableness, and empathy (Bekkers, 2010; Snipes et al., 2010; Shier and Handy, 2012; Kitchen, 1992). In our context of university donations, prior work has looked at predicting how likely it is for an alumnus to donate a substantial amount of money based on their educational and professional background (Dong et al., 2020). While this shed light on signals of individual capacity and general inclination to donate, this did not look at which specific causes donors choose to give to.

There is substantially less insight into which specific charitable causes donors are likely to choose. Studies have primarily focused on giving among one or two types of charities, such as secular and religious causes (Helms and Thornton, 2012), or international and national causes (Rajan et al., 2009; Micklewright and Schnepf, 2009). These are mainly based on surveys (Breeze, 2013) asking people to recount their recent donations and describe personal dispositions such as values (Sneddon et al., 2020), empathy (Neumayr and Handy, 2019), and beliefs about the cause (Bachke et al., 2014). Most such studies are limited in the number of donors, donations, and charities observed.

In our work, we model donor behavior and donation choices using a large dataset of donations to

Entity type	Number
Alumni	5883
Funds	1644
Articles	283
Majors	251

Table 1: Statistics of entities in the alumni donation dataset.

different causes, connected with known histories of donor interactions with engagement efforts that indicate personal interests.

3 University Alumni Dataset

We conduct our experiments on a dataset of alumni information maintained by a large, public university in the Midwestern region of the United States. Each alumnus is tied to their educational history; we primarily use their major during their highest level of study at the university. The language used in the data is English.

We focus on those who have donated any amount back to their alma mater and who have also engaged with engineering alumni online newsletters, which are typically distributed by email on a regular basis. We have 2 years of newsletter content from January 2018 to March 2020, accompanied by the interaction history of alumni. The interaction history consists of when and how many times a click occurred, as well as what article was specifically clicked in the newsletter.

Likewise, we also have a history of donations that individual alumni have made to various causes at the university. Given our focus on those who have engaged with newsletters, the corresponding history of donations for these alumni span between January 2015 to June 2020. We show statistics about entities in our dataset in Table 1.

3.1 Donation Funds

At this university, alumni typically donate to funds with designated purposes. For instance, the "Engineering Student Emergency Fund" supports emergency needs related to the well-being of Engineering students. They have a title and an optional textual description of the fund's purpose. Examples of funds and their descriptions are shown in Table 2. We see that fund descriptions can range from short and generic to lengthier and more detailed. Similarly, titles can also range in their descriptiveness of the fund's purpose.

The set of all funds span different schools and countless initiatives. In our work, we consider only the 1644 funds (Tab. 1) that have been donated to by people who have clicked on engineering alumni engagement newsletters.

3.2 Engagement Newsletters

The university under consideration sends online newsletters to their alumni on a regular basis. These newsletters contain university news, such as student accomplishments, novel research findings, and alumni events. They consist of links to articles with an accompanying graphic and a short summary.

User actions are recorded, such as clicking on a particular article within the newsletter. Engagement with a newsletter is indicative of what alumni are interested in beyond their formal studies. For instance, a computer science graduate may primarily read articles about the solar car racing team or the university's efforts to lower its carbon footprint, showing that this alumnus has personal interests in sustainability. This would not necessarily be apparent in their educational or employment history. Therefore, we utilize user interaction with engagement newsletters to model personal user interests. There are 283 articles in our dataset (Tab. 1), drawn from 49 total newsletters.

4 Representing Alumni and Funds

We aim to represent each alumnus primarily with their clicks. As seen in the previous section, every article linked within a newsletter has an accompanying short preview or summary that is displayed in the newsletter. Since this is what alumni initially see and what prompts their clicks, we use this text in our experiments, rather than the full article text.

4.1 Text Representation

Prior work has successfully represented entities in a graph as the average of the word vectors corresponding to its name (Socher et al., 2013). We therefore also encode our entities using word vectors. We represent an alumnus as their history of newsletter article clicks, which indicates their interests. We construct an alumnus embedding that is the averaged GloVe embedding of all newsletter article summaries that they have clicked on. We first compute an average GloVe embedding for each article snippet and then average over all of the article snippet embeddings to get the overall alumnus

Fund Name	Fund Description
Engineering Diversity, Equity, and Inclusion Initiatives	This fund helps provide a vibrant and inclusive climate, which leverages our strengths, broadens our perspectives and paves the way for innovation.
Engineering Student Emergency Fund	This expendable fund supports the emergency needs related to the health, safety and well-being of our Engineering students, especially during the current coronavirus pandemic.
Jane Doe Dance Scholarship Fund	This endowment provides scholarship support for undergraduate dance majors.

Table 2: Examples of funds and descriptions.

embedding. Similarly, we represent a fund using the average GloVe embedding of the words in the fund's name, department, and description.

4.2 Graph Representation

We construct a graph to encapsulate the connections between alumni, alumni majors, funds, and newsletter articles. Each unique alumnus, major, fund, and newsletter article are nodes in the graph. We include an edge between an alumnus and a fund if they have donated to it, weighted by the value of the total amount of donations they've given to this fund. We also connect an alumnus to a newsletter article if they have clicked on it, with the edge weighted by the number of clicks the person made. Funds included in the graph are only those associated with donations in the training set of our experiments. All newsletter clicks made by alumni are included, as was done in the text-only setting.

We then use a graph representation learning method to create embedding representations of the nodes. Specifically, we use the node2vec model proposed by (Grover and Leskovec, 2016). We also conducted experiments using LINE (Tang et al., 2015), but found that they yielded similar results, and therefore we only show results for node2vec.

4.2.1 Similarity Edges

While the explicit connections between entities through actions such as clicking and donating can contain a lot of information, there can still be additional connections made with additional info. Since it's unlikely that many alumni donate and click on exactly the same funds and articles, it may be difficult to capture all relations between them based on alumni behavior alone. For instance, two articles may contain very similar content but not have many overlapping clicks due to the sparseness of click data. Given the graph we have currently, the graph embedding model likely would not capture that the articles are similar based only on clicks. Similarly, two funds may be similar in their purpose and descriptions but have few overlapping donors, resulting in embeddings that do not capture their relevance to each other.

Graph edge type	Number
Alumni - Fund Edges	15,604
Alumni - Article Edges	20,184
Alumni - Major Edges	7,625
Fund - Fund Edges	72,136
Article - Article Edges	3,020

Table 3: Statistics of the graph derived from alumni clicks and donations, enhanced with implicit textual similarity edges.

To better capture these relations among articles and funds, respectively, we propose the addition of similarity edges. The addition of the proposed edges can add these relevance connections that we know inherently exist. This can allow the graph to encode that two funds are related even in the absence of explicit evidence, such as someone donating to both funds or two people clicking on the same article and donating to the same fund.

In preliminary experiments, we found that connecting all pairs of entities weighted by similarity results in lower performance embeddings, as well as much longer training times. We suspect this is due to adding too much noise to the representation through extraneous connections.

To minimize this, we only add edges if the similarity is above a certain threshold. We also give every such edge an equal weight of 1. For every pair of articles, we compute the cosine similarity between their average GloVe embeddings and add an edge between the corresponding nodes if their similarity is above 0.7. We do the same for every pair of funds, adding an edge if the similarity is above 0.8. We choose these thresholds empirically by looking at the distribution of similarities for all pairs of articles and funds, respectively, approximately keeping the upper quartile of similarity values. We give the numbers of different types of edges in the resulting graph in Table 3.

4.3 Analysis: Similarity between Alumni and Newsletter Articles

To gain further insights into the donor behavior graph model, we perform an analysis of the relationships between alumni and funds using their graph representations. We would expect the embeddings for alumni to be more similar to the embeddings of funds that they are more likely to donate to. This graph could then be used for querying for relevant entities. For instance, we could find the top funds that may be of interest to an alum.

To examine this, we compute the cosine similarity between pairs of alumni and funds where the alumnus has donated to the fund, and compare with pairs where the alumnus did not donate to the fund. We use node2vec embeddings based on the graph that has all similar edges incorporated. Further, we ensure that the model is not simply remembering known donations in this analysis by focusing on the subset of donations that occur in 2020 and *removing links between alumni and funds corresponding to these donations* from the graph, no matter which year the donation was made during. This way, we are looking at similarity of alumni and funds that are known to be related, but *that the model does not explicitly have knowledge about*; their similarity therefore comes solely from other alumni behavior and semantic connections. We show the distribution of similarities in Figure 1. Using a two-sided T-test, we calculate the statistical significance between the donation and non-donation samples of similarity values; we designate those with a significance level of $p < 0.1$.

Notably, we see that the GloVe-based similarities do not distinguish well between alumnus-fund pairs where a donation occurred and where a donation did not occur. In fact, the non-donation pairs actually have higher similarity than the donation pairs. This implies that it is not sufficient to use only textual semantic similarity between alumni and funds for determining donation interest.

However, we see significantly higher similarities

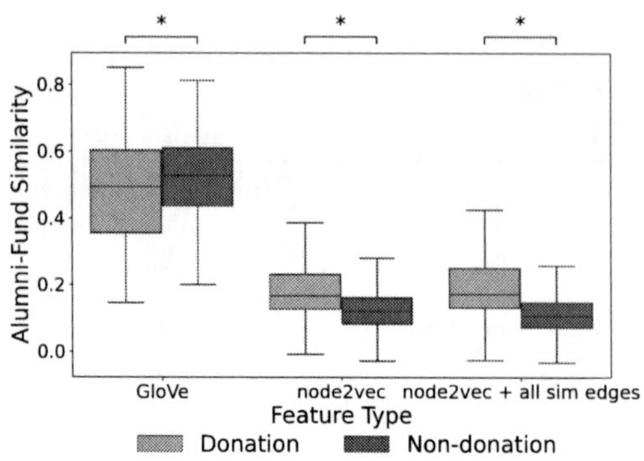

Figure 1: Distribution of similarities between pairs of alumni and funds where alumni have either donated to the fund or not. We show distributions of embedding cosine similarity based on text-only GloVe features and node2vec graph features with and without the addition of similarity edges. Statistical significance is determined using a two-sided T-test, and designated with a star (*) if $p < 0.1$.

between alumni and funds that they have donated to than between negative samples of alumni and funds when using graph embeddings. Further, this is more pronounced when similarity edges are included in the graph, yielding greater separation between pairs who have and have not donated, respectively. This shows that the graph embeddings are indeed encoding alumni behavior and interest.

5 Predicting User Behavior

We have seen that the alumni behavior graph model encapsulates relationships between entities in the resulting embedding space. We evaluate the alumni behavior graph model for downstream predictive use in the context of donation prediction. We construct a task where we predict whether an alumnus is likely to donate to a particular fund, showing that we can distinguish *which funds* someone is likely to donate to.

5.1 Experimental Setup

We focus on alumni who have both clicked on newsletter articles and have made donations. We conduct our experiments on this set of alumni, along with the funds that they have donated to, their majors (only as graph nodes), and the newsletter articles they have clicked on. We look at all pairs of alumni and the particular funds they've donated to as data samples. Donations made prior to the beginning of 2020 are considered training data and donations made in 2020 are test data. Splitting our

Alumnus-Fund Pairs	# Train	# Test
Complete	19,882	3,236
Unique	18,888	3,058

Table 4: Number of samples in the training and test sets of our task. The training samples are donations that were made prior to 2020. The test samples are donations made in 2020.

data by time reflects the real task that universities face, where we know an alumnus' history and want to predict their future donation behavior.

Funds that do not appear prior to 2020 are not included, as our graph representation models are based solely on the training data and would not be able to produce a representation for a previously unseen entity. Similarly, alumni who only appear in 2020 would be excluded from the experiments as they have no prior history and therefore would have no corresponding representation features.

We then use negative sampling to construct sample pairs where the alumnus has not donated to the fund. The training set includes an equal number of such negative samples to obtain a balanced dataset. When looking at accuracy, a balanced test set can better show the model's performance. We therefore also balance the test set. To construct a negative sample, we randomly select an alumnus and a fund from those considered in our dataset. Then, we check if the alumnus-fund pair appears as a positive sample in the corresponding data split and keep the pair if it does not appear.

Donation prediction with unique alumnus-fund pairs. We also conduct experiments in a modified setting where we predict the donation interests of alumni without knowledge of their past donations to the same funds they've donated to in 2020. We remove all alumnus-fund pairs from the training set that occur in the test set, which corresponds to removing past donations that are identical to ones in 2020. Other prior donations that alumni have made are kept. This is a more difficult task, as prior donations to a fund can be highly indicative of future donations to the same fund. Therefore, we must rely more on alumni background and the implicit relationships between different funds as well as between newsletter articles and funds.

5.2 Classification

We train a logistic regression classifier to predict whether an alumnus has donated to a given fund in 2020, based on the described data. As classification model input, we concatenate the feature representations for the alumnus and fund in a given pair. When using text-only representations, we concatenate the averaged GloVe embeddings derived from text corresponding to the alumnus and the fund in a pair, respectively (Sec. 4.1). Similarly, when we use graph-based representations, we concatenate the node2vec embeddings of the nodes corresponding to the alumnus and the fund in a pair, respectively (Sec. 4.2).

There are funds that receive thousands of donations while others receive far fewer individual donations. This can be due to the fund being very general, such as a general scholarship fund, or a popular interest, such as a sports-related fund. On the other hand, funds with more specific or niche subjects may receive fewer donations. Such large data imbalances can lead predictive models to simply memorize the most frequently occurring funds, rather than using the embedded features to make more complex connections between alumni and funds. We empirically find that less than 1% of the funds we consider have received over 200 donations. Therefore, we downsample the number of unique donations each fund has to 200 samples.

Although we implement this downsampling, there are likely still funds or types of funds that are inherently more popular. For instance, funds supporting certain sports draw many donations from alumni of diverse backgrounds. For these types of funds, the alumnus-fund fit may not be as crucial for predicting whether someone will donate; classification models are likely to capture this. Therefore, we also predict donations where we use only features representing the fund, excluding all alumni features. Comparison with this setting can show whether pairwise alumnus-fund fit is indeed useful.

6 Results

We compare the use of text-only GloVe features and graph-based node2vec features in our experiments to evaluate the benefit of our alumni behavior graph model. Further, we evaluate our graph representations both when enhanced with text similarity-based edges and without to show the effects of this adding this implicit information to the graph. We show our alumni donation interest prediction results in Table 5.

In the results, we see that the graph embedding features generally perform better than the text-only

Features	Complete Donation Pairs		Unique Donation Pairs	
	Fund Only	Alumni + Fund	Fund Only	Alumni + Fund
Text-only	0.782	*0.784*	*0.799*	0.798
Graph representations	0.781	*0.812*	*0.791*	0.778
+ *article sim edges*	0.774	*0.817*	*0.789*	0.778
+ *fund sim edges*	0.804	*0.846*	0.816	*0.824*
+ *article and fund sim edges*	0.798	*0.841*	0.816	*0.830*
All (GloVe + node2vec w/ all edges)	0.824	***0.856***	0.848	***0.855***

Table 5: Results from the donation behavior prediction task. Left: Training set contains the complete prior donation history of alumni in test set. Right: Donations made in 2020, in the test set, are removed from the training set. Italicized values designate the highest performance for a given feature type and experimental setting. Bold values designate the highest performance in the experimental setting overall.

features. This is in line with our hypothesis, since the text only contains information about the semantic content, but nothing about how it is related to any other entities. Further, such relations would be difficult for the machine learning model to pick up through the prediction task, as alumni generally do not individually donate to many funds and there is likely little overlap between different people. This sparsity of connections are typical in many recommendation systems contexts. Our framework of encoding user behavior into a graph could therefore be applied to other types of downstream tasks that aim to predict future behavior.

We see that adding implicit edges derived from the textual content of the funds and articles generally improves performance over only having explicit action edges that designate donations and clicks. Similarity links between articles are more helpful when we have knowledge of an alumnus' entire prior donation history.

Accuracy based on using only fund features is much higher than random, showing that the model is indeed learning trends in which types of funds, in terms of content and theme, are generally more well-received. We know the classifier isn't simply picking up on specific popular funds, since we downsampled frequently occurring funds.

Notably, when we use both features from alumni and funds, we generally see better performance, especially when using graph features and with fund edges added. This shows that the prediction model is capturing learning relationships between alumni and funds, and how compatible a given alumnus is as a potential donor for a fund.

When we use only unique donation pairs, we see that the results remain largely comparable with using complete donation pairs. However, the performance is lower than with the use of complete donation pairs when using only features derived from alumni, showing that the complete donation pairs prediction model learned more about donation trends of specific alumni whereas the unique donation pairs model has to understand more of the implicit relatedness between funds and articles.

Finally, we see that combining text-only GloVe features with graph-based node2vec features yields the highest performance. This implies that there is still use in having both the semantic content of the entities and their relational information, and that they are complementary to each other.

Qualitative Analysis

For a qualitative analysis, we use the node2vec model that includes all similarity edges, built from the training data with unique donations. We analyze how the model is able to retrieve relevant alumni and funds for a given alum.

Retrieving relevant funds. In Table 6, we show examples of funds that alumni have previously donated to and the funds that the model determined to have the highest cosine similarity. In the first example, the model retrieves funds that are related to the medical field and supporting research and education in the fields, which matches well with the alum's actual prior donations to funds supporting student scholarships and an endowed professorship. The second and third examples similarly show that the given alum's previous donations and most similar funds share common themes of aerospace engineering and natural history, respectively.

Retrieving relevant alumni. In Table 7, we show examples of click and donation activities of alumni and their highest (cosine) similarity alumni

Prior Donations	Top 3 Similar Funds (Similarity Score)
Engineering General Scholarship Fund Professorship in Rheumatology	Professorship in Gastroenterology and Hepatology Fund (0.40) Gastroenterology Nurse Education Fund (0.36) Gastroenterology Education and Research Fund (0.32)
Aerospace Engineering Support Aerospace Engineering Centennial Fund	Aerospace Engineering Junior Faculty Support Fund (0.47) Aerospace Graduate Research Excellence Fellowship (0.42) Aerospace Graduate Teaching Award and Scholarship (0.38)
Iconic Mastodons Movement Fund Majungasaurus Exhibit Fund	Mammoth Museum Exhibit Fund (0.44) Museum of Natural History Discretionary Fund (0.42) Museum of Natural History Membership (0.39)

Table 6: Prior donations made by a given alumnus the top 3 most similar funds with respect to the alum, determined by embedding cosine similarity. To preserve anonymity, we remove all names and specific details from fund titles. Text of the fund descriptions are not shown for brevity.

Alum's Prior Donations and Clicks	Nearest Alum's Donations and Clicks
F: Engineering General Scholarship Fund F: Mechanical Engineering Special Gifts Fund A: A high altitude long endurance aircraft	F: Engineering General Scholarship Fund F: Mechanical Engineering Special Gifts Fund A: Second place finish for the solar car team A: 3D printing 100 times faster with light
F: Engineering Entrepreneurship Fund F: Engineering Faculty Scholar Award A: Autonomous car preventing traffic jams A: Nobel Prize nomination for powerful laser pulse	F: Engineering Dean's Discretionary Fund A: Driverless future A: Solar car test A: Smart wearables improving elderly mobility

Table 7: Examples of the most similar alumnus for a given alum. To preserve anonymity, we do not show names and remove all identifying information within fund descriptions and article titles. We show the donations and clicks made by the alumni. F - Fund; A - Article

neighbors. In the first example, the chosen alum's donations and clicks are related to mechanical engineering. The most similar alumnus has also donated to mechanical engineering funds and clicked on mechanical engineering-related articles, which shows that nearest alumni neighbors' interests and behaviors match well with the chosen alumni. Likewise, the alumnus in the second example and their most similar alumnus both share interest in autonomous vehicles and research advancements.

7 Conclusion

In this work, we explored the use of text-aware graph representations for user behavior prediction. Using a large dataset consisting of university alumni donations and their interests as expressed through click-throughs on a university newsletter, we showed that the use of a graph framework to explicitly encode the relations between user behaviors and user interests leads to significant improvements over simple linear representations.

Moreover, we showed how further improvements can be obtained by enhancing the graph with implicit links inferred from the semantic distance between graph entities' associated textual data. Our results demonstrate the role played by graph representations using explicit and implicit relations for the prediction of user behavior.

Future work can expand upon our results and explore how textual semantic links behave with different datasets with heterogeneous graph algorithms, as well as in larger-scale data settings combined with transformer-based algorithms.

Acknowledgments

This material is based in part upon work supported by the University of Michigan Fellowship program and by the John Templeton Foundation (grant #61156). Any opinions, findings, and conclusions or recommendations expressed in this material are those of the authors and do not necessarily reflect the views of the University of Michigan or the John Templeton Foundation.

References

Maren Elise Bachke, Frode Alfnes, and Mette Wik. 2014. Eliciting Donor Preferences. *Voluntas*, 25(2):465–486.

René Bekkers. 2010. Who gives what and when? A scenario study of intentions to give time and money. *Social Science Research*, 39(3):369–381.

Nicholas J Belkin and W Bruce Croft. 1992. Information filtering and information retrieval: Two sides of the same coin? *Communications of the ACM*, 35(12):29–38.

Beth Breeze. 2013. How donors choose charities: the role of personal taste and experiences in giving decisions. *Voluntary Sector Review*, 4(2):165–183.

Hongyun Cai, Vincent W. Zheng, and Kevin Chen Chuan Chang. 2018. A Comprehensive Survey of Graph Embedding: Problems, Techniques, and Applications. *IEEE Transactions on Knowledge and Data Engineering*, 30(9):1616–1637.

MeiXing Dong, Rada Mihalcea, and Dragomir Radev. 2020. Extending sparse text with induced domain-specific lexicons and embeddings: A case study on predicting donations. *Computer Speech and Language*, 59.

MeiXing Dong, Xueming Xu, Yiwei Zhang, Ian Stewart, and Rada Mihalcea. 2021. Room to Grow: Understanding Personal Characteristics Behind Self Improvement Using Social Media. In *Proceedings of the Ninth International Workshop on Natural Language Processing for Social Media*, pages 153–162. Association for Computational Linguistics (ACL).

Palash Goyal and Emilio Ferrara. 2018. Graph embedding techniques, applications, and performance: A survey. *Knowledge-Based Systems*, 151:78–94.

Aditya Grover and Jure Leskovec. 2016. node2vec: Scalable Feature Learning for Networks. *KDD : proceedings. International Conference on Knowledge Discovery & Data Mining*, 2016:855–864.

Sara E. Helms and Jeremy P. Thornton. 2012. The influence of religiosity on charitable behavior: A COPPS investigation. *The Journal of Socio-Economics*, 41(4):373–383.

Harry Kitchen. 1992. Determinants of charitable donations in Canada: A comparison over time. *Applied Economics*, 24(7):709–713.

Juzheng Li, Jun Zhu, and Bo Zhang. 2016. Discriminative Deep Random Walk for network classification. In *54th Annual Meeting of the Association for Computational Linguistics, ACL 2016 - Long Papers*, volume 2, pages 1004–1013.

Pierre-Emmanuel Mazare, Samuel Humeau, Martin Raison, , and Antoine Bordes. 2018. Training millions of personalized dialogue agents. In *Proceedings of the Conference in Empirical Methods in Natural Language Processing*.

John Micklewright and Sylke V. Schnepf. 2009. Who gives charitable donations for overseas development? *Journal of Social Policy*, 38(2):317–341.

Michaela Neumayr and Femida Handy. 2019. Charitable Giving: What Influences Donors' Choice Among Different Causes? *Voluntas*, 30(4):783–799.

Enrico Palumbo, Giuseppe Rizzo, Raphaël Troncy, Elena Baralis, Michele Osella, and Enrico Ferro. 2018. Knowledge graph embeddings with node2vec for item recommendation. In *European Semantic Web Conference*, pages 117–120. Springer.

Bruno Pradel, Savaneary Sean, Julien Delporte, Sébastien Guérif, Céline Rouveirol, Nicolas Usunier, Françoise Fogelman-Soulié, and Frédéric Dufau-Joel. 2011. A case study in a recommender system based on purchase data. In *Proceedings of the 17th ACM SIGKDD international conference on Knowledge discovery and data mining*, pages 377–385.

Jiarui Qin, Weinan Zhang, Xin Wu, Jiarui Jin, Yuchen Fang, and Yong Yu. 2020. User behavior retrieval for click-through rate prediction. In *Proceedings of the 43rd International ACM SIGIR Conference on Research and Development in Information Retrieval*, pages 2347–2356.

Suja S Rajan, George H Pink, and William H Dow. 2009. Sociodemographic and personality characteristics of Canadian donors contributing to international charity. *Nonprofit and Voluntary Sector Quarterly*, 38(3):413–440.

Paul Resnick and Hal R Varian. 1997. Recommender systems. *Communications of the ACM*, 40(3):56–58.

Micheal L. Shier and Femida Handy. 2012. Understanding online donor behavior: the role of donor characteristics, perceptions of the internet, website and program, and influence from social networks. *International Journal of Nonprofit and Voluntary Sector Marketing*, 17(3):219–230.

Joanne N Sneddon, Uwana Evers, and Julie A Lee. 2020. Personal Values and Choice of Charitable Cause: An Exploration of Donors' Giving Behavior. *Nonprofit and Voluntary Sector Quarterly*, 49(4):803–826.

Robin L Snipes, Sharon L Oswald, Robin L Snipes, and Sharon L Oswald. 2010. Charitable giving to not-for-profit organizations: factors affecting donations to non-profit organizations.

Richard Socher, Danqi Chen, Christopher D Manning, and Andrew Y Ng. 2013. Reasoning with neural tensor networks for knowledge base completion. In *Advances in Neural Information Processing Systems*.

Jian Tang, Meng Qu, Mingzhe Wang, Ming Zhang, Jun Yan, and Qiaozhu Mei. 2015. LINE: Large-scale information network embedding. In *WWW 2015 - Proceedings of the 24th International Conference on World Wide Web*.

Kristina Toutanova, Danqi Chen, Patrick Pantel, Hoifung Poon, Pallavi Choudhury, and Michael Gamon. 2015. Representing text for joint embedding of text and knowledge bases. In *Conference Proceedings - EMNLP 2015: Conference on Empirical Methods in Natural Language Processing*, pages 1499–1509. Association for Computational Linguistics.

Xiang Wang, Xiangnan He, Yixin Cao, Meng Liu, and Tat-Seng Chua. 2019. Kgat: Knowledge graph attention network for recommendation. In *Proceedings of the 25th ACM SIGKDD International Conference on Knowledge Discovery & Data Mining*, pages 950–958.

Zhen Wang, Jianwen Zhang, Jianlin Feng, and Zheng Chen. 2014. Knowledge Graph Embedding by Translating on Hyperplanes. *Proceedings of the AAAI Conference on Artificial Intelligence*, 28(1).

Steven R Wilson and Rada Mihalcea. 2020. Predicting human activities from user-generated content. In *ACL 2019 - 57th Annual Meeting of the Association for Computational Linguistics, Proceedings of the Conference*, pages 2572–2582.

Han Xiao, Minlie Huang, Lian Meng, and Xiaoyan Zhu. 2017. SSP: Semantic space projection for knowledge graph embedding with text descriptions. In *31st AAAI Conference on Artificial Intelligence, AAAI 2017*, pages 3104–3110.

Zhentao Xu, Verónica Pérez-Rosas, and Rada Mihalcea. 2020. Inferring Social Media Users' Mental Health Status from Multimodal Information.

Hongzhi Yin, Bin Cui, Ling Chen, Zhiting Hu, and Zi Huang. 2014. A temporal context-aware model for user behavior modeling in social media systems. In *Proceedings of the ACM SIGMOD International Conference on Management of Data*, pages 1543–1554.

Yuyu Zhang, Hanjun Dai, Chang Xu, Jun Feng, Taifeng Wang, Jiang Bian, Bin Wang, and Tie-Yan Liu. 2014. Sequential Click Prediction for Sponsored Search with Recurrent Neural Networks. *Proceedings of the AAAI Conference on Artificial Intelligence*, 28(1).

Yu Zhao, Zhiyuan Liu, and Maosong Sun. 2015. Representation learning for measuring entity relatedness with rich information. In *IJCAI International Joint Conference on Artificial Intelligence*, volume 2015-Janua, pages 1412–1418.

Word Sense Disambiguation of French Lexicographical Examples Using Lexical Networks

Aman Sinha, Sandrine Ollinger, Mathieu Constant
ATILF, Université de Lorraine, Nancy, France
{firstname.lastname}@atilf.fr

Abstract

This paper focuses on the task of word sense disambiguation (WSD) on lexicographic examples relying on the French Lexical Network (*fr-LN*). For this purpose, we exploit the lexical and relational properties of the network, that we integrated in a feedforward neural WSD model on top of pretrained French BERT embeddings. We provide a comparative study with various models and further show the impact of our approach regarding polysemic units.

1 Introduction

Word sense disambiguation is a long-standing research field in NLP investigating supervised, unsupervised, knowledge-based and mixed approaches (Navigli, 2009). Lexical resources have always played a crucial role not only serving as sense inventories, but also as sources of information to help the disambiguation process (a.o. Wilks and Stevenson (1998)). In particular, the structure and lexical content of lexical networks have been successfully exploited for this task with graph-based algorithms (a.o. Agirre et al. (2006)).

With the deep learning revolution, supervised approaches relying on neural networks and pretrained word embeddings have quickly gained popularity. In such framework, WSD is often seen as a token classification task, where tokens are assigned a sense label among an exist set of senses. Classical supervised models are built on a MultiLayer Perceptron (MLP) for predicting a sense label for the target tokens (Raganato et al., 2017) and lately the use of pretrained contextualized word embedding has become standard (ex. Vial et al. (2019)).

Such supervised systems are dependent on sense-annotated datasets that tend to have limited coverage due to the manual annotation cost. Furthermore, in these systems, rare senses are often disadvantaged towards more frequent ones. To tackle this problem, more and more research works propose approaches integrating lexical network knowledge to such models. Several strategies have been proposed: either integrating lexical knowledge – e.g. glosses (Huang et al., 2019) –, or integrating structural properties – e.g. use of graph-based algorithms such as Personalized PageRank (El Sheikh et al., 2021), use of hyperonym/hyponym/synonym relations in a lexical network to compress the sense tagset and then make the labeling task easier (Vial et al., 2019) –. Other models such as EWISE (Kumar et al., 2019) and EWISER (Bevilacqua and Navigli, 2020) enhance the WSD system with explicit and implicit knowledge using graph structure information from lexical knowledge networks and existing sense embeddings.

In this paper, we are interested in adapting the EWISER model to specific lexical data: the data from the French Lexical Network (*fr-LN*, Polguère (2014)) and its derived database of lexicographical usage examples (DBLE-LN-fr). In particular, we exploited the linguistic richness of its relation types, by integrating trainable weighted relations. Our system gets better or comparable results than the original system.

This paper is organized as follows. Section 2 presents our dataset and its particularities. Section 3 introduces the model and its adaptations. Sections 4 and 5 are respectively devoted to introducing the experimental setup and discussing and comparing the results.

2 The French Lexical Network and its database of lexicographical examples

2.1 A linguistically-rich lexical network

Lexical networks used as lexical knowledge in NLP are generally variants of WordNet (Miller, 1995). In this paper, we rely on the French lexical network *fr-LN*[1], which is under construction. It is based on the model of lexical systems (Polguère,

[1]The data are available on the ORTOLANG platform: `https://hdl.handle.net/11403/lexical-system-fr/v2.1`

Proceedings of TextGraphs-16: Graph-based Methods for Natural Language Processing, pages 70–76
October 16, 2022.

2014) and is in line with the research projects conducted in the framework of Explanatory and Combinatorial Lexicology (Mel'čuk, 2006). It contains among others syntagmatic, paradigmatic, copolysemic and phraseological relations. The complete *fr-LN* contains 29,220 word senses and 80,036 relations between them. In this paper, we focus only on the 62,641 paradigmatic and syntagmatic links, which are standardized using the system of 686 distinct Meaning-Text lexical functions (LFs) (Polguère, 2007). Table 1 shows statistics on *fr-LN*. It differs from WordNet (WN) in several dimensions: WN has much larger coverage, contains few relation types that are mainly paradigmatic relations and is built on synset nodes. fr-LN relations mainly involve senses of different part-of-speech tags, whereas WN relations quasi-exclusively involve nodes of the same part-of-speech. For instance, less than 6% of the relations involving verbs are between two verbs. WN and fr-LN have comparable polysemy rates. Contrary to WN, fr-LN does not include glosses and the lexicographic definitions are still prototypical. An interesting feature of fr-LN is that relations are associated manually crafted semantic weights (three possible values: 0, 1 and 2) depending to what extent the semantic content of the source node includes the semantic content of the target one.

Graph	#Word Senses	#Lemmas	#LF-Arcs	#LFs
Complete	29,220	18,400	62,641	686
Verbs-only	5,237	2,559	9,854	399
Nouns-only	14,044	8,639	21,580	501

Table 1: Statistics on the *fr-LN* network.

2.2 The *DBLE-LN-Fr* database of lexicographical examples

The fr-LN lexical network comes with lexicographical usage examples for each word sense, that have been gathered in the *DBLE-LN-Fr* database[2]. The examples come from three main sources: *Frantext*[3], *FrWaC* (Baroni et al., 2009), the *Est-Républicain* newspaper corpus (ATILF and CLLE, 2020). They have been selected because they display interesting use cases for distinguishing meanings. They should enable speakers to appropriate the lexicographic descriptions of the lexical units they illustrate. Coupled with these descriptions, they provide all the information needed to use correctly each lexical unit described.

Corpus	#examples	#targets	#Word Senses	#Lemmas
Complete	31,131	51,347	27,343	17,161
Verbs-only	8,169	9,428	5,141	2,483
Nouns-only	19,644	27,105	13,601	8,131

Table 2: DBLE-LN-fr dataset. # targets stands for the number of occurrences of target words in the dataset.

Each example contains from one to eleven occurrences of lexical entities present in the fr-LN. These occurrences are marked and associated with the part-of-speech tag of the lexical entity and a link to visualize the lexical entity in the spiderlex web application[4]. For this work, we selected the examples which contain an occurrence of verb/noun word senses, excluding the examples that contain an occurrence of a verb/noun that is itself included in an occurrence of a multiword unit (locution, idioms, etc.). The table (2) synthesizes the composition of the resulting corpora. Figure 2 (resp. Figure 3) represents a subgraph for the lemma `ping-pong` from the lexical network fr-LN with all lexical function relations (resp. with relations with nouns only).

3 A model integrating graph knowledge

The proposed model is a variant of EWISER (Bevilacqua and Navigli, 2020) that we adapted using some specific features of fr-LN, namely the richness of its relation types, and the semantic weights associated to relations (cf. section 2). EWISER can be seen as a token classification system. It takes as input a sequence of words that feeds a BERT layer. For each target word, a feedforward module is then applied to predict its sense label given the input sequence. The exact modelling is depicted by the equation 1 taken and derived directly from the original paper[5].

$$\begin{aligned} H_0 &= \texttt{BatchNorm}(B) \\ H_1 &= \texttt{swish}(H_0 W + b) \\ Q &= H_1 A^T + H_1 \end{aligned} \quad (1)$$

In the above equation, B corresponds to the sum of the last four *BERT* hidden layer, which

[2]The data are available on the ORTOLANG platform: `https://hdl.handle.net/11403/examples-ls-fr/v2`

[3]`https://www.frantext.fr`

[4]`https://spiderlex.atilf.fr/`

[5]We removed from the original paper the use of external preexisting semantic embeddings as our aim was to rely entirely on the database of lexicographic examples and the French lexical network to evaluate their impact on the WSD task.

is given as input to a 2-layer feedforward to compute the logits H_1. This output is encoded with graph information from the lexical network using A which is the corresponding adjacency matrix. Each node corresponds to a possible word sense in the training dataset. In the original EWISER paper, matrix A encodes hypernym and hyponyms relations from Wordnet, whereas in our case it encodes paradigmatic and syntagmatic relations from fr-LN. The parameters of A may be frozen or trainable (Bevilacqua and Navigli, 2020).

In this paper, we use two strategies to compute the elements $a_{i,j}$ of A relying on some features of *fr-LN*. Every node pair (i, j) have a set $S_{i,j}$ of present relations between i and j. Each relation r has a weight $w(r)$, and $a_{i,j}$ is the sum of the weights of the relations between i and j: $a_{i,j} = \sum_{r \in S_{i,j}} w(r)$.

We consider two weighing schemes for every relation r: (1) $w(r) = 1$, the element $a_{i,j}$ being the cardinality of $S_{i,j}$ [STRUCT]; (2) $w(r) = s_r + 1$ where $s_r \in 0, 1, 2$ is the semantic weight of r, $a_{i,j}$ determining to what extent the semantic content of i is included in the one of j [SEM]. The STRUCT strategy is taken from (Bevilacqua and Navigli, 2020), whereas SEM is a contribution of this paper.

For each weighting scheme, we experimented three settings: (a) the element $a_{i,j}$ is frozen, (b) $a_{i,j}$ is trainable, (c) $w(r)$ is trainable, the weight of each relation being learnt from the training dataset. The setting (c) is a proposal of this paper, whereas (a) and (b) are taken from (Bevilacqua and Navigli, 2020).

4 Experimental Setup

4.1 Dataset

As stated in section 2, we experiment our models on the database of lexicographic examples DBLE-LN-fr built on the French lexical network Fr-LN (Polguère, 2014) focusing on nouns and verbs.

We performed a strategy-based data splitting using the following rules :

1. If the lemma has only one sense, we keep it in the train set, in order to prevent from having straightforward cases in the evaluation;
2. All lemma in test/dev should be in train;
3. Unseen senses can be in test/dev;
4. The distribution of senses between train and test/dev is proportional;
5. Any example with multiple senses to disambiguate should be in the same data split.

4.2 Baselines

We compare our variants of EWISER with various standard baselines. These include Most/Least Frequent Sense per lemma (MFS/LFS) baseline; a random sense (RS) baseline; a cosine-based similarity of the sense representations from BERT-based language model as (Barycenter) baseline (Le et al., 2020) and H_1 representation (refer eqn 1) as MLP baseline.

4.3 Implementation

We used contextual embeddings of two French language models namely, FlauBERT (Le et al., 2020) and CamemBERT (Martin et al., 2020). We use hidden layer size of 3000 and 8000 by rough estimate of number of unique lemmas in the verb and noun corpora respectively. We use `Adam` optimizer with learning rate 0.001 as a common setting for both sets of experiments. We use negative log likelihood (NLL) as our loss function. For each experiment, we used the following decoding strategy selecting the most probable sense among the possible senses for the target word in the fr-LN sense inventory. The code of this implementation is available on GitHub (`https://github.com/ATILF-UMR7118/GraphWSD`).

System	VERB		NOUN	
	Dev	Test	Dev	Test
MFS	0.1145	0.1427	0.2026	0.2016
LFS	0.1178	0.1091	0.1973	0.1939
RS	0.1578	0.1654	0.2444	0.2357
BARYC.	0.3189	0.3178	0.5390	0.5454
MLP	0.2648	0.2822	0.5091	0.5163
STRUCT	0.3513	0.3751	0.5061	0.5171
STRUCT*	0.3502	0.3708	**0.5521**	**0.5615**
STRUCT**	0.3372	0.347	0.5444	0.5516
SEM	0.3416	0.3676	0.5260	0.5309
SEM*	0.3556	0.3546	0.5379	0.5362
SEM**	**0.3610**	**0.3838**	0.5103	0.5274

Table 3: WSD results on DBLE-LN-fr. STRUCT and SEM are the two strategies to compute A matrix. By default, $a_{i,j}$ are frozen. * indicates that $a_{i,j}$ is trainable. ** indicates that the relation weights w are trainable.

5 Results and discussion

To evaluate our models, we used the accuracy of the system predictions, i.e. the percentage of correct

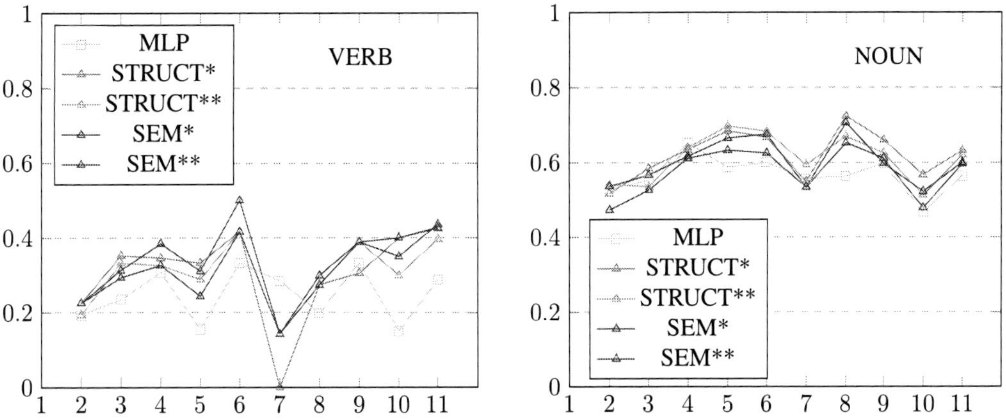

Figure 1: Polysemic performance analysis on dev set; x-axis: `sense-count` and y-axis : `accuracy`

predictions. The system was preliminary tuned on the dev dataset. The MLP-baseline obtained better performances using the CamemBERT embeddings, whereas the Barycenter performances were better using FlauBERT.

5.1 Global system performances

Table 3 shows results on both dev and test sets for all experimented systems both for nouns and verbs. Results are consistent across test and dev sets. MFS/LFS baselines results are on par with the random baseline, due to the uniform distribution of senses in our dataset coming from the use of lexicographic examples instead of standard annotated texts on which MFS is traditionally quite high. It is also worth noting that the simple Barycenter baseline consistently outperforms the MLP baseline. Our experiments consolidate the results of Bevilacqua and Navigli (2020), showing the integration of lexical network knowledge systematically tends to improve the WSD performances. Regarding the two strategies to compute the A matrix, SEM weights tend to perform better than STRUCT weights for verbs, whereas this is the other way around for nouns. In both cases, the use of trainable weights is favourable. The better performance of SEM for verbs can be attributed to the #LF-Arcs – #Lemma ratio (refer Table:1) which is more for verbs (3.85) than nouns (2.49) implying the semantic richness of the verb subgraph.

Overall, WSD on our dataset for French verbs is harder than for nouns (1/3 vs. 1/2 accuracy). We compared these results using those obtained for other French datasets. In particular, we applied the barycenter baseline on the French SemEval data (FSE) for verbs (Segonne et al., 2019) and on the FLUE benchmark for nouns (Le et al., 2020) to get a rough comparison (though datasets are quite different): for nouns, we reach comparable results (0.5353 accuracy), whereas the difference is quite large for verbs (0.5034 accuracy). One may partly explain this by the way annotated verbs were selected: medium frequency and medium rate of polysemy.

5.2 Analysis by degree of polysemy

Figure 1 shows the performance comparison for the different models in our experimental setup for disambiguating polysemic lemmas with respect to the number of senses per lemma. We observe that our proposed models tend to more effectively disambiguate polysemic lemmas with more than three-four senses than the MLP baseline (with some exceptions), showing the interest of using lexical network knowledge for those cases. For instance, for the verb *aller* (to go), our models predicted 8 distinct senses out of the 13 expected, while MLP baseline predicted 4 senses only.

6 Conclusion

We presented a preliminary study of various word sense disambiguation systems on the French dataset, DBLE-LN-fr-V2. We proposed a weighted training model in order to incorporate the richness of lexical and semantic information from the fr-LN network effectively and showed comparable performance to state of the art systems.

A first path of future research would be to enhance the scarcity of A matrix: e.g. adding neighbors of various POS, or including transitive closures of relations. We would like to explore the incorporation of sense embeddings using various graph representation learning algorithms. Furthermore, we would like to experiment tagset compression like in (Vial et al., 2019).

Acknowledgement

This work has been partly funded by the CPER Langues, Connaissances & Humanités Numériques (2014 - 2020).

References

Eneko Agirre, David Martínez, Oier López de Lacalle, and Aitor Soroa. 2006. Two graph-based algorithms for state-of-the-art WSD. In *Proceedings of the 2006 Conference on Empirical Methods in Natural Language Processing*, pages 585–593, Sydney, Australia. Association for Computational Linguistics.

ATILF and CLLE. 2020. Corpus journalistique issu de l'est républicain. ORTOLANG (Open Resources and TOols for LANGuage) –www.ortolang.fr.

Marco Baroni, Silvia Bernardini, Adriano Ferraresi, and Eros Zanchetta. 2009. The wacky wide web: a collection of very large linguistically processed web-crawled corpora. *Language Resources and Evaluation*, 43(3):209–226.

Michele Bevilacqua and Roberto Navigli. 2020. Breaking through the 80% glass ceiling: Raising the state of the art in word sense disambiguation by incorporating knowledge graph information. In *Proceedings of the 58th Annual Meeting of the Association for Computational Linguistics*, pages 2854–2864, Online. Association for Computational Linguistics.

Ahmed El Sheikh, Michele Bevilacqua, and Roberto Navigli. 2021. Integrating personalized PageRank into neural word sense disambiguation. In *Proceedings of the 2021 Conference on Empirical Methods in Natural Language Processing*, pages 9092–9098, Online and Punta Cana, Dominican Republic. Association for Computational Linguistics.

Luyao Huang, Chi Sun, Xipeng Qiu, and Xuanjing Huang. 2019. GlossBERT: BERT for word sense disambiguation with gloss knowledge. In *Proceedings of the 2019 Conference on Empirical Methods in Natural Language Processing and the 9th International Joint Conference on Natural Language Processing (EMNLP-IJCNLP)*, pages 3509–3514, Hong Kong, China. Association for Computational Linguistics.

Sawan Kumar, Sharmistha Jat, Karan Saxena, and Partha Talukdar. 2019. Zero-shot word sense disambiguation using sense definition embeddings. In *Proceedings of the 57th Annual Meeting of the Association for Computational Linguistics*, pages 5670–5681, Florence, Italy. Association for Computational Linguistics.

Hang Le, Loïc Vial, Jibril Frej, Vincent Segonne, Maximin Coavoux, Benjamin Lecouteux, Alexandre Allauzen, Benoît Crabbé, Laurent Besacier, and Didier Schwab. 2020. Flaubert: Unsupervised language model pre-training for french. In *Proceedings of The 12th Language Resources and Evaluation Conference*, pages 2479–2490, Marseille, France. European Language Resources Association.

Louis Martin, Benjamin Muller, Pedro Javier Ortiz Suárez, Yoann Dupont, Laurent Romary, Éric de la Clergerie, Djamé Seddah, and Benoît Sagot. 2020. CamemBERT: a tasty French language model. In *Proceedings of the 58th Annual Meeting of the Association for Computational Linguistics*, pages 7203–7219, Online. Association for Computational Linguistics.

Igor Mel'čuk. 2006. Explanatory Combinatorial Dictionary. In *Open Problems in Linguistics and Lexicography*, polimetrica, monza edition, pages 225–355.

George A. Miller. 1995. Wordnet: A lexical database for english. *Communications of the ACM*, 38:39–41.

Roberto Navigli. 2009. Word sense disambiguation: A survey. *ACM Comput. Surv.*, 41(2).

Alain Polguère. 2014. From Writing Dictionaries to Weaving Lexical Networks. *International Journal of Lexicography*, 27(4):396–418.

Alain Polguère. 2007. Lexical function standardness. In *Selected Lexical and Grammatical Issues in the Meaning–Text Theory*. John Benjamins.

Alessandro Raganato, Claudio Delli Bovi, and Roberto Navigli. 2017. Neural sequence learning models for word sense disambiguation. In *Proceedings of the 2017 Conference on Empirical Methods in Natural Language Processing*, pages 1156–1167, Copenhagen, Denmark. Association for Computational Linguistics.

Vincent Segonne, Marie Candito, and Benoît Crabbé. 2019. Using Wiktionary as a resource for WSD : the case of French verbs. In *Proceedings of the 13th International Conference on Computational Semantics - Long Papers*, pages 259–270, Gothenburg, Sweden. Association for Computational Linguistics.

Loïc Vial, Benjamin Lecouteux, and Didier Schwab. 2019. Sense vocabulary compression through the semantic knowledge of WordNet for neural word sense disambiguation. In *Proceedings of the 10th Global Wordnet Conference*, pages 108–117, Wroclaw, Poland. Global Wordnet Association.

Yorick Wilks and Mark Stevenson. 1998. Word sense disambiguation using optimised combinations of knowledge sources. In *36th Annual Meeting of the Association for Computational Linguistics and 17th International Conference on Computational Linguistics, Volume 2*, pages 1398–1402, Montreal, Quebec, Canada. Association for Computational Linguistics.

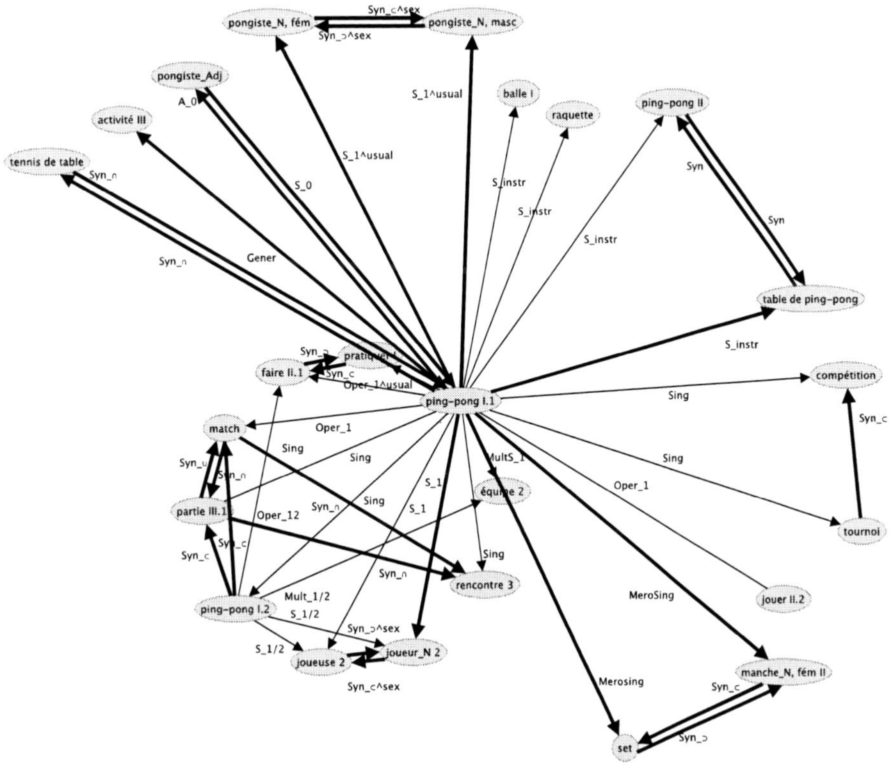

Figure 2: Extract of the *fr-LN* subgraph around the sense *ping-pong#I.1*. Only Lexical Function (LF) links are provided. The thickness of the lines reflects the semantic weight of the relation between two senses.

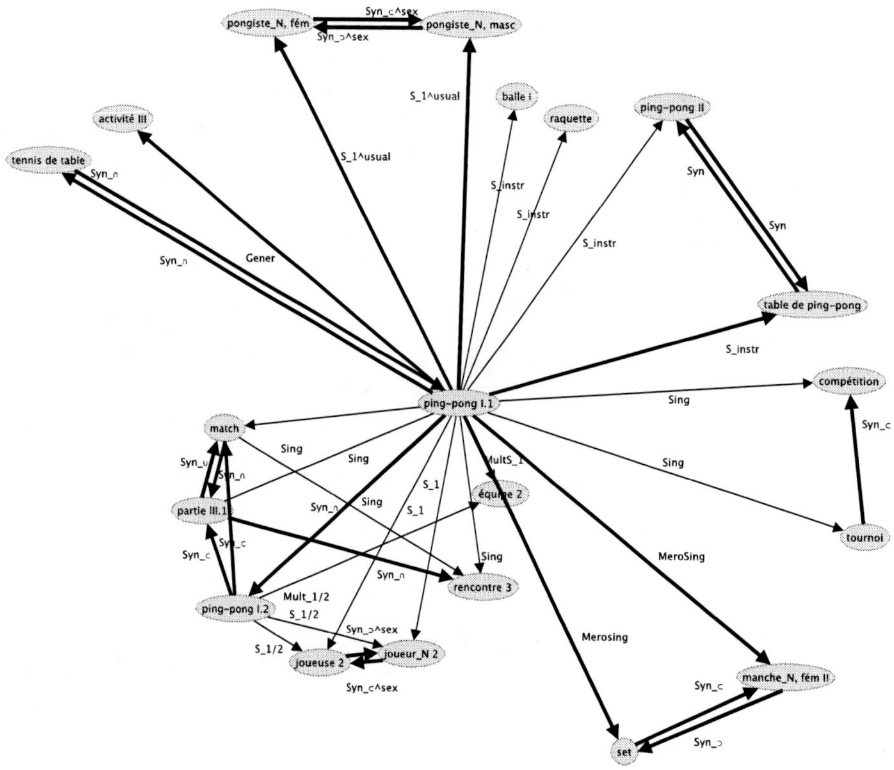

Figure 3: Extract of the *fr-LN* subgraph around the sense *ping-pong#I.1*. Only nouns and Lexical Function (LF) links are provided. The thickness of the lines reflects the semantic weight of the relation between two senses.

RuDSI: graph-based word sense induction dataset for Russian

Anna Aksenova
National Research University
Higher School of Economics
Russia
a.aksenova@hse.ru

Ekaterina Gavrishina, Elisey Rykov
National Research University
Higher School of Economics
Russia
eigavrishina@edu.hse.ru
esrykov@edu.hse.ru

Andrey Kutuzov
University of Oslo
Norway
andreku@ifi.uio.no

Abstract

We present RuDSI, a new benchmark for word sense induction (WSI) in Russian. The dataset was created using manual annotation and semi-automatic clustering of Word Usage Graphs (WUGs). Unlike prior WSI datasets for Russian, RuDSI is completely data-driven (based on texts from Russian National Corpus), with no external word senses imposed on annotators. Depending on the parameters of graph clustering, different derivative datasets can be produced from raw annotation. We report the performance that several baseline WSI methods obtain on RuDSI and discuss possibilities for improving these scores.

1 Introduction

Word sense induction (WSI) is among the most challenging problems in computational linguistics. The difficulty lies not only in the character of the task itself but also in the lack of datasets properly designed for it. We have developed such a dataset for the Russian language by means of manual annotation and clustering of the obtained senses. We dub it *Russian Data-driven Sense Induction* dataset (RuDSI)[1]. Its annotation was based on so-called Word Usage Graphs (WUGs), where word usages in context are nodes connected by edges with weights corresponding to semantic proximity (Schlechtweg et al., 2020). This workflow has been already used to create diachronic semantic change datasets for Russian (Rodina and Kutuzov, 2020; Kutuzov and Pivovarova, 2021), but it is the first time it is employed for designing synchronic WSI benchmarks.

Graphs representing semantic relations between word usages were crucial for the creation of RuDSI. Communities or clusters induced from these graphs correspond to lexical senses; the number and composition of clusters for each word depends not only on human annotation, but also on the particular clustering procedure. Since we provide raw annotators' judgments, other researchers can apply their preferred graph processing techniques and obtain slightly different sense assignments.

The rest of the paper is organized as follows. In Section 2, we talk about the WSI datasets created earlier and their limitations. In Section 3, we present and analyze RuDSI and describe our annotation workflow. In Section 4, we show how graph clustering parameters affect the dataset. Section 5 reports the performance of several baseline WSI methods. In Section 6, we describe to whom and how RuDSI will be useful.[2]

2 Related work

In this section, we give a brief overview of word sense induction datasets for English developed as a part of SemEval competition, take a look at RUSSE'18 dataset and discuss the approaches towards WSI dataset creation.

2.1 SemEval datasets

Existing sense-annotated corpora like SemCor (Miller et al., 1993) allow for building competitive word sense disambiguation (WSD) models since they provide sufficient amount of training data. However, the major problem of such sources is the fact that word sense inventories vary depending on text domain and time period. Thus, WSD models are never universal. To solve this issue, word sense induction task was created. WSI systems aim to infer word senses from the given corpus.

In 2010, a WSI dataset was introduced during the SemEval competition (Manandhar et al., 2010). Compared to SemEval 2007 (Agirre and Soroa, 2007), it was more balanced in terms of nouns and

[1] https://github.com/kategavrishina/RuDSI

[2] This research was supported in part through computational resources of HPC facilities at HSE University (Kostenetskiy et al., 2021).

Proceedings of TextGraphs-16: Graph-based Methods for Natural Language Processing, pages 77–88
October 16, 2022.

verbs distribution (50 verbs and 50 nouns in English). The main difference was in the evaluation procedure. The authors assumed that although WSI task is unsupervised, evaluating the methods on unseen test set of contexts would be more realistic. Different metrics for the clustering quality evaluation were inspected (V-measure, paired F-score) and all of them turned to be biased by number of senses predicted by WSI algorithms.

In 2013, another task setting was suggested by Jurgens and Klapaftis (2013). They claimed that there are contexts where multiple sense tags might be used. Therefore, the setup required predicting the weighted distribution of word senses for each context, i.e., perform *graded* word sense induction. To evaluate this task, two novel measures were introduced: fuzzy B-Cubed and fuzzy normalized mutual information. We should emphasize that our RuDSI dataset is aimed to test systems for *non-graded* word sense induction, although it could be transformed into graded setup (see Section 3.3).

2.2 Russian WSI datasets

Despite the fact that word sense induction task was well-developed for English, there were no manually annotated data for Russian until recently. In the last years, the interest to WSI and WSD tasks in Russian has increased due to the appearance of the first Russian WSI dataset. It was created as a part of RUSSE-18 shared task (Panchenko et al., 2018) and contains three subsets:

1. **wiki-wiki** (automatically extracted examples and senses from Wikipedia articles, mainly homonyms and homographs)

2. **bts-rnc** (examples from the Russian National Corpus (RNC), labeled with senses from the 'Big Explanatory dictionary')

3. **active-dict** (examples and senses from the 'Active dictionary of the Russian language' by Yuri Apresjan (Apresjan, 2014))

The training sections contained a total of about 17 thousand contexts. The key metric for the competition was Adjusted Rand Index (ARI) score (Hubert and Arabie, 1985). The Rand Index calculates the similarity between two clusterings by counting object pairs that were assigned the same or different clusters in golden labeling and in predictions. ARI adds adjustment for chance and gives score close to 0 for random labeling and 1 for identical clusterings. When the clustering is worse than random, ARI is negative.

2.3 Limitations of previous datasets

Unfortunately, RUSSE-18 shared task data has a number of significant limitations. Linguistically, it includes homonyms, polysemous words and homographs, which does not correspond to the original WSI task setting: inducing senses of lexemes with the same set of word forms. In addition, some of the contexts in RUSSE-18 are noisy: there are cases where the target word is actually a root of a composite or a derivation (e.g., 'луковица' *bulb* is suggested as one of the words in context set for target word 'лук' *onion/bow*). The key issue is that word sense cannot be induced in these cases since derivations are mostly non-compositional and do not necessarily maintain the ambiguity relations of parent word. Finally, none of the target words of RUSSE-18 are monosemous, hence the dataset does not test WSI systems for polysemy detection, which is a critical issue in terms of developing a universal algorithm.

All the datasets for both Russian and English SemEval discussed above were automatically or manually tagged with dictionary-based sense inventories. We believe that it might be more realistic to derive word sense inventories for WSI pipelines evaluation not from linguistic sources, but directly from corpora, since the sets of senses vary in different corpora and domains (Kilgarriff, 1997).

2.4 Graph-based WSI datasets

A possible solution comes from combining word-in-context disambiguation and graph clustering. Conceptualization of semantic relationships as graphs empowered the approaches that represent the ambiguous lexeme as a central node in graph where nodes are the words and edge weights represent the measure of association between those words. Hope and Keller (2013) suggests calculating edge weights as a frequency measure for word co-occurrence similarity: the more similar are the contexts of the node lexemes, the higher will be the edge weight bridging them. Such co-occurence graphs are calculated automatically. The similarity networks are afterwards clustered to induce word senses (Hope and Keller, 2013; Sherstuk, 2020).

McCarthy et al. (2016) highlighted the problem of using fixed sets of senses for word sense inventory representation. Graphs used in the paper were derived from word in context disambiguation annotation. They suggested treating annotators' judgements as graph edges and investigated different clusterability measures of such graphs.

Graph clustering has been successfully employed in annotating datasets for semantic change detection task (Schlechtweg et al., 2020, 2021). The annotation process is essentially word-in-context disambiguation: the annotators have to decide whether a pair of sentences represent the same target word sense or not. The annotation forms a *word usage graph* combining the uses from each pair of word contexts, where the nodes are the contexts themselves (sentences), and edges are weighted with the medians of annotators' judgments for a particular pair. Then, using correlation clustering, the graph is separated into clusters (communities of nodes) that correspond to the senses. The method is simple yet quite efficient as the annotators do not assign sense labels directly and the resulting clusters represent a set of data-driven senses[3]. Such a method does not only represent the relations between word usages, but also allows for choosing the granularity of the final word sense inventory. Moreover, the resulting senses are derived from data and not biased by lexicographic information; also, the number of clusters is determined automatically (Schlechtweg et al., 2021).

3 RuDSI dataset

3.1 Target words selection

To create RuDSI, it was first necessary to select a limited number of target words for further manual annotation. As we aimed at having words of different degree of polysemy presented in the final dataset, we extracted the total number of senses for each word in three distinct resources: Russian National Corpus (RNC)[4], representative collection of texts in Russian with linguistic annotation; Wiktionary[5], web-based free dictionary; and RuWordNet(Loukachevitch et al., 2016), a thesaurus of the Russian language created in the format of English WordNet (Miller, 1995). All non-noun words were discarded from this set.

Since the purpose of the annotation was to create a dataset with a balanced number of mono- and polysemous lexemes, we selected eight most frequent words (according to the dictionary by Lyashevskaya and Sharov (2009)) in each of three groups: words with one sense, words with 2-4 senses (moderately polysemous), words with five or more senses (highly polysemous). The value of eight was chosen because of our limitations on the volume of annotation. The final number of senses was calculated as the average[6] between RNC, Wiktionary and RuWordNet for each target word. Note that we did not consider these values as any sort of a gold standard, and they did not affect our human judgements in any way: annotators were not aware about the polysemy groups which the target words belonged to.

Thus, 24 target nouns were prepared for the annotation. For each word from the resulting set, 35 sentences containing this word were randomly sampled from the RNC. Next, annotators were given pairs of these sentences to estimate the relatedness of target word senses between each element in the pair.

3.2 Annotation

The annotation was performed using the DURel web service[7], which allows to annotate pairs of contexts for each word from the loaded sample. At each step of the annotation, a human is offered a pair of sentences to judge. For each pair, the columns 'Sentence 1' and 'Sentence 2' are presented with contexts containing the target word, which is highlighted in bold. The task is to assess how close in meaning the occurrences of the target word are in the two presented sentences on the scale from 1 (Unrelated) to 4 (Identical). The scores of 2 (Distantly Related) and 3 (Closely Related) are more subjective. In general, the 2 rating is for the uses that have different senses, but are somewhat related, and the 3 rating is for the cases when two uses have the same sense with some variation. So, a score of 1 is implied in the following example with the target word 'сторона' which is presented in the Figure 2, indicating that there is no connection between the senses (direct and figurative meaning of the lexeme):

[3]As opposed to dictionary-based senses, since the obtained senses are not taken from any resources, they are the result of automatic clustering.

[4]`https://ruscorpora.ru`; in particular, we used the RNC semantic markup (Rahilina et al., 2009) which includes parts of speech and semantic classes for a large number of lexemes (for example, *fruit/food* for the word 'apricot').

[5]`http://www.wiktionary.org`

[6]The average was preferable to minimum and maximum, since they would give more weight to one of the resources: in Wiktionary, words usually have few senses (1-2), but in RNC, same words can have a lot more senses (6 on average).

[7]`https://durel.ims.uni-stuttgart.de`

(1) a. 'При этом важны не только масштабы производства, но и его качественная сторона, то есть эффективное управление активами...' (the meaning of *'component, element'*)
At the same time, not only the scale of production is important, but also its qualitative ***side****, that is, effective asset management...*

b. 'Так, донеся государю императору Александру о занятии Реймса, полки разошлись на пространстве от города вёрст до тридцати на квартиры в разные стороны.' (the meaning of *'space, direction'*)
So, having informed the Emperor Alexander about the occupation of Reims, the regiments dispersed in the space from the city to thirty versts to apartments in different ***directions****.*

The next example presents the case of two uses with identical senses for the word 'день' (*day*) requiring the score of 4:

(2) a. 'Вещи не были еще расставлены, рамы были частью без стекол, частью с остатками расколотых, и (был дождливый день) с потолка текло.'
Things were not yet arranged, the window frames were partly without glass, partly with the remains of splintered ones, and (it was a rainy ***day****) the ceiling was flowing.*

b. 'Каждый день с раннего утра до обеда и с обеда до вечера я занят был работою или в доме, или в саду, или в огороде'
Every ***day****, from early morning to lunch and from lunch to evening, I was busy working either in the house, or in the garden, or in the vegetable garden.*

For each of the 24 words, as mentioned earlier, 35 sentences were sampled from the RNC. The DURel platform automatically generated random sentence pairs, and at the first stage of our workflow, 180 pairs were annotated for each target word[8]. As a result, 24 separate word usage graphs with 35 nodes each were obtained.

[8] Annotation was performed by a subset of the authors of the article as native Russian speakers.

3.3 Aggregation of senses via graph clustering

Clustering of the sentences obtained as a result of the annotation for each lexeme was performed using the pipeline from (Schlechtweg et al., 2021) based on the variation of correlation clustering (Bansal et al., 2004; Schlechtweg et al., 2020). The DURel relatedness scale from 1 to 4 was derived from continuum of semantic proximity (Blank, 1997): Homonymy - Proximity - Context Variance - Identity. Based on the continuum, the authors rescaled the annotators' judgements for clusterization to represent the idea of usage pairs with 1 and 2 scores belonging to different senses, and with 3 and 4 scores — to the same sense. For this purpose they created the *threshold* parameter which was used to calculate the resulting edge weight: $W'(e) = W(e) - threshold$, and equated it to 2.5 (e.g., a score of 1 became -1.5). The division into clusters is based on the similarity between the target word senses within the sentences in a pair: clustering algorithm minimizes the sum of positive edge weights (3 and 4 scores in the original) across clusters and the sum of negative edge weights (1 and 2 scores) within clusters. Correlation clustering yields only one cluster label for a node (sentence), but by replacing it with a fuzzy graph clustering algorithm like the one in (Peng et al., 2021), it is possible to come up with a graded variation of RuDSI.

As a result of clustering, sense clusters were obtained, which contain examples for each target word, labeled with sense number and connected by edges (the edge weight depends on the number and values of annotators' judgements).

After the first round of annotation, we analyzed the number of *uncompared clusters* — those clusters whose sentences have never been compared in the process of annotation. The existence of uncompared clusters indicates that the graph is not connected enough. We decided that for the five words with the number of uncompared clusters exceeding the average (2.75) additional annotation is required. After the second annotation round (60 extra pairs of sentences for each of five words) there were still four words left for which the number of uncompared clusters has remained almost the same and still exceeded the average number. For these words, sentences from the corresponding clusters were manually selected, organized into pairs and annotated following our regular workflow. After all the annotation rounds, the number of uncompared clusters is not more than two for any target word, and the average number of annotated sentence pairs per word is 215.

Initially, we got a large number of singleton clusters (1.13 on average across words). These are clusters containing only one node (context, usage example). They may appear when the target word is used in a specific context, for example, in an idiomatic expression. Singleton clusters are problematic, since in these cases it is difficult to tell legitimate exotic senses from clustering errors. We planned to filter them out in one of the following ways: not to consider examples from singleton clusters or to attach singleton examples to the largest cluster of a particular word, reducing the total number of senses. However, after reviewing the clusters manually, we noticed that in some lexemes singleton clusters can be aggregated with a larger one, but not with the largest one, and in other lexemes singleton clusters, on the contrary, express a very specific idiomatic expression that can neither be attached to another cluster nor removed from the sample without loss of representative power. So, we decided to leave the singleton clusters untouched and did not filter them out.

Figure 1 shows the distribution of the number of senses for the target words yielded by the annotation procedure (per-word numbers can be found in the Appendix). As can be seen, most words tend to end up having 3-5 senses.

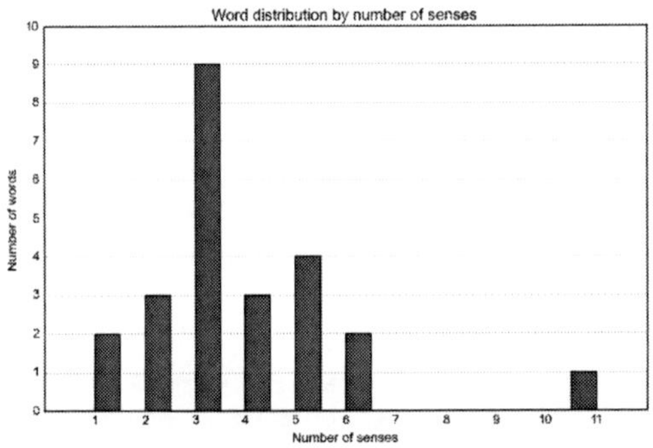

Figure 1: Word distribution by the number of senses obtained in RuDSI.

3.4 Important statistics

Based on the results of clustering, we computed some statistics presented in this subsection. In particular, the ratios of words by the number of senses was calculated. As it turned out, RuDSI contains 8.3% of monosemous words, 62.5% of words with 2-4 senses (moderately polysemous), and 29.2% of words with five or more senses (highly polysemous). Note that these values are different from the original percentages obtained from our linguistics sources. This is expected, since our senses are fully data-driven.

It was also interesting to consider the correlation of these 'data-driven' sense numbers and the degree of lexical polysemy yielded by the RNC, Wiktionary and RuWordNet, on which we relied during the selection of the target words. The Table 1 shows Spearman correlation between the number of clusters in the RuDSI word usage graphs and the number of senses in the sources mentioned above. 'Mean number of senses' is the average between the RNC, Wiktionary and RuWordNet. All the correlations are strong and significant at $p = 0.05$: that is, the resulting clusters based on data-driven sense induction roughly correspond to sense numbers from external linguistic sources.

Source	***Spearman*** ρ	***p value***
RNC	0.84	0.000
Wiktionary	0.43	0.034
RuWordNet	0.73	0.000
Mean number of senses	0.90	0.000

Table 1: Correlation of the word sense numbers between RuDSI and other resources.

In addition, we calculated the Spearman correlation between the number of senses in RuDSI and the target word frequencies from the Lyashevskaya and Sharov (2009) dictionary (based on the RNC). Its value is 0.53 ($p = 0.007$). Therefore, the number of word senses in RuDSI is significantly correlated with word frequencies in the RNC. This is expected, since it is known that frequent words tend to be more polysemous (Zipf, 1945; Hernández-Fernández et al., 2016). It also means than in many cases it is possible to predict the number of RuDSI senses for a word by looking at its RNC frequency.

3.5 Format and technical details

As a result of the steps described above, each example sentence (usage) for each target word was assigned an index of the cluster to which it belongs. We aggregated this data in order to compile a dataset in a format similar to RUSSE-18 (Panchenko et al., 2018). The structure of the RuDSI dataset is presented in the Table 2: word, context (sentence), positions of the word in the context and the gold identifier of the cluster (sense).

word	context	positions	sense_id
'тысяча'	'...тысяча пятьсот запорожцев...'	76-82	0
'тысяча'	'...вмещает 12 тысяч зрителей.'	34-39	0
'тысяча'	'...около 5 тыс. вагонов...'	49-52	0
'тысяча'	'...ну, сотни тысяч.'	34-39	0
'тысяча'	'...на пытки тысячи ни в чем...'	28-34	1

Table 2: RuDSI dataset sample for the word 'тысяча' (*thousand*).

We encourage evaluating state-of-the-art WSI approaches with RuDSI, this is why it was important for the texts in the dataset to not exceed 512 tokens in length. The maximum sequence length is always added to the Transformers architecture models due to the attention layers, which are quadratically scaled with increasing sequence length. 512 tokens is the popular maximum sequence length, which was first specified in BERT. The only sentence in RuDSI (out of 840) which has been longer than this value has been truncated to 512 tokens.

4 Robustness of clustering

In order to verify the stability of clustering algorithm we experimented with changing the default hyperparameters and analyzed the resulting data in comparison with the default sense clusters presented in RuDSI. In the pipeline (Schlechtweg et al., 2021), there were two parameters that could affect the obtained clusters: the threshold used to rescale the annotators' judgements and the number of clustering iterations. The threshold parameter was previously described in 3.3: it affects the resulting weights on the graph edges. Originally, the threshold was 2.5 causing 1 and 2 scores ('Unrelated' and 'Distantly Related') to transform to negative values, and 3 and 4 scores ('Closely Related' and 'Identical') to remain positive to represent the contrast between different senses and the same sense of the word. We reviewed two other options: the threshold equaled to 1.5 (so that a score of 1 became negative (-0.5) and contrasted with 2, 3 and 4 scores that were matched to 0.5, 1.5 and 2.5 respectively) and equaled to 3.5 (1, 2 and 3 scores were opposed to a score of 4; only the sentences marked us 'Identical' were considered as containing the same sense of the word).

The number of clustering iterations ('iters' parameter) stands for the number of passes through the same graph given that the input graph is the result of the previous iteration. Each pass performs the clustering algorithm and minimizes the loss of the obtained clusters.

In Table 3, are presented the mean and standard deviation of ARI score among words between the default clustering and clusterings with modified hyperparameters. We can conclude that the number of iterations does not greatly affect the resulting clusters, even as a result of a single iteration ('iters' = 1) approximately the same clustering is obtained. However the threshold parameter strongly influences the obtained clusters as it reforms the original idea of similarity of different judgements during the annotation.

iters	threshold	*Mean ARI*	*SD ARI*
5	2.5	–	–
5	1.5	0.12	0.29
5	3.5	0.27	0.26
1	2.5	0.95	0.13
3	2.5	0.95	0.10
4	2.5	0.95	0.11
6	2.5	0.94	0.13

Table 3: Similarity (by ARI) of the default RuDSI clustering and clusterings obtained by changing hyperparameters. 'SD' stands for standard deviation.

We also examined the change in the number of singleton clusters depending on clustering hyperparameters. Similarly, the threshold parameter has a much stronger effect than the number of iterations. The threshold of 1.5 causes merging of most senses into one cluster (sense) and separation of the minimal number of singleton clusters (0.13 on average). In turn, the threshold of 3.5 generates division into a larger number of clusters most of which are singleton clusters (6.33 on average). Notably, the iterations parameter is inversely proportional to the number of singleton clusters: the more iterations, the more singleton clusters are attached to larger clusters (the more senses are considered the same). A summary of singleton clusters analysis can be found in Table 4.

5 Baseline WSI methods performance

In this section, we show how the existing WSI methods perform on RuDSI. We deliberately did not experiment with the state-of-the-art lexical substitution method (Amrami and Goldberg, 2019). The goal is to report the results of the baseline approaches, leaving more advanced methods for future research.

iters	threshold	*# Singletons*	*SD*
5	2.5	1.13	0.74
5	1.5	0.13	0.45
5	3.5	6.33	4.43
1	2.5	1.21	0.83
3	2.5	1.13	0.8
4	2.5	1.13	0.95
6	2.5	1.08	0.88

Table 4: Statistics for singleton clusters in the default RuDSI clustering and clusterings obtained by changing hyperparameters. 'Singletons' is the average number of singleton clusters among words. 'SD' stands for standard deviation.

5.1 Naive baselines

Two naive baselines were implemented for WSI problem solution, namely assignment of the same sense for all target words, and a random choice of two senses for each target word.

5.2 Birch

Next, we applied more advanced embedding-based approaches. One of the methods top-rated in the RUSSE-18 shared task is static embeddings clustering (Panchenko et al., 2018). After testing different clustering algorithms, we settled on Birch (Zhang et al., 1996), which provided the best results. We used the following pipeline: first, we calculated sentence embeddings as an average over word embeddings for each context, second, all embeddings within each target context were divided into two clusters. For word embedding extraction we used *ruwikiruscorpora-func_upos_skipgram_300_5_2019* Word2Vec model trained on RNC and Wikipedia from the RusVectores web service (Kutuzov and Kuzmenko, 2017).

5.3 Jamsic

Jamsic method was also included in the list of the best systems in the RUSSE-18 shared task description paper (Panchenko et al., 2018). Using the Word2Vec model specified above, the nearest neighbor for each target word is extracted. The embedding of this word represents the first sense of the target word. Then this embedding is subtracted from the embedding of the target word and the embedding of the second sense is obtained. Finally, we get an average embedding for each sentence and determine to which sense it is closer by cosine similarity. This method works with one word sense and its nearest one, so it always distributes contexts into only two senses.

5.4 Egvi

This is a relatively new approach that has successfully proved itself in solving the WSI problem for different languages. For this method, we used Russian sense inventories pre-generated by processing ego graphs (Logacheva et al., 2020), and for each target word we received an average embedding of each sense from sense inventories. For word embeddings, we used the same *ruwikiruscorpora-func_upos_skipgram_300_5_2019* model. Then we removed the target word from RuDSI contexts, received average word embeddings and clustered them with the KMeans algorithm, passing embeddings of values from sense inventories as cluster centers. The parameter of number of clusters for each target word was equal to number of senses in sense inventories for this word.

5.5 BERT KMeans

BERT-based embeddings proved to be efficient in solving RUSSE-18 too (Slapoguzov et al., 2021). We took the *sbert_large_nlu_ru* model[9] as a feature extractor and used token embeddings from its last layer. For calculating the representation of words split during tokenization, mean pooling was used. Word vectors were clustered by the KMeans algorithm into two senses.

We also tried to do KMeans clustering of BERT embeddings by taking the number of clusters from Egvi sense inventories.

5.6 Results

The mean and standard deviation of ARI score among words are presented in Table 5. The ARI metric takes into account randomness when clustering, so the ARI of the Random sense method is 0.0. The approaches that became the best in the RUSSE-18 shared task do not gain values higher than 0.05 on RuDSI. The simplest One sense baseline is better than BERT clustering. Arguably, the low BERT results are caused by the number of clusters parameter of the KMeans algorithm, which was equal to 2, while only two target words (out of 24) actually had two senses. Egvi algorithm proved to be the best. This method was based on the pre-generated

[9] https://huggingface.co/sberbank-ai/sbert_large_nlu_ru

sense inventories, in which the number of senses often was identical to RuDSI, so it worked better than BERT KMeans. The number of Egvi senses improved the quality of clustering of BERT embeddings, but not enough to exceed the native Egvi.

For comparison, the table shows the results of the methods on the RUSSE-18 dataset. Due to a number of limitations described earlier, a wiki-wiki dataset was taken for comparison. It is noticeable that the values of the ARI metric for the basic methods on wiki-wiki are much higher.

We also found no correlation between the density of the word graph and the values of the ARI metric, with the exception of the Jamsic method, for which the correlation results are significant at a significance level of $p = 0.05$.

Method	RuDSI		RUSSE	
	Mean ARI	SD ARI	Mean ARI	SD ARI
One sense	0.08	0.28	0.00	0.00
Random sense	0.00	0.00	0.01	0.00
Birch	0.03	0.14	0.93	0.10
Jamsic	0.04	0.10	0.58	0.47
BERT KMeans	0.03	0.14	0.85	0.06
BERT KMeans + Egvi	0.08	0.31	0.64	0.31
Egvi	**0.17**	0.22	0.59	0.16

Table 5: Performance of WSI methods on RuDSI and RUSSE. 'SD' stands for standard deviation.

6 Intended RuDSI audience

Our vision is that RuDSI might be of use for three different communities.

1. Researchers analyzing NLP systems in terms their WSD and WSI abilities for Russian. It is especially important for evaluating contextualized language models trained on large-scale corpora using deep neural architectures, from RNNs to Transformers and beyond. RussianSuperGLUE benchmark (Shavrina et al., 2020) already includes the RUSSE dataset (cast as a binary classification task). We believe RuDSI might be a useful addition, representing a more difficult task related to lexical senses. As was shown in 5, it cannot be solved with trivial baselines (Iazykova et al., 2021), which makes it an interesting NLP challenge.

2. Graph theory researchers and all those interested in applications of graphs to real world tasks. Word usage graphs we are providing are representative of contextual semantic similarity judgments by humans. These graphs can be processed and clustered in different ways, yielding different 'views' of Russian word sense inventories. In addition, the properties of word usage graphs themselves can bring new insights for both graph theory and Russian linguistics.

3. Finally, our work on RuDSI is a part of a larger project of implementing WSI features into the RNC web interface. RuDSI is based on RNC data, so it will be used to evaluate various WSI solutions and choose the best one. Thus, it is going to be directly or indirectly used by the large RNC audience, consisting of both linguists and general population.

7 Conclusion

We have presented RuDSI, a novel graph-based word sense induction dataset for Russian, obtained by clustering word usage graphs produced by human annotation. It includes words with different degrees of polysemy (monosemous, moderately polysemous and highly polysemous words). The sense inventories are generated in a completely data-driven way as well. Importantly, depending on what graph processing workflow is used, slightly different datasets can be produced from the same raw RuDSI human judgments.

We report the RuDSI performance for only the simplest and most basic approaches to WSI, so a possible future work would be to apply some more advanced methods to it. Also we have considered only nouns, so it would be interesting to experiment with other parts of speech as well (this will require a new round of annotation). Since most of the target words in RuDSI have 3-5 senses, the addition of highly polysemous words may become another future improvement. In addition, it would be beneficial to extend the list of contexts for each word, however extra annotation would be required.

References

Eneko Agirre and Aitor Soroa. 2007. SemEval-2007 task 02: Evaluating word sense induction and discrimination systems. In *Proceedings of the Fourth International Workshop on Semantic Evaluations (SemEval-2007)*, pages 7–12, Prague, Czech Republic. Association for Computational Linguistics.

Asaf Amrami and Yoav Goldberg. 2019. Towards better substitution-based word sense induction. *arXiv preprint arXiv:1905.12598*.

Juri Apresjan. 2014. Active dictionary of russian. *Meaning-Text Theory*, 2014.

Nikhil Bansal, Avrim Blum, and Shuchi Chawla. 2004. Correlation clustering. *Machine learning*, 56(1):89–113.

Andreas Blank. 1997. *Prinzipien des lexikalischen Bedeutungswandels am Beispiel der romanischen Sprachen.* Niemeyer, Tübingen.

Antoni Hernández-Fernández, Bernardino Casas, Ramon Ferrer-i Cancho, and Jaume Baixeries. 2016. Testing the robustness of laws of polysemy and brevity versus frequency. In *International Conference on Statistical Language and Speech Processing*, pages 19–29. Springer.

David Hope and Bill Keller. 2013. Maxmax: a graph-based soft clustering algorithm applied to word sense induction. In *International Conference on Intelligent Text Processing and Computational Linguistics*, pages 368–381. Springer.

Lawrence Hubert and Phipps Arabie. 1985. Comparing partitions. *Journal of classification*, 2(1):193–218.

Tatyana Iazykova, Denis Kapelyushnik, Olga Bystrova, and Andrey Kutuzov. 2021. Unreasonable effectiveness of rule-based heuristics in solving Russian SuperGLUE tasks. *Komp'yuternaya Lingvistika i Intellektual'nye Tekhnologii: Dialog conference.*

David Jurgens and Ioannis Klapaftis. 2013. SemEval-2013 task 13: Word sense induction for graded and non-graded senses. In *Second Joint Conference on Lexical and Computational Semantics (*SEM), Volume 2: Proceedings of the Seventh International Workshop on Semantic Evaluation (SemEval 2013)*, pages 290–299, Atlanta, Georgia, USA. Association for Computational Linguistics.

Adam Kilgarriff. 1997. I don't believe in word senses. *Computers and the Humanities*, 31(2):91–113.

P. S. Kostenetskiy, R. A. Chulkevich, and V. I. Kozyrev. 2021. HPC resources of the higher school of economics. *Journal of Physics: Conference Series*, 1740(1):012050.

Andrey Kutuzov and Elizaveta Kuzmenko. 2017. Webvectors: A toolkit for building web interfaces for vector semantic models. In *Analysis of Images, Social Networks and Texts: 5th International Conference, AIST 2016, Yekaterinburg, Russia, April 7-9, 2016, Revised Selected Papers*, pages 155–161, Cham. Springer International Publishing.

Andrey Kutuzov and Lidia Pivovarova. 2021. Three-part diachronic semantic change dataset for Russian. In *Proceedings of the 2nd International Workshop on Computational Approaches to Historical Language Change 2021*, pages 7–13, Online. Association for Computational Linguistics.

Varvara Logacheva, Denis Teslenko, Artem Shelmanov, Steffen Remus, Dmitry Ustalov, Andrey Kutuzov, Ekaterina Artemova, Chris Biemann, Simone Paolo Ponzetto, and Alexander Panchenko. 2020. Word sense disambiguation for 158 languages using word embeddings only. In *Proceedings of the 12th Language Resources and Evaluation Conference*, pages 5943–5952, Marseille, France. European Language Resources Association.

Natalia V Loukachevitch, German Lashevich, Anastasia A Gerasimova, Vladimir V Ivanov, and Boris V Dobrov. 2016. Creating russian wordnet by conversion. In *Computational Linguistics and Intellectual Technologies: papers from the Annual conference "Dialogue*, pages 405–415.

Ol'ga Nikolaevna Lyashevskaya and Sergej Aleksandrovich Sharov. 2009. *Chastotny'j slovar' sovremennogo russkogo yazy'ka: na materialax Nacional'nogo korpusa russkogo yazy'ka.* Azbukovnik.

Suresh Manandhar, Ioannis Klapaftis, Dmitriy Dligach, and Sameer Pradhan. 2010. SemEval-2010 task 14: Word sense induction &disambiguation. In *Proceedings of the 5th International Workshop on Semantic Evaluation*, pages 63–68, Uppsala, Sweden. Association for Computational Linguistics.

Diana McCarthy, Marianna Apidianaki, and Katrin Erk. 2016. Word sense clustering and clusterability. *Computational Linguistics*, 42(2):245–275.

George A Miller. 1995. Wordnet: a lexical database for english. *Communications of the ACM*, 38(11):39–41.

George A Miller, Claudia Leacock, Randee Tengi, and Ross T Bunker. 1993. A semantic concordance. In *Human Language Technology: Proceedings of a Workshop Held at Plainsboro, New Jersey, March 21-24, 1993.*

Alexander Panchenko, Anastasia Lopukhina, Dmitry Ustalov, Konstantin Lopukhin, Nikolay Arefyev, Alexey Leontyev, and Natalia Loukachevitch. 2018. RUSSE'2018: A Shared Task on Word Sense Induction for the Russian Language. In *Computational Linguistics and Intellectual Technologies: Papers from the Annual International Conference "Dialogue"*, pages 547–564, Moscow, Russia. RSUH.

Yong Peng, Xin Zhu, Feiping Nie, Wanzeng Kong, and Yuan Ge. 2021. Fuzzy graph clustering. *Information Sciences*, 571:38–49.

Ekaterina Rahilina, Galina Kustova, Ol'ga Lyashevskaya, Tatyana Reznikova, and Ol'ga Shemanayeva. 2009. Zadachi i principy semanticheskо'j razmetki leksiki v nkrya. In *Russian National Corpus: 2006-2008. New results and perspectives*, pages 215–240. Nestor-Istorija.

Julia Rodina and Andrey Kutuzov. 2020. RuSemShift: a dataset of historical lexical semantic change in Russian. In *Proceedings of the 28th International Conference on Computational Linguistics*, pages 1037–1047, Barcelona, Spain (Online). International Committee on Computational Linguistics.

Dominik Schlechtweg, Barbara McGillivray, Simon Hengchen, Haim Dubossarsky, and Nina Tahmasebi. 2020. SemEval-2020 task 1: Unsupervised lexical semantic change detection. In *Proceedings of the Fourteenth Workshop on Semantic Evaluation*, pages 1–23, Barcelona (online). International Committee for Computational Linguistics.

Dominik Schlechtweg, Nina Tahmasebi, Simon Hengchen, Haim Dubossarsky, and Barbara McGillivray. 2021. DWUG: A large resource of diachronic word usage graphs in four languages. In *Proceedings of the 2021 Conference on Empirical Methods in Natural Language Processing*, pages 7079–7091, Online and Punta Cana, Dominican Republic. Association for Computational Linguistics.

Tatiana Shavrina, Alena Fenogenova, Emelyanov Anton, Denis Shevelev, Ekaterina Artemova, Valentin Malykh, Vladislav Mikhailov, Maria Tikhonova, Andrey Chertok, and Andrey Evlampiev. 2020. RussianSuperGLUE: A Russian language understanding evaluation benchmark. In *Proceedings of the 2020 Conference on Empirical Methods in Natural Language Processing (EMNLP)*, pages 4717–4726, Online. Association for Computational Linguistics.

Leonid Sherstuk. 2020. Context-based text-graph embeddings in word-sense induction tasks. Master's thesis, HSE.

Aleksandr Slapoguzov, Konstantin Malyuga, and Evgenij Tsopa. 2021. Word sense induction for Russian texts using BERT. In *Proceedings of the 28th Conference of Fruct Association, Moscow, Russia*, pages 25–29.

Tian Zhang, Raghu Ramakrishnan, and Miron Livny. 1996. Birch: An efficient data clustering method for very large databases. In *Proceedings of the 1996 ACM SIGMOD International Conference on Management of Data*, SIGMOD '96, page 103–114, New York, NY, USA. Association for Computing Machinery.

George Kingsley Zipf. 1945. The meaning-frequency relationship of words. *The Journal of general psychology*, 33(2):251–256.

A Annotation interface

B Word usage graph

C Detailed performance

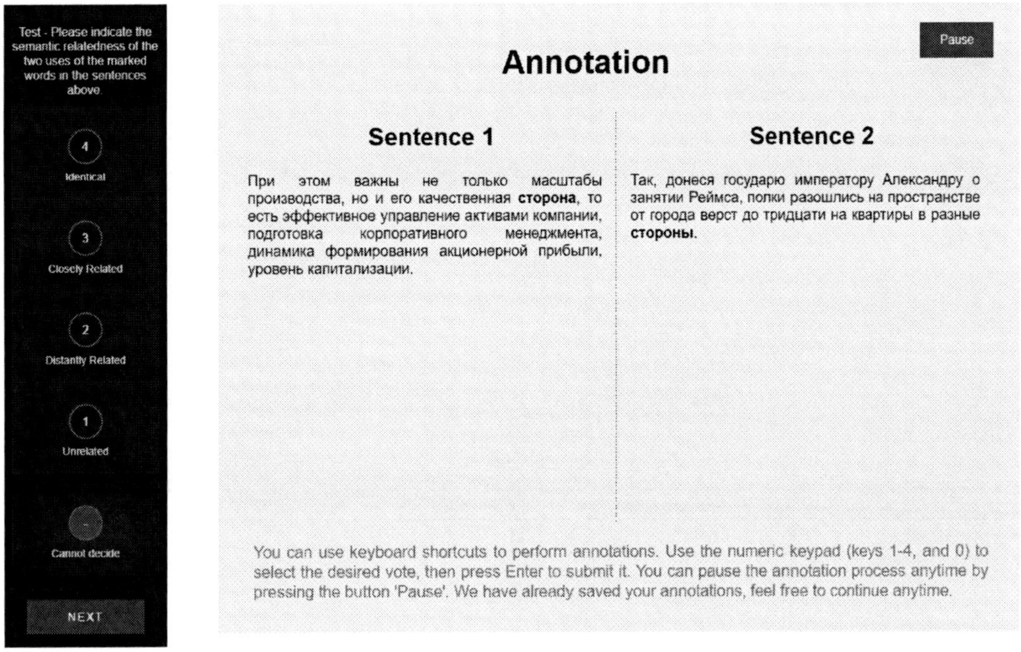

Figure 2: Example of the word 'сторона' (*side, direction*) annotation in the DURel interface.

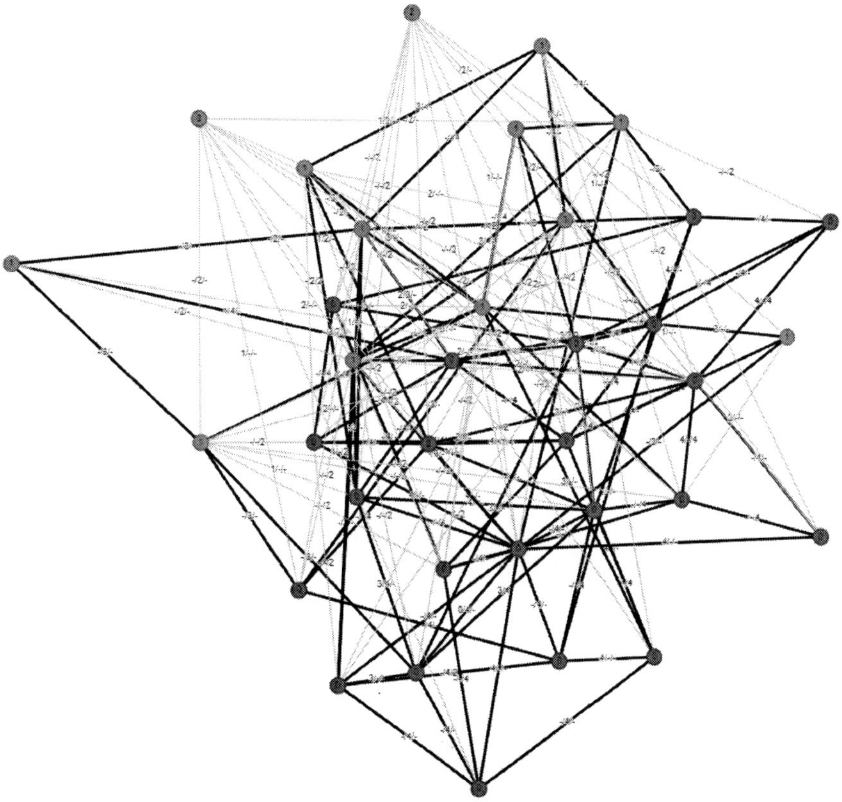

Figure 3: Word usage graph for the word 'голова' (*head*) as a result of clustering (four clusters, marked with node color).

Word	One sense	Random sense	Birch	Jamsic	BERT KMeans	Egvi	BERT KMeans + Egvi	№ of clusters
'Бог' (God)	0.00	-0.02	-0.04	0.13	-0.04	-0.04	0.01	3
'Время' (time)	0.00	-0.03	0.02	0.00	-0.07	-0.01	-0.04	6
'Год' (year)	0.00	0.06	-0.03	0.01	-0.02	-0.04	0.13	3
'Голова' (head)	0.00	-0.03	0.51	-0.02	0.20	0.61	-0.02	4
'Город' (city)	0.00	-0.01	-0.03	0.01	-0.01	1.00	0.00	2
'Государство' (state)	-0.06	0.02	-0.04	-0.06	-0.05	-0.04	-0.05	3
'Дело' (business)	0.00	0.03	-0.01	0.00	0.01	0.02	0.08	11
'День' (day)	0.00	0.11	-0.05	0.08	-0.02	-0.05	0.00	5
'Друг' (friend)	0.00	-0.02	0.25	-0.04	-0.09	0.12	-0.01	3
'Жена' (wife)	0.00	-0.03	0.00	-0.03	-0.04	0.00	0.0	2
'Женщина' (woman)	1.00	0.00	0.00	0.00	0.00	1.00	1.0	1
'Жизнь' (life)	0.00	0.00	0.33	-0.01	-0.13	-0.04	0.04	4
'Лицо' (face)	0.00	-0.02	0.05	0.50	0.39	0.00	0.61	3
'Место' (place)	0.00	0.05	-0.10	0.09	0.01	-0.04	-0.02	4
'Мир' (world)	0.00	-0.01	0.13	0.14	0.04	0.20	0.00	5
'Ночь' (night)	1.00	0.00	0.00	0.00	0.00	0.00	0.00	1
'Работа' (work)	0.00	-0.01	-0.04	-0.04	-0.04	0.15	0.05	5
'Результат' (result)	0.00	0.01	-0.07	0.04	0.01	0.63	-0.03	2
'Рука' (hand)	0.00	0.00	-0.08	0.06	0.38	0.16	0.05	3
'Сила' (power)	0.00	-0.01	-0.02	-0.02	0.22	-0.02	0.04	6
'Слово' (word)	0.00	-0.03	0.01	0.01	0.19	0.00	0.00	3
'Сторона' (side)	0.00	-0.01	-0.04	0.21	0.30	0.41	0.20	5
'Тысяча' (thousand)	0.00	0.00	-0.08	-0.01	-0.05	-0.04	-0.01	3
'Человек' (human)	0.00	0.00	-0.04	-0.06	-0.00	0.00	0.00	3

Table 6: Detailed performance of WSI methods.

Temporal Graph Analysis of Misinformation Spreaders in Social Media

Joan Plepi[*†] and **Flora Sakketou**[*†] and **Henri-Jacques Geiß**[‡] and **Lucie Flek** [†]
[†]Conversational AI and Social Analytics (CAISA) Lab
Department of Mathematics and Computer Science, University of Marburg
[‡]Department of Computer Science, Technical University of Darmstadt
{flora.sakketou, joan.plepi, lucie.flek}@uni-marburg.de,
henri-jacques.geiss@stud.tu-darmstadt.de
* These authors contributed equally to this work

Abstract

Proactively identifying misinformation spreaders is an important step towards mitigating the impact of fake news on our society. Although the news domain is subject to rapid changes over time, the temporal dynamics of the spreaders' language and network have not been explored yet. In this paper, we analyze the users' time-evolving semantic similarities and social interactions and show that such patterns can, on their own, indicate misinformation spreading. Building on these observations, we propose a dynamic graph-based framework that leverages the dynamic nature of the users' network for detecting fake news spreaders. We validate our design choice through qualitative analysis and demonstrate the contributions of our model's components through a series of exploratory and ablative experiments on two datasets.

1 Introduction

With the popularity of social media platforms constantly increasing, the dissemination of false online information becomes a major hurdle, having catastrophic effects on our society (McKay and Tenove, 2021). It is essential to address this issue early on; to efficiently and rapidly identify misinformation spreaders and spurious accounts which are likely to propagate posts from unreliable news sources. To this end, we introduce an early warning model that distinguishes authors who have repeatedly shared news from unreliable sources in the past, from those that share news from reliable sources. We use the terms 'misinformation spreaders' and 'real news spreaders' for each user class, respectively. In this paper, the term *misinformation* is used as an umbrella term that covers *misinformation, disinformation, partisan news and satirical content*. Figure 1 depicts examples of the posting activity for each user class.

Recently, significant attention has garnered towards graph representational learning methods (Wu et al., 2021) due to their advances in various NLP domains. Kim and Ko (2021) use a graph-based approach to model the semantic relationship between sentences in a document for fake news detection. Rath et al. (2021) apply graph neural networks to explore the social network of misinformation spreaders and show that interpersonal trust plays a significant role in differentiating them from real news spreaders. Such graph approaches are able to model user-to-user relationships and therefore provide a promising underexplored research direction for identifying misinformation spreaders.

The impact of time on fake news prediction has made the task even more challenging, as the content-based differences of news sources change due to the highly dynamic nature of the news topics (Horne et al., 2019). Most of the fake news detection methods that use static features need to be continuously updated with new annotated data to stay relevant (Kwon et al., 2017). We argue that this hypothesis can be generalized for detecting misinformation spreaders. Similarly to feature-based methods, existing graph modeling approaches are not specifically designed for learning the time-evolving similarities of the users' interactions. Addressing these limitations of existing research, we propose an approach accounting for the temporal dynamics of user-to-user relationships instead. We introduce a model that extracts features from users' content similarities and social interactions and models the temporal evolution of these connections in order to identify misinformation spreaders. In addition, our study aims to answer the following research questions:

RQ1: Do the users' semantic similarities and social interactions fluctuate over time?

RQ2: Are temporal relationships indicative of misinformation spreading behavior?

For the first exploration, we formulate the problem as a binary classification task, with a potential for a more fine-grained approach in the future. We

Proceedings of TextGraphs-16: Graph-based Methods for Natural Language Processing, pages 89–104
October 16, 2022.

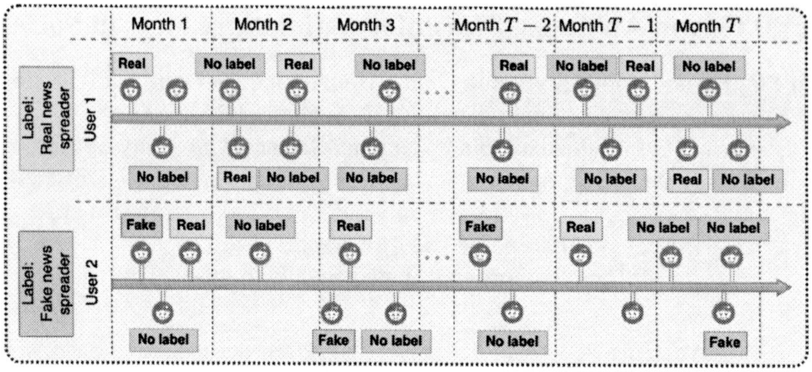

Figure 1: **Examples of the user classes.**

first build dynamic linguistic and social graphs, which are constructed based on the users' posting behaviour within consecutive time-windows. Subsequently, the generated temporal graph representations are treated as a sequence of features for the final classification. To the best of our knowledge, dynamic graph modelling has not been utilized for identifying misinformation spreaders in other works. We conduct a series of exploratory analyses in the user-to-user relationships. Through ablative experiments, we show the effectiveness of our model's components for profiling misinformation spreaders. Our contributions are as follows:

- We provide a comprehensive qualitative and quantitative analysis of the users' temporal semantic and social similarities and investigate the different types of dynamic graph connections.
- We develop a dynamic graph neural network framework for (a) predicting the users' future misinformation spreading behavior, (b) predicting the behavior of unseen users, and (c) predicting misinformation spreading behavior in a zero-shot scenario.
- We show that our proposed dynamic framework outperforms the baseline content-based models as well as the static graph model.
- We release our code to encourage future research.

2 Background and Related Work

While user profiling approaches have been investigated for various tasks, it wasn't until after the PAN 2020 competition (Bevendorff et al., 2020) that the problem of misinformation spreaders identification gained the attention of the research community. Most recent studies are focused on analyzing emotional signals (Giachanou et al., 2021), personality and linguistic patterns (Mu and Aletras, 2020; Giachanou et al., 2020). These methods rely on the assumption that the content, and therefore the features that are extracted, remains constant over time. While static linguistic patterns have proven to be useful features for misinformation spreader detection, none of the current methods explore temporal aspects of their behavior. Our model utilizes the users' contextualized content embeddings as user (node) representations and simultaneously leverages their content similarities over time and social interactions dynamically (via edges in the temporal graph).

In the context of user modelling, graph representational learning approaches (Kipf and Welling, 2016; Veličković et al., 2018; Chami et al., 2019) have made significant advances in enhancing NLP models for various tasks (Mishra et al., 2019; Chopra et al., 2020; Sawhney et al., 2021; Kacupaj et al., 2021; Plepi and Flek, 2021). Rath et al. (2020, 2021) identified misinformation spreaders by extracting features from a network that is built based on interpersonal trust metrics. Despite their success, a limitation of the existing approaches is that they do not account for the temporal dynamics of the semantic and social connections.

We argue that the users' characteristics and interactions change dynamically over time due to the dynamic nature of the news cycle, therefore temporal graphs are more suitable to model the evolution of the user-to-user relationships (Wu et al., 2021). Our hypothesis, inspired by Bahns et al. (2017), is that both the social and the content similarity patterns of misinformation spreaders differ from those of other users.

The concept of temporal graphs has been around for some years (Rossi et al., 2020; Seo et al., 2016; Han et al., 2014) with numerous applications (Guo et al., 2019; Li et al., 2018; Yan et al., 2018). The most relevant to our work is the model proposed by Sawhney et al. (2020), leveraging signals from financial data, social media, and inter-stock relationships via a graph neural network in a hierarchical temporal fashion. We draw inspiration from these approaches and propose a dynamic temporal graph for misinformation spreader detection.

3 Datasets

FACTOID Dataset (Reddit). We utilized the FACTOID dataset published by (Sakketou et al., 2022), which includes a sufficient amount of user history, and, more importantly, simultaneous information on the users' social behavior (Pardo et al., 2020). To the best of our knowledge, this is the only dataset that contains a sufficient amount of social connections to build dense temporal graphs. FACTOID contains a total of 3.3M posts authored by 4.1K users, with 73.8% of the users being "real news spreaders" while the rest 26.2% being misinformation spreaders, determined by the factuality of the news sources they link to. The data covers the period before and after the US elections (from January 2020 to April 2021), making it an ideal dataset for investigating temporal relationships since this time period includes significant events regarding the political scene.

Twitter Dataset. To generalize our content similarity dynamics findings, we utilize in addition the Twitter dataset released by Mu and Aletras (2020). Since the dataset contained the labels and the user IDs, we re-crawled the users' posting history. After filtering the users whose handles were deleted or had insufficient data, the resulting dataset contained 3.5K users and 2.6M posts with roughly 40:60 class distribution of fake and real news spreaders respectively. Since there are practically no social interactions between the users in this dataset, we report results only with the semantic similarity graphs. We split the dataset into train (70%), development (20%) and test (10%) as in the original paper.

	FACTOID	Twitter
Total number of posts	3,354,450	2,626,176
Total number of users	4,150	3,541
# of misinformation spreaders	3,064	1,455
# of real news spreaders	1,086	2,086

Table 1: Summary of dataset statistics for FACTOID and Twitter.

4 Temporal Graph Construction

4.1 Encoding Users

Each user u^i is associated with a posting history $\mathcal{H}^i$. We partition the complete posting time period in equal discrete time frames τ, containing the users' posts that were posted within these time frames.

User2Vec. We adopt User2Vec (Amir et al., 2016) to compute each user's representation $E^i_\tau \in \mathbb{R}^{200}$ based on their corresponding historical posts within the time frame τ, by optimizing the conditional probability of texts given the author.

UBERT. In addition, we use Sentence-BERT (SBERT) (Reimers and Gurevych, 2019) to encode each user's individual historical posts, and we obtain each user's temporal historical encoding $E^i_\tau \in \mathbb{R}^{768}$ by averaging over the posting history length within a corresponding time frame τ.

4.2 Individual Graph construction

We model the user's temporal relationships by constructing a sequence of graphs $\mathcal{G}_1, \mathcal{G}_2, \ldots, \mathcal{G}_T$ corresponding to each time frame τ. Each graph $\mathcal{G}_\tau$ is comprised by a set of user nodes $\mathcal{V}_\tau$ that have posted at least once within the time frame τ and a set of edges $\mathcal{E}_\tau$ between these users. We construct the following types of graphs.

Semantic graph. The user embeddings E^i_τ represent each user's context within the time period τ. Users with semantically similar content are close in the vector space (Reimers and Gurevych, 2019) since they have similar context encoding. To construct the users' semantic graphs $\mathcal{G}^{sem}_\tau = (\mathcal{V}_\tau, \mathcal{E}^{sem}_\tau)$, we calculate all the pairwise cosine similarities between the users' embeddings within a time period τ; $cos(E^i_\tau, E^j_\tau)$. We form connections between two users only if their cosine similarity is above a high threshold θ, representing the semantic similarity between two users.

Social graph. On Reddit, users engage in various discussions with their peers. Social science argues that like-minded people tend to interact more with each other (Bahns et al., 2017), therefore, for the FACTOID dataset, we are able to construct the social graph $\mathcal{G}^{soc}_\tau = (\mathcal{V}_\tau, \mathcal{E}^{soc}_\tau)$ in a way that captures the users' social interactions with each other. We define as social interaction the replies and mentions in a post thread. For each thread of posts, we connect all the chain of replies to the root (i.e.

the original post) of the conversation and all mentions/replies to each other. Next, these post connections are translated to user connections in the social graph (Appendix A.2). In the Twitter dataset, the social connections are too few therefore we were unable to build dense temporal graphs.

4.3 Temporal Analysis of Graphs

To answer the *RQ1*, we wish to monitor the temporal evolution of the users' semantic similarities and social interactions between different groups of users over time and associate those temporal fluctuations to the political landscape. We group the users by their credibility label (misinformation spreaders, real news spreaders) and define three different *edge types*: (1) edges between misinformation spreaders ('m2m'), (2) edges between real news spreader ('r2r') and (3) edges between misinformation spreaders and real news spreaders ('m2r'). We partition the users' total posting period (from the start of January 2020 until the end of April 2021) to 16 monthly time periods, and we compute the connections' percentage within each time period for all edge types. The connections' percentage can be interpreted as the normalized edge count of a particular edge type during a time period τ (see Appendix A.4 for more details). For the temporal semantic graphs, an increase in this metric essentially shows an increase in the language usage similarity between different user groups. Correspondingly, for the social graphs, an increase would show that two user groups engage in discourse and share opinions in a thread.

Can we detect different temporal relationship patterns depending on the users' credibility?

Figure 2 depicts the connections' percentage on the semantic graph and the social graph. For both graphs, we can observe that the 'm2r' connections percentage is consistently the lowest for all time periods, indicating that on an aggregate level, misinformation spreaders and real news spreaders do not have as much context similarity to each other and avoid socially interacting with each other. On the other hand, misinformation spreaders seem to be more densely connected with each other and tend to exchange information regularly.

How do the users' temporal semantic and social relationships fluctuate based on the political scene?

Interestingly, we observe peaks in the connections' percentage during January 2020 (event 1), November 2020 (event 2) and January 2021 (event 3) for both graphs. The percentage fluctuations are more obvious in the semantic graph compared to the social graph, this is the first indication that the temporal context similarities might be more useful for the model compared to the social interactions. We provide a list of pivotal political events in Table 2 which evidently explain the increase in the connections' percentage and provide an intuition behind the users' behavior.

Date	Event Description
Feb 5	Trump is acquitted on the charges of abuse of power and obstruction of Congress. (event 1)
Aug 11	Joe Biden chooses Senator Kamala Harris (D-CA) as his running mate
Nov 3	2020 United States elections (event 2)
Jan 6	US Capitol is attacked by supporters of Trump (event 3)

Table 2: **Major political events**[1]. These events are referenced in Figure 2.

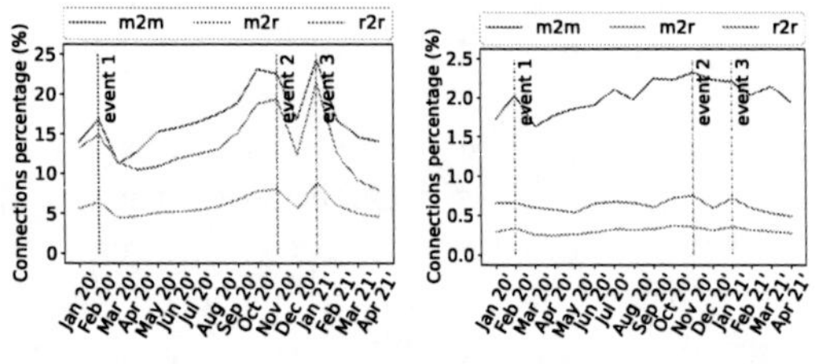

Figure 2: **Connection percentage** of per month for the semantic (left) and social graphs (right). The events shown in this Figure correspond to the events mentioned in Table 2.

5 Neural Network Design

5.1 Graph Neural Network Layer

We utilize three different types of Graph Neural Network (GNN) layers in order to demonstrate the robustness and predictability of the users' connections. The input to the GNN layer is a set of user embeddings E^i_τ for each time frame τ. The GNN layer is shared across the time frames and produces new representations $\widetilde{E^i_\tau}$ which are learned by utilizing either the semantic or social graphs.

Graph Convolutional Neural Network. To embed the nodes in our graph, we employ Graph Convolutional Networks (GCN) (Kipf and Welling, 2016). GCN is a commonly used, powerful graph embedding method that encodes both local graph structure and features of the nodes, by using a layer-wise propagation rule.

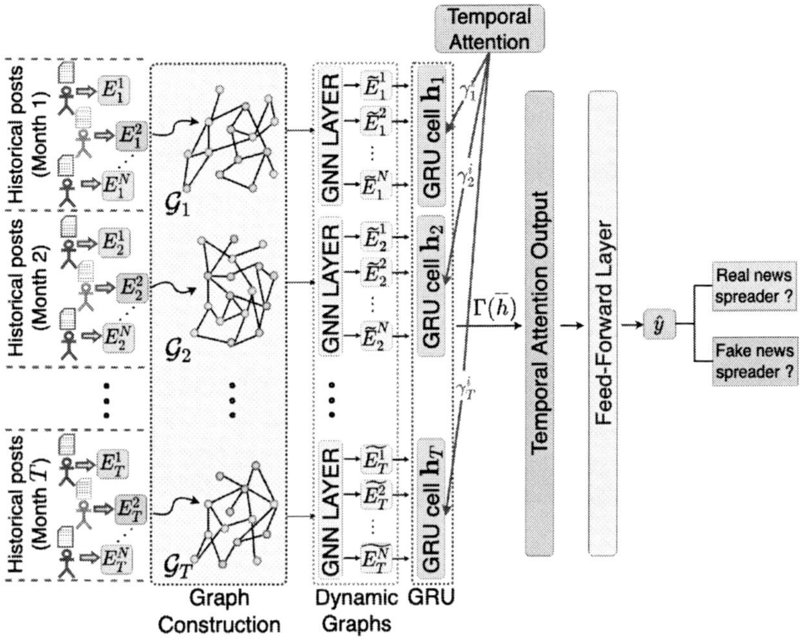

Figure 3: **Overview of the proposed framework.** We first obtain the user embeddings for each time frame and construct the temporal graphs. Next, we feed the graphs to a GNN to extract neighbourhood features. For each user, we use a GRU with temporal attention to compute an overall representation of the user, which is finally forwarded to a classification layer.

Graph Attention Network. As users have a different influence on one another, we need to focus on users that have more relevant connections with higher influence. To model the importance of the influences of the neighbourhood to a node, we use Graph Attention Networks (GAT) (Veličković et al., 2018). GAT attends to the neighborhood of each user and assigns an importance score to the connections that contribute more to the detection of misinformation spreaders.

Hyperbolic Graph Convolutional Neural Networks. Research has shown that GCNs often do not generalize well to hierarchical, tree-like networks such as the social graphs constructed from social media threads (Chen et al., 2012b), since they operate in the Euclidean space. Building on the scale-free nature of the users' social graphs, we utilize Hyperbolic Graph Neural Networks (HGCN) (Chami et al., 2019) which employ graph convolutions in the hyperbolic space as opposed to the standard graph convolutions. The HGCN layer projects the user embeddings in the hyperbolic space to minimize distortions and learn better representations.

5.2 Temporal Neural Network Layer

Temporal Encoding. We investigate the users' behavior over a long time-period, and we wish to encode the dynamic changes between the users' interactions over time. We argue that simply compressing the users' semantic and social connections into one static graph, would introduce too much noise and the information regarding the temporal fluctuations of the semantic and social relationships would be lost. To this end, we model the sequential dependencies through time for each user, with a Gated Recurrent Unit (GRU) (Cho et al., 2014). The GRU encodes the dynamic user graph representations across the time axis, producing hidden states for each time frame τ.

Temporal Attention and Network Optimization. The GRU models the sequential dependencies of the temporal graph user representation, however during the long time span of the users' posting activity, certain socio-political events, such the election seasons, the release date of a new vaccine, etc., may cause the outburst of misinformation spreading. Therefore, we wish to model the contributions of these important time periods to the users' overall representation. To this end, we employ an attention mechanism (Bahdanau et al., 2016) to compute an overall representation for the user with adaptive weights over the aggregated GRU hidden states.

We formulate the author profiling problem as a binary classification task to predict the class y^i of the user, where $y^i \in \{$misinformation spreader, real news spreader$\}$. The overall learned representations for each user are forwarded into a linear layer, and we use cross-entropy loss to calculate the difference between the true and predicted labels.

6 Experimental Setup

To answer the *RQ2*, we need to investigate the reliability of the temporal semantic and social connections as features for identifying misinformation spreaders in various scenarios.

Predicting future user behavior. We analyze whether the past user behavior, represented through temporal graphs, can be used to predict their future user behavior. To this end, we use the whole set of users in the training, validation and test, but each set contains data from different time periods. Specifically, the training set consists of 8 months (Jan-Aug 20'), and the validation (Sep-Dec 20') and test sets (Jan-Apr 21') 4 months each, resulting in a consecutive 50:25:25 *time split* of the user's posting history. This stands for both datasets since they were collected around the same time period. We provide a visual depiction of this split in Appendix A.5 in Figure 8a.

Generalizing to unseen users. We examine which types of relationships have the ability to generalize to unseen users. In this setup we utilize a *user split*, where we divide the users into a train:validation:test sets of ratio 70:10:20 using all of their posting history. This split is also visually depicted in Appendix A.5 in Figure 8b.

Performance on unseen users in the future. We also aim to test whether the temporal graph features generalize on both unseen users and future content, to this end we utilize the *mixed split*. We split the users into a train:validation:test sets of ratio 70:10:20, where the train set contains users who have posted the first half (Jan-Aug 20') of the whole time period, while the validation and test sets contain a different set of users who post on the second half (Sep 20'-Apr 21'). With this setup, we evidently demonstrate the reliability of the proposed model of detecting misinformation spreaders on unseen data. A visual depiction of this split is provided in Appendix A.5 in Figure 8c.

7 Experimental Results

7.1 Performance results

Feature baselines First, we compare the proposed model to simple, yet strong content-based baselines by utilizing interpretable classifiers; Support Vector Machines (SVM), Logistic Regression (LR), and Random Forest (RF) using the following features:

ngrams: While word ngrams are considered as simple features, they have been used successfully in the past for identifying misinformation spreaders (Vogel and Meghana, 2020). In this case, we utilized the word bi-grams.

statistical-emotional (StEm): We employ a feature vector ($n = 22$) with standard statistical linguistic variables (such as min, max, average number of tokens and characters, lexical diversity, etc.) (Buda and Bolonyai, 2020; Pardo et al., 2020). Additionally, we added 8 emotional dimensions to this baseline feature (Fersini et al., 2020; Mohammad and Turney, 2013).

UBERT: We use the SBERT embeddings of the documents averaged over the whole time frame as feature vectors.

U2V: We also utilized the User2Vec embeddings to represent the users as feature vectors.

Table 3 shows the accuracy results of the baseline models compared to the dynamic graph models on the FACTOID and Twitter datasets. Note that we utilized both the social and the semantic graph and two initialization methods for the FACTOID dataset - in this table we report the best performing variant (for all variants see Table 4). For the Twitter dataset, we experiment only with the semantic graph since there are no social connections between users, and we obtained the temporal graphs with UBERT. We observe that all the proposed models significantly outperform all baseline models for both datasets. For the FACTOID dataset, the best performing dynamic graph model showed higher macro F_1-score compared to the baseline models in all splits, which was on average 10.47% higher on the time split, 15.3% on the user split and 14.08% on the mixed split. For the Twitter dataset, the best performing dynamic graph model showed on average 8% better performance on the time split, 10.8% on the user split and 16.8% on the mixed split.

The results on both datasets validate our claim

	FACTOID									Twitter								
	Time Split			User Split			Mixed Split			Time Split			User Split			Mixed Split		
	SVM	LR	RF	SVM	LR	RF	SVM	LR	RF	SVM	LR	RF	SVM	LR	RF	SVM	LR	RF
ngrams	43.6	56.4	55.4	43.4	58.4	59.5	42.5	42.5	57.6	73.9	75.2	76.9	61.7	65.5	66.6	52.37	42.6	64.81
StEm	52.5	51.6	56.8	49.1	54.9	60.6	54.1	52.1	60.3	61.4	60.8	70.2	59.4	57.3	63.9	43.0	43.5	63.6
UBERT	42.5	47.9	56.1	53.9	58.6	49.7	42.3	45.7	54	62.6	77.3	71.9	64.1	64.7	64.3	36.2	59.4	65.8
U2V	47.6	52.1	61.3	50.2	55.1	56.5	46.4	53.0	59.6	-	-	-	-	-	-	-	-	-
DyGAT		**64.56***			63.59			63.22			**78.2***			67.30			**69.2***	
DyGCN		64.18			65.75			**64.23***			66.9			65.60			66.1	
DyHGCN		64.24			**66.75***			58.58			67.7			**73.90***			65.3	

Table 3: **Baseline experimental results on the FACTOID and Twitter datasets.** Bold indicates the best macro F_1-score. All results are in percentages. We show that the DyGNN framework outperforms all baselines for each split in both datasets. The results with the asterisk (*) are statistically significant based on the Wilcoxon signed rank test ($p = 0.001$) compared to all the baseline methods.

		Semantic			Social		
		Time	User	Mixed	Time	User	Mixed
UBERT	DyGAT	**64.56***	57.26	60.46	62.91	61.66	63.12
	DyGCN	63.57	58.67	61.60	64.18	61.08	59.44
	DyHGCN	55.39	**66.75**	55.25	56.38	62.02	58.58
U2V	DyGAT	63.03	63.59	62.88	63.50	63.01	**63.22***
	DyGCN	62.28	65.75	**64.23***	62.76	64.21	61.35
	DyHGCN	42.51	42.52	47.39	**64.24***	**66.09***	56.10

Table 4: **Comparative analysis of two embedding methods** for semantic graph construction and DyGNN initialization (social graph). Reported macro F_1-score for the FACTOID dataset. All results are in percentages. Bold indicates best result. The results with the asterisk (*) are statistically significant based on the Wilcoxon signed rank test ($p = 0.001$) compared to the second best performing method.

that the specific language features become quickly outdated, while temporal semantic similarities and social interactions are more robust and constitute a better tool for (a) predicting future behavior (time split), (b) predicting the behavior of unseen users (user split), and (c) identifying misinformation spreaders on unseen data (mixed split).

Comparison of dynamic graph models. Table 4 shows the performance results on the three different experimental setups (see Appendix A.6.1 for more detailed results). We analyze the results of the dynamic graph models, based on the utilized graph type (semantic and social), initialization method (UBERT and User2Vec) and graph neural network type (GAT, GCN and HGCN).

Comparing graph types. We observe that the model obtains a slightly better performance by utilizing the semantic similarity graphs compared to utilizing the social graphs for all three setups. Figure 2 shows that the percentage of temporal connections is higher, and fluctuates more, on the semantic graphs compared to the social graphs. This may represent users sharing similar opinionated news regarding the same event, with patterns changing for a new event, while social connections stay similar.

Comparing initialization methods. When UBERT and User2Vec are used in the social graphs, they simply act as initialization vectors, since the social graph construction does not depend on the embedding method. When the models use the social graphs, User2Vec initialization produces better results than UBERT in all setups, despite its lower dimensionality. This performance is expected since User2Vec yields better results than UBERT when it is utilized as a baseline method (Table 3).

The semantic similarity graphs, on the other hand, differ when constructed with UBERT or with User2Vec. In the time split evaluation setup, the semantic graph model achieves the best performance with UBERT, while in the mixed split, the best performance is obtained with User2Vec. This is likely due to UBERT particular suitability for capturing meaningful user similarities even with a small amount of user history, since SBERT (from which we obtain UBERT) is tailored for producing sentence embeddings comparable using cosine-similarity. User2Vec requires a significant amount

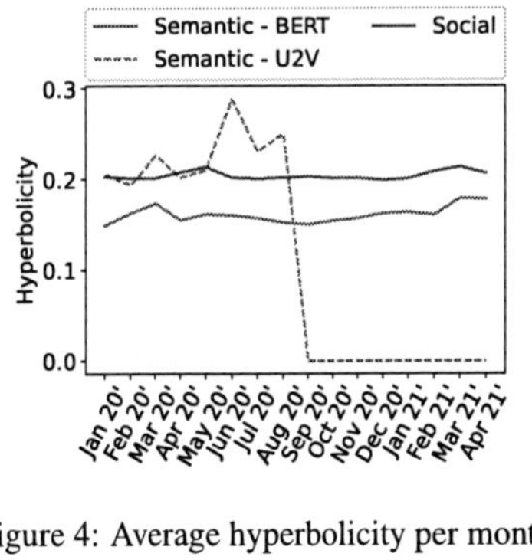

Figure 4: Average hyperbolicity per month

	Semantic			Social		
	Time	User	Mixed	Time	User	Mixed
DyGNN	**64.56***	66.75	**64.23***	**64.24***	**66.09***	**63.22***
no temporal	55.14	53.53	60.24	62.64	59.37	56.54
no attention	62.27	**66.78***	61.97	61.01	64.51	56.32

Table 5: **Ablation study - temporal dynamics.** In this study we remove the temporal component (keeping simple "static" GNN approach) and the attention. Results show that both components play a significant role to the model's performance. Bold indicates the best macro F_1-score. All results are in percentages. The results with the asterisk (*) are statistically significant based on the Wilcoxon signed rank test ($p = 0.001$).

of documents in order to obtain high-quality user representations however, it leads to a stronger generalizability on unseen data.

Comparing dynamic graph neural networks. We observe that the hyperbolic DyHGCN obtains the best performing results in 3/6 combinations of split and graph type. However, it performs poorly when it utilizes the User2Vec semantic graphs. Figure 4 shows the average hyperbolicity of the dynamic graphs for each month. As is known, high hyperbolicity values indicate a tree-like structure of the network Chen et al. (2012a); Aparicio et al. (2015). Due to the lower posting activity during the last months, and thus higher sparsity of the topics represented by one user, users are more dissimilar, resulting in fewer edges. This in turn leads to lower hyperbolicity during this time period, which explains the DyHGCN's poor performance with User2Vec semantic graphs. The social graph shows high hyperbolicity for all months, therefore DyHCGN achieves superior performance when utilizing the social graphs. DyGAT and DyGCN obtain the best performance once, but in contrast to DyHGCN, they both achieve results within a certain range which is neither too low nor too high.

Discussion. In conclusion, based this comparative analysis, dynamic semantic similarity graphs lead to better results than dynamic social graphs, and given a large amount of user history, User2Vec is preferred for constructing these. In addition, the use of DyHGCN is recommended only when the hyperbolicity of the graph is high, alternatively, DyGAT or DyGCN provide comparable results.

7.2 Ablation Study - Temporal Components

We perform an ablation study on the components of the best performing dynamic graph model to demonstrate the effect of each layer on the overall performance, namely the temporal attention and the temporal graphs:

No attention. We remove the temporal attention layer from our dynamic graph model. Intuitively, this component should focus on the time periods with high misinformation spreading activity and highest differences between user groups.

No temporal dynamics. We average each user's representations across all time frames to obtain a single user representation, and remove the dynamic part of our model by merging all the graphs constructed for every discrete time frame. Specifically, we construct a single graph that includes all the user connections from all time periods and replace the GRU layer, with a linear layer. This model captures the overall semantic and social interactions of the users over their whole posting timeline, and could also be considered as a graph-based baseline.

Table 5 shows the ablative results over the components of the best performing dynamic graph models for all setups. We observe that removing the temporal information has a significant detrimental effect on the performance in all cases, which is on average 7.53%. This demonstrates the strong predictive power of temporal patterns in semantic and social relationships for identifying misinformation spreaders and validates our proposed framework for dynamically modeling the users' semantic and social graphs. In addition, except for the semantic graph on the user split, adding the temporal attention over the users' timeline increases significantly the performance, reinforcing our hypothesis that the similarity of language use during important socio-political events is strongly indicative of misinformation spreading. We have seen that for the semantic graph using the user split, the attention weights through different time slots are the same. Due to this reason, the overall user representation is just a simple average of the GRU states. One reason why this is happening, is because the temporal attention is not capturing temporal patterns of the users, that can generalize to unseen ones.

7.3 Error Analysis

We conducted an analysis of users that consistently get the same prediction *by at least half* of the GNN models. We identify two groups of users; consistently correctly classified, and consistently misclassified. The following error analysis is based on the results obtained on the FACTOID dataset on the user split, however similar results were observed for the rest of the splits.

Approximately 72% of the consistently misclassified users are misinformation spreaders, which can be attributed to the class imbalance decreasing the recall.

It is harder to identify users that are borderline fake news spreaders. Table 6 shows, for the correctly classified and misclassified fake news (FNS) and real news spreaders (RNS), the average number of fake and real news posts, average science and factual level provided in Sakketou et al. (2022) and the average no. of months of active posting. The science level of each user $\in [-1, 1]$ is the normalized weighted average of non-scientific (-1) and scientific (1) articles and the factual level $\in [-3, 3]$ is the normalized weighted average factuality of the news domains, manually labeled by journalists from very low (-3) to very high (3). [2]

		fake posts	real posts	science level	factual level	activity (months)
correctly	**FNS**	9.66	39.45	0.13	0.59	12.99
classified	**RNS**	0.29	9.95	0.70	1.76	12.57
mis-	**FNS**	3.76	22.88	0.16	0.83	11.21
classified	**RNS**	0.60	22.67	0.42	1.59	12.37

Table 6: **Error analysis.** Correctly classified fake news spreaders (FNS) post more often than misclassified ones, and post more consistently over time.

As we can see, the misclassified FNS have posted a considerably lower number of fake news on average compared to the correctly classified FNS. While they also posted a lower number of real news posts, their (annotated) factual level is quite high - the source quality plays a role. For the correctly classified FNS, high number of real news combined with low factual level indicates that the real news sources these users are posting are borderline credible - their credibility level is only 'mostly factual'(+1), whereas the credibility level of the fake news sources is from 'low'(-2) to 'very low'(-3). The correctly classified RNS tend to post significantly more scientific articles and articles with higher factuality on average than the misclassified RNS. Overall, correctly classified users of both classes post more consistently over the months compared to the misclassified users.

Since our data heuristics might include wrongly labeled posts and, by extension, users, we manually labeled 210 posts of consistently misclassified users. In this small sample we found that approximately 14% of the posts were wrongly labeled, however less than 1% of the users would obtain a different label because of these posts. We show two examples of mislabeled posts in Table 7.

Mislabeled as fake news
(...) These pieces rely on discredited sources who have peddled debunked theories about Dominion's supposed ties to Venezuela (...) These statements are completely false and have no basis in fact. (...) [link to non-credible source posting fake news]
Mislabeled as real news
The CCP (Chinese Communist Party) controls Google from within. Change my mind. [link to credible source posting real news]

Table 7: Mislabeled news posts.

8 Conclusion

In this study we proposed a dynamic graph neural network framework that generates temporal graph representations from the users' semantic similarities and social interactions through time.

Our extensive experiments and ablation study demonstrated that the temporal graphs are more efficient than content-based models or simple static graphs for predicting (a) the future misinformation spreading behavior, (b) the behavior of unseen users, and (c) misinformation spreading behavior in a zero-shot scenario. These results indicate that a model utilizing temporal user relationships is more robust and more efficient for misinformation spreader detection compared to topic-sensitive or time-agnostic models, e.g. talking about Trump doesn't make one a misinformation spreader and it is quite normal near election time.

Through exploratory experiments, we analyzed the various aspects of the framework in order to provide an insight into its usability. These experiments showed that dynamic semantic similarities lead to better results than the social ones. The ablation study on the components of the model revealed that the temporal modelling of the users' semantic similarities and social interactions significantly contributes to identifying misinformation spreaders effectively. Our error analysis indicated that the misclassified fake news spreaders tend to post a very low number of fake news posts and a high number of real news posts from highly credible sources. Yet, the proposed framework is applicable as a human moderator-assistance tool for identifying users that post fake news more consistently.

[2]When embedding the users, we erased the URLs from the text, so that no information about the number of links, or the names of the domains was leaked in the user embeddings, therefore none of the models could have had any prior knowledge of these factors.

Acknowledgements

This work has been supported by the German Federal Ministry of Education and Research (BMBF) as a part of the Junior AI Scientists program under the reference 01-S20060.

Ethical Considerations and Limitations

Ethical considerations. The ability to automatically approximate personal characteristics of online users in order to improve natural language classification algorithms requires us to consider a range of ethical concerns. Use of any user data for personalization shall be transparent, and limited to the given purpose (Hewson and Buchanan, 2013). Any user-augmented classification efforts risk invoking stereotyping and essentialism, as the algorithm labels people as misinformation spreaders or not. Such stereotypes can cause harm even if they are accurate on average differences (Rudman and Glick, 2012). These can be emphasized by the semblance of objectivity created by the use of an algorithm (Koolen and van Cranenburgh, 2017).

We acknowledge that our research could be used in order to identify gullible individuals that are susceptible to fake news, which enables malicious parties to promote their propaganda. However, the intended use of this research is to limit the misinformation spread by addressing this problem at its origin, therefore our data and the code implementation provided in this work, should only be used for research purposes.

Other limitations. Automatically labelled datasets should be utilized with caution since they might include wrongly labeled posts and, by extension, wrongly labeled users. For example, a number of posts contained multiple links from mixed sources (credible and non-credible). In this paper, we utilized the same labeling method of such posts as Sakketou et al. (2022), where a post is considered misinformation when there is at least one non-credible news source cited. This includes cases where the number of real news sources overcomes the number of fake news sources within one post. We argue that the ratio of the non-credible to credible news sources posted in one post should be considered as a labeling threshold instead. More specifically, if more than half the sources within one post are non-credible, only then should it be labeled as misinformation.

We acknowledge that there is a very thin line separating real news spreaders and misinformation spreaders, however in future works a new class of "potential misinformation spreaders" could be introduced for the users that are on the fence.

References

Silvio Amir, Byron C. Wallace, Hao Lyu, Paula Carvalho, and Mário J. Silva. 2016. Modelling context with user embeddings for sarcasm detection in social media. In *Proceedings of The 20th SIGNLL Conference on Computational Natural Language Learning*, pages 167–177, Berlin, Germany. Association for Computational Linguistics.

Sofía Aparicio, Javier Villazón-Terrazas, and Gonzalo Álvarez. 2015. A model for scale-free networks: Application to twitter. *Entropy*, 17(8):5848–5867.

Dzmitry Bahdanau, Kyunghyun Cho, and Yoshua Bengio. 2016. Neural machine translation by jointly learning to align and translate.

Angela Bahns, Chris Crandall, Omri Gillath, and Kristopher Preacher. 2017. Similarity in relationships as niche construction: Choice, stability, and influence within dyads in a free choice environment. *Journal of Personality and Social Psychology*, 11:329–355.

Janek Bevendorff, Bilal Ghanem, Anastasia Giachanou, Mike Kestemont, Enrique Manjavacas, Ilia Markov, Maximilian Mayerl, Martin Potthast, Francisco Rangel, Paolo Rosso, Günther Specht, Efstathios Stamatatos, Benno Stein, Matti Wiegmann, and Eva Zangerle. 2020. Overview of pan 2020: Authorship verification, celebrity profiling, profiling fake news spreaders on twitter, and style change detection. In *Experimental IR Meets Multilinguality, Multimodality, and Interaction*, pages 372–383, Cham. Springer International Publishing.

Jakab Buda and Flora Bolonyai. 2020. An Ensemble Model Using N-grams and Statistical Features to Identify Fake News Spreaders on Twitter–Notebook for PAN at CLEF 2020. In *CLEF 2020 Labs and Workshops, Notebook Papers*. CEUR-WS.org.

Daniel Cer, Mona Diab, Eneko Agirre, Inigo Lopez-Gazpio, and Lucia Specia. 2017. Semeval-2017 task 1: Semantic textual similarity multilingual and crosslingual focused evaluation. *Proceedings of the 11th International Workshop on Semantic Evaluation (SemEval-2017)*.

Ines Chami, Zhitao Ying, Christopher Ré, and Jure Leskovec. 2019. Hyperbolic graph convolutional neural networks. *Advances in neural information processing systems*, 32:4868–4879.

Wei Chen, Wenjie Fang, Guangda Hu, and Michael W. Mahoney. 2012a. On the hyperbolicity of small-world and tree-like random graphs.

Wei Chen, Wenjie Fang, Guangda Hu, and Michael W. Mahoney. 2012b. On the hyperbolicity of small-world networks and tree-like graphs. *CoRR*, abs/1201.1717.

Kyunghyun Cho, Bart van Merriënboer, Dzmitry Bahdanau, and Yoshua Bengio. 2014. On the properties of neural machine translation: Encoder–decoder approaches. In *Proceedings of SSST-8, Eighth Workshop on Syntax, Semantics and Structure in Statistical Translation*, pages 103–111, Doha, Qatar. Association for Computational Linguistics.

Shivang Chopra, Ramit Sawhney, Puneet Mathur, and Rajiv Ratn Shah. 2020. Hindi-english hate speech detection: Author profiling, debiasing, and practical perspectives. In *The Thirty-Fourth AAAI Conference on Artificial Intelligence, AAAI 2020, The Thirty-Second Innovative Applications of Artificial Intelligence Conference, IAAI 2020, The Tenth AAAI Symposium on Educational Advances in Artificial Intelligence, EAAI 2020, New York, NY, USA, February 7-12, 2020*, pages 386–393. AAAI Press.

E. Fersini, Justin Armanini, and Michael D'Intorni. 2020. Profiling fake news spreaders: Stylometry, personality, emotions and embeddings. In *CLEF*.

Anastasia Giachanou, Esteban A. Ríssola, Bilal Ghanem, Fabio Crestani, and Paolo Rosso. 2020. The role of personality and linguistic patterns in discriminating between fake news spreaders and fact checkers. In *Natural Language Processing and Information Systems*, pages 181–192, Cham. Springer International Publishing.

Anastasia Giachanou, Paolo Rosso, and Fabio Crestani. 2021. The impact of emotional signals on credibility assessment. *Journal of the Association for Information Science and Technology*.

Shengnan Guo, Youfang Lin, Ning Feng, Chao Song, and Huaiyu Wan. 2019. Attention based spatial-temporal graph convolutional networks for traffic flow forecasting. *Proceedings of the AAAI Conference on Artificial Intelligence*, 33(01):922–929.

Isabelle Guyon, Jason Weston, Stephen Barnhill, and Vladimir Vapnik. 2002. Gene selection for cancer classification using support vector machines. *Machine learning*, 46(1-3):389–422.

Wentao Han, Youshan Miao, Kaiwei Li, Ming Wu, Fan Yang, Lidong Zhou, Vijayan Prabhakaran, Wenguang Chen, and Enhong Chen. 2014. Chronos: A graph engine for temporal graph analysis. In *Proceedings of the Ninth European Conference on Computer Systems*, EuroSys '14, New York, NY, USA. Association for Computing Machinery.

Claire Hewson and Tom Buchanan. 2013. Ethics guidelines for internet-mediated research. The British Psychological Society.

Benjamin D. Horne, Jeppe Nørregaard, and Sibel Adali. 2019. Robust fake news detection over time and attack. *ACM Trans. Intell. Syst. Technol.*, 11(1).

Endri Kacupaj, Joan Plepi, Kuldeep Singh, Harsh Thakkar, Jens Lehmann, and Maria Maleshkova. 2021. Conversational question answering over knowledge graphs with transformer and graph attention networks. In *Proceedings of the 16th Conference of the European Chapter of the Association for Computational Linguistics: Main Volume*, pages 850–862, Online. Association for Computational Linguistics.

Gihwan Kim and Youngjoong Ko. 2021. Graph-based fake news detection using a summarization technique. In *Proceedings of the 16th Conference of the European Chapter of the Association for Computational Linguistics: Main Volume*, pages 3276–3280, Online. Association for Computational Linguistics.

Diederik P Kingma and Jimmy Ba. 2015. Adam, a method for stochastic optimization. In *Proceedings of the 3rd International Conference on Learning Representations (ICLR)*, volume 1412.

Thomas N Kipf and Max Welling. 2016. Semi-supervised classification with graph convolutional networks. *arXiv preprint arXiv:1609.02907*.

Corina Koolen and Andreas van Cranenburgh. 2017. These are not the stereotypes you are looking for: Bias and fairness in authorial gender attribution. In *Proceedings of the First ACL Workshop on Ethics in Natural Language Processing*, pages 12–22, Valencia, Spain. Association for Computational Linguistics.

Sejeong Kwon, Meeyoung Cha, and Kyomin Jung. 2017. Rumor detection over varying time windows. *PLOS ONE*, 12(1):1–19.

Yaguang Li, Rose Yu, Cyrus Shahabi, and Yan Liu. 2018. Diffusion convolutional recurrent neural network: Data-driven traffic forecasting.

Spencer McKay and Chris Tenove. 2021. Disinformation as a threat to deliberative democracy. *Political Research Quarterly*, 74(3):703–717.

Pushkar Mishra, Marco Del Tredici, Helen Yannakoudakis, and Ekaterina Shutova. 2019. Abusive language detection with graph convolutional networks. *CoRR*, abs/1904.04073.

Saif M Mohammad and Peter D Turney. 2013. Crowdsourcing a word–emotion association lexicon. *Computational intelligence*, 29(3):436–465.

Yida Mu and Nikolaos Aletras. 2020. Identifying twitter users who repost unreliable news sources with linguistic information. *PeerJ Comput. Sci.*, 6:e325.

Francisco M. Rangel Pardo, Anastasia Giachanou, Bilal Ghanem, and Paolo Rosso. 2020. Overview of the 8th author profiling task at PAN 2020: Profiling fake news spreaders on twitter. In *Working Notes of CLEF 2020 - Conference and Labs of the Evaluation Forum, Thessaloniki, Greece, September 22-25, 2020*, volume 2696 of *CEUR Workshop Proceedings*. CEUR-WS.org.

Joan Plepi and Lucie Flek. 2021. Perceived and intended sarcasm detection with graph attention networks. In *Findings of the Association for Computational Linguistics: EMNLP 2021*, pages 4746–4753, Punta Cana, Dominican Republic. Association for Computational Linguistics.

Bhavtosh Rath, Xavier Morales, and Jaideep Srivastava. 2021. SCARLET: explainable attention based graph neural network for fake news spreader prediction. *CoRR*, abs/2102.04627.

Bhavtosh Rath, Aadesh Salecha, and Jaideep Srivastava. 2020. Detecting fake news spreaders in social networks using inductive representation learning.

Nils Reimers and Iryna Gurevych. 2019. Sentence-BERT: Sentence embeddings using Siamese BERT-networks. In *Proceedings of the 2019 Conference on Empirical Methods in Natural Language Processing and the 9th International Joint Conference on Natural Language Processing (EMNLP-IJCNLP)*, pages 3982–3992, Hong Kong, China. Association for Computational Linguistics.

Emanuele Rossi, Ben Chamberlain, Fabrizio Frasca, Davide Eynard, Federico Monti, and Michael Bronstein. 2020. Temporal graph networks for deep learning on dynamic graphs.

Laurie A Rudman and Peter Glick. 2012. *The social psychology of gender: How power and intimacy shape gender relations*. Guilford Press.

Flora Sakketou, Joan Plepi, Riccardo Cervero, Henri-Jacques Geiss, Paolo Rosso, and Lucie Flek. 2022. Factoid: A new dataset for identifying misinformation spreaders and political bias.

Ramit Sawhney, Shivam Agarwal, Arnav Wadhwa, and Rajiv Ratn Shah. 2020. Deep attentive learning for stock movement prediction from social media text and company correlations. In *Proceedings of the 2020 Conference on Empirical Methods in Natural Language Processing (EMNLP)*, pages 8415–8426, Online. Association for Computational Linguistics.

Ramit Sawhney, Harshit Joshi, Rajiv Ratn Shah, and Lucie Flek. 2021. Suicide ideation detection via social and temporal user representations using hyperbolic learning. In *Proceedings of the 2021 Conference of the North American Chapter of the Association for Computational Linguistics: Human Language Technologies*, pages 2176–2190, Online. Association for Computational Linguistics.

Youngjoo Seo, Michaël Defferrard, Pierre Vandergheynst, and Xavier Bresson. 2016. Structured sequence modeling with graph convolutional recurrent networks. *CoRR*, abs/1612.07659.

Petar Veličković, Guillem Cucurull, Arantxa Casanova, Adriana Romero, Pietro Liò, and Yoshua Bengio. 2018. Graph attention networks.

Inna Vogel and Meghana Meghana. 2020. Fake news spreader detection on twitter using character n-grams. notebook for pan at clef 2020.

Zonghan Wu, Shirui Pan, Fengwen Chen, Guodong Long, Chengqi Zhang, and Philip S. Yu. 2021. A comprehensive survey on graph neural networks. *IEEE Transactions on Neural Networks and Learning Systems*, 32(1):4–24.

Sijie Yan, Yuanjun Xiong, and Dahua Lin. 2018. Spatial temporal graph convolutional networks for skeleton-based action recognition.

A Appendix

A.1 Dataset

A.1.1 Analysis of the linguistic differences

To get an intuition for the actual linguistic differences between the two user groups of misinformation spreaders and real news spreaders, we extracted the learned token weights from the SVM model in order to study the predictiveness of the tokens for each class (Guyon et al., 2002). The most predictive tokens are shown in Table 8. It can be seen that there's a tendency for misinformation spreaders to reference politically left-leaning groups as "liber", "dem", "left" or "blm" (referring to the Black Lives Matter movement), while real news spreaders use the terms "fascist" and "republican" with higher frequency.

Label	Tokens
Misinformation Spreaders	china, video, come, offici, blm, corrupt, media, away, liber, order, new, trump's, seem, wrong, kill, left, dem, riot
Fact Checkers	public, first, week, understand, trial, fascist, republican, war, one, forced-birth, health, pleas, power, let, shock, view, service

Table 8: Top-ranked tokens for each label.

A.2 Social graph construction

Figure 5 shows the transformation of the thread structure into a social graph.

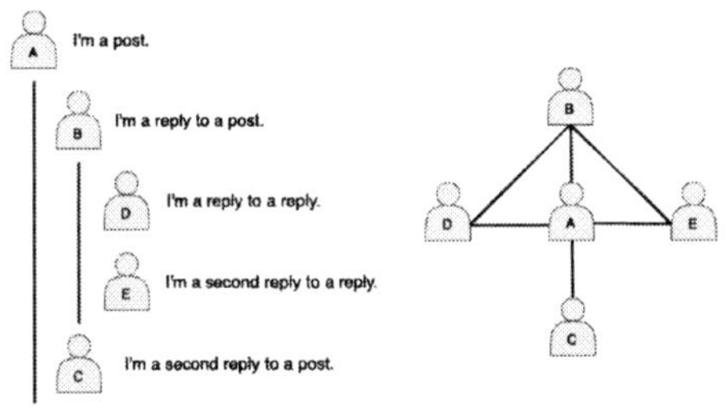

Figure 5: Transforming a post/reply tree in social media into a social graph network.

A.3 Temporal Analysis of Nodes

Centrality. Figure 6 depicts the graph centrality normalized by the number of posts. This metric helps in identifying important nodes in a graph. We can see that, in the linguistic graph, the centrality of the misinformation spreaders and real news spreaders follows a similar pattern but fluctuates a lot over time. Interestingly, there's an obvious increase in the centrality of both classes during August, right after former President Trump announced the possibility of postponing the US elections (see Table 2). This increase is more obvious in the misinformation spreaders, meaning that they are discussing a particular topic more extensively compared to the real news spreaders. In the social graph, we observe a great difference in the values of centrality between misinformation spreaders and real news spreaders. This metric shows that misinformation spreaders are gathered in the center of the graph, while real news spreaders are in the periphery of the graph and are not that densely connected to each other. This essentially indicates that misinformation spreaders form a densely connected "community" and marginalize real news spreaders. The centrality of the misinformation spreaders decreases over time, while in the case of real news spreaders it fluctuates but still stays within a specific range. This apparent dynamically changing behavior of the nodes supports our choice of temporal modelling of the graphs.

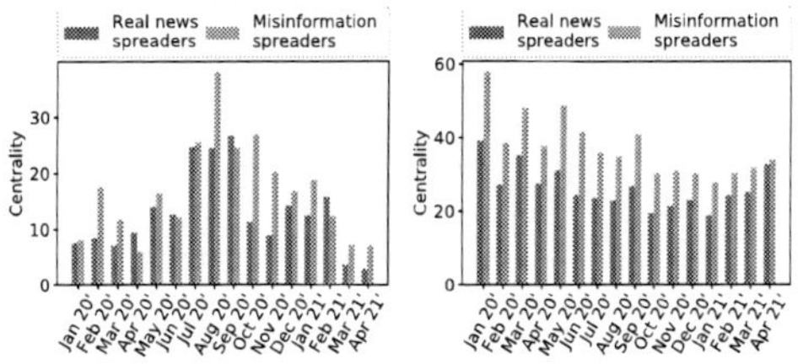

Figure 6: Approximated (k=1000) graph centrality normalized by post amount calculated for all time spans for the semantic (left) and social (right) graph.

Homophily. In Figure 7, we show the amount of homophily observed for both semantic and social graphs, which is defined as the percentage of edges that connect users with the same label. Interestingly, we observe that in the semantic graph the homophily follows different patterns in misinformation spreaders and real news spreaders, and it is fluctuating over time. In the social graph, the misinformation spreaders have consistently higher homophily than real news spreaders, which means that they tend to interact and exchange opinions more with each other compared to real news spreaders. These results complement the edge analysis from Section 4.3 which shows that users from the same credibility group tend to socially interact more with each other, which is more apparent in misinformation spreaders.

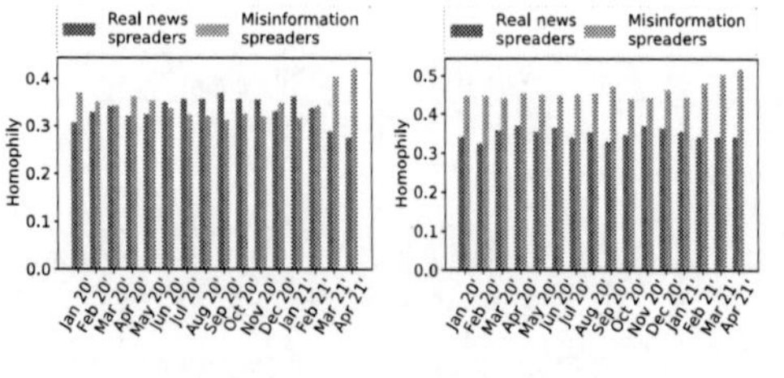

Figure 7: Amount of homophily observed through time for both semantic (left) and social graph (right).

A.4 Connections' percentage

We define the connections' percentage of a certain edge type as $\rho_{\text{edge type}} = r^{(\tau)}_{\text{edge type}} / R^{(\tau)}_{\text{edge type}}$, where $r^{(\tau)}_{\text{edge type}}$ is the number of edges (of that edge type) that exist between two users during the time period τ and $R^{(\tau)}_{\text{edge type}}$ is the number of all possible connections (of that edge type) at the time period τ, computed as follows:

$$R^{(\tau)}_{m2m} = N^{(\tau)}_{m}(N^{(\tau)}_{m} - 1)/2$$
$$R^{(\tau)}_{r2r} = N^{(\tau)}_{r}(N^{(\tau)}_{r} - 1)/2$$
$$R^{(\tau)}_{m2r} = (N^{(\tau)}_{m} + N^{(\tau)}_{r})(N^{(\tau)}_{m} + N^{(\tau)}_{r} - 1)/2$$

where $N^{(\tau)}_{m}$ is the number of misinformation spreaders and $N^{(\tau)}_{r}$ is the number of real news spreaders that have posted at least one post at time period τ.

A.5 Training Setup

We use the pretrained model `'all-mpnet-base-v2'` from SBERT[3], which achieved the best performance on various challenging similarity datasets (Cer et al., 2017). This model has max length set to 512, uses mean pooling and has the output dimension $d_b = 768$. The users' historical representations are obtained as described in Section 4.1 For each post in the user history, we masked the links so that the cosine similarity is not attributed based on the links. We run experiments with $\delta \in 15, 30, 60, 360$ (δ is the number of days spanned by each that each time period τ). In each sample, we randomly sample $n \in 200, 400, 800, 1200$ users, and we build a subgraph of those users for each discrete time window. In the semantic graph, we connect users with each other based on the hyperparameter $\theta \in [0, 1]$ (as defined in Section 4.2). We find

[3] `https://www.sbert.net/docs/pretrained_models.html`

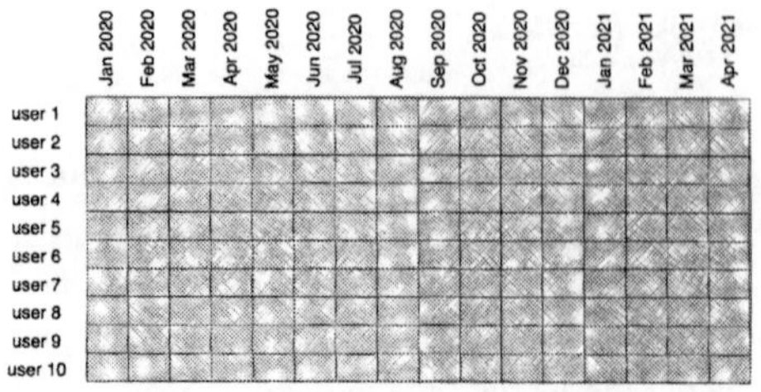

(a) Time split. Splitting the time periods in order to predict future user behavior.

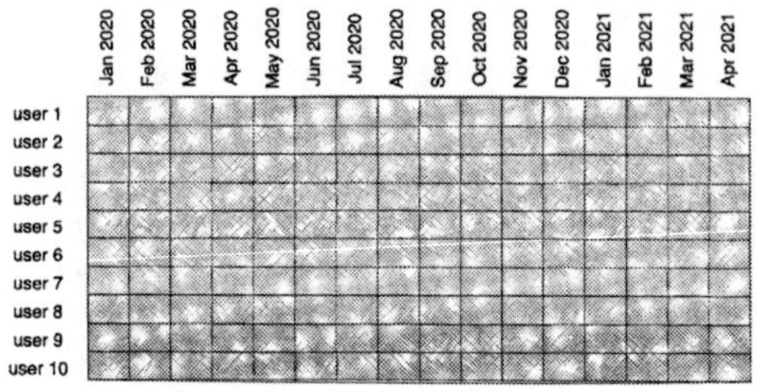

(b) User split. Splitting the users in order to predict the behavior of unseen users.

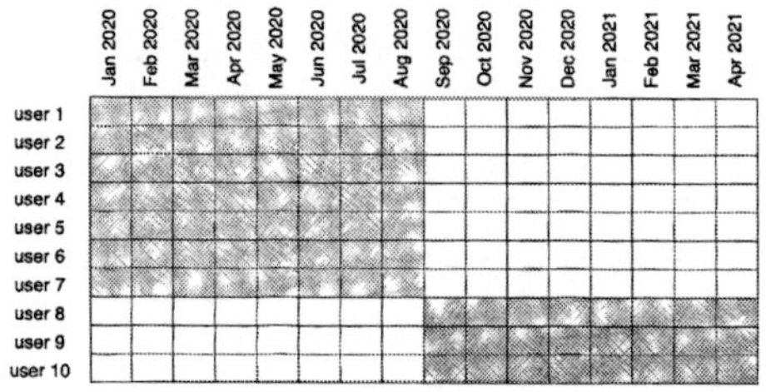

(c) Mixed split. Splitting the users and the time periods in order to predict the behavior of unseen users in the future.

Figure 8: Visual demonstration of the (a) Time split, (b) User split and (c) Mixed split.

out that our model works best with the following hyperparameters: $n = 200$, $\delta = 30$, $\theta = 0.8$. For the models initialized with User2Vec embeddings, we use the dimensions $d_g = 100$ for our graph layer and $d_r = 50$ for our GRU sequential layer. On the other hand, for the models initialized with UBERT embeddings we use the dimensions $d_g = 256$ for our graph layer and $d_r = 128$ for our GRU sequential layer. We use Adam optimizer (Kingma and Ba, 2015) with learning rate $5e-5$, weight decay $1e-2$, and train the model for 100 epochs using early stopping with patience 20 on the validation set. We run each experiment with 5 random seeds and report the mean result on the test set in Tables 3, 4 and 5. DyGAT model using User2Vec embeddings as initialization has 116K parameters, while DyGCN and DyHGCN have 55K parameters. On the other hand, DyGAT

		Semantic graph								
		Time Split			User Split			Mixed Split		
		F_1-score	Precision	Recall	F_1-score	Precision	Recall	F_1-score	Precision	Recall
UBERT	DyGAT	**49.64**	**45.09**	**55.22**	33.44	40.46	28.49	43.18	40.09	46.77
	DyGCN	46.55	45.52	47.63	36.8	41.06	33.33	44.44	41.9	47.31
	DyHGCN	45.97	34.3	69.65	**52.45**	**48.2**	**57.53**	44.81	33.88	66.13
U2V	DyGAT	47.85	42.89	54.11	42.86	54.1	35.48	44.44	45.98	43.01
	DyGCN	41.47	49.56	35.65	52.09	45.9	60.22	**49.77**	**44.17**	**56.99**
	DyHGCN	0	0	0	0	0	0	10.38	42.31	5.91

Table 9: Reported F_1-score, Precision and Recall on the fake news spreader class for the FACTOID dataset utilizing the semantic graph. All results are in percentages. Bold indicates the best macro F_1-score on both classes.

		Social graph								
		Time Split			User Split			Mixed Split		
		F_1-score	Precision	Recall	F_1-score	Precision	Recall	F_1-score	Precision	Recall
UBERT	DyGAT	47.14	43.07	52.05	41.42	46.05	37.63	46.43	44.17	48.92
	DyGCN	44.97	51.28	40.04	39.5	47.37	33.87	39.89	40	39.78
	DyHGCN	47.39	35.25	72.29	51.99	40.18	73.66	32.71	53.01	23.66
U2V	DyGAT	57.24	41.84	90.61	43.24	48.98	38.71	**48.36**	**42.92**	**55.38**
	DyGCN	41.85	51.54	35.23	48.9	44.84	53.76	44.05	41.63	46.77
	DyHGCN	**46.74**	**47.74**	**45.78**	**54.47**	**45.07**	**68.82**	46.21	34.78	68.82

Table 10: Reported F_1-score, Precision and Recall on the fake news spreader class for the FACTOID dataset utilizing the social graph. All results are in percentages. Bold indicates the best macro F_1-score on both classes.

using UBERT embeddings as initialization has 1M parameters, while DyGCN and DyHGCN have 427K parameters. Our experiments for each model take around 1 hour to run on NVIDIA A100-PCIE 40GB GPU. Our implementation, the annotated dataset, and the results are publicly available to facilitate reproducibility and reuse.

A.6 Detailed Experimental Results

A.6.1 Comparison of the graph types

Tables 9 and 10 show the F_1-score, Precision and Recall on the fake news spreader class for the FACTOID dataset utilizing the semantic and social graphs respectively. Given the same combination of setups, i.e different splits, GNN and embedding initialization, we qualitatively compared the results obtained by utilizing the semantic and social graphs. We report the findings regarding the cases with the best macro F_1-scores (in bold).

In the time split, for the DyGAT+UBERT model, we observed that the results are not significantly different when comparing the utilization of semantic and social graphs. In the same split, for the DyHGCN+User2Vec model, we note that 24.99% of the users were classified differently by the semantic and social models, this difference is expected since the difference between the F_1-scores obtained by each graph type is more than 20%. When the semantic graph is utilized, we observe that DyHGCN+User2Vec fails to recognize any of the misinformation speaders, however it achieves an impressively high performance with the social graph. This result is justified due to the low hyperbolicity values of the semantic User2Vec graph as mentioned in Section 7.1.

In the user split, for the DyHGCN+UBERT model, we note that 32.54% of the users were classified differently from the semantic and social models, even though the difference between their macro F_1-scores is only 4%. By utilizing the semantic graph, the model yields to a worse Recall for the fake news spreader class, but higher Recall for the real news spreader class. In the same split, for the DyHGCN+User2Vec model, we note that 39.72% of the users were classified differently, however this difference is expected since the F_1-scores obtained by the semantic and social models have more than 20% difference between them. Once more we observe a staggering difference between the F_1-scores obtained from semantic and social models, with the social model achieving the highest score.

In the mixed split, for the DyGCN+User2Vec

model, we note that 27.55% of the users were classified differently. We observe that the model obtains higher recall on the fake news spreader class when the semantic relationships are utilized, instead of the social ones. In the same split, for the DyHGCN+UBERT model, we observe that 7.82% of the users were calculated differently. By utilizing the social graph, the model achieves higher Recall on the fake news spreader class.

TextGraphs 2022 Shared Task on Natural Language Premise Selection

Marco Valentino[1,2], **Deborah Ferreira**[2], **Mokanarangan Thayaparan**[1,2],
André Freitas[1,2], **Dmitry Ustalov**[3]
[1]Idiap Research Institute, Switzerland
[2]University of Manchester, United Kingdom
[3]Toloka, Serbia

Abstract

The Shared Task on *Natural Language Premise Selection (NLPS)* asks participants to retrieve the set of premises that are most likely to be useful for proving a given mathematical statement from a supporting knowledge base. While previous editions of the TextGraphs shared tasks series targeted multi-hop inference for explanation regeneration in the context of science questions (Thayaparan et al., 2021; Jansen and Ustalov, 2020, 2019), NLPS aims to assess the ability of state-of-the-art approaches to operate on a mixture of natural and mathematical language and model complex multi-hop reasoning dependencies between statements. To this end, this edition of the shared task makes use of a large set of approximately 21k mathematical statements extracted from the PS-ProofWiki dataset (Ferreira and Freitas, 2020a). In this summary paper, we present the results of the 1st edition of the NLPS task, providing a description of the evaluation data, and the participating systems. Additionally, we perform a detailed analysis of the results, evaluating various aspects involved in mathematical language processing and multi-hop inference. The best-performing system achieved a MAP of 15.39, improving the performance of a TF-IDF baseline by approximately 3.0 MAP.[1]

1 Introduction

The articulation of mathematical language represents a core feature of human intelligence, requiring complex reasoning capabilities and abstraction as well as a correct evaluation of the semantics of mathematical structures and its internal components (Greiner-Petter et al., 2019). Moreover, mathematical language consists in a combination of words and symbols, which act following different rules and alphabets, but preserving, at the same time, mutual dependencies that are necessary for the comprehension of mathematical discourse (Ganesalingam, 2013).

Theorem

> For every integer n such that $n > 1$, n can be expressed as the product of one or more primes, uniquely up to the order in which they appear.

Proof

> In Integer is Expressible as Product of Primes it is proved that every integer n such that $n > 1$, n can be expressed as the product of one or more primes.
>
> In Prime Decomposition of Integer is Unique, it is proved that this prime decomposition is unique up to the order of the factors.

Figure 1: Given a mathematical statement s, that requires a mathematical proof, and a collection of premises P, the task of Natural Language Premise Selection (NLPS) consists in retrieving the premises in P that are most likely to be useful for proving s (Ferreira and Freitas, 2020a).

These features provide a unique set of opportunities for the evaluation of state-of-the-art models in Natural Language Processing (NLP) (Ferreira and Freitas, 2020a,b; Welleck et al., 2021). To encourage new lines of research at the intersection of natural language and mathematics, we propose the 1st Shared Task on *Natural Language Premise Selection (NLPS)*.

The NLPS task asks participants to retrieve the premises that are most likely to be useful for proving a given mathematical statement from a supporting knowledge base (see Figure 1). Specifically, NLPS is designed to assess the capabilities and behaviours of state-of-the-art approaches in dealing with a mixture of natural language and mathematical text along with the modelling of complex multi-hop dependencies between statements. To this end, this edition of the shared task makes use of a large set of approximately 21k mathematical statements extracted from the PS-ProofWiki dataset (Ferreira and Freitas, 2020a).

In this summary paper, we present the results of

[1]Data and code available online: `https://github.com/ai-systems/tg2022task_premise_retrieval`.

Proceedings of TextGraphs-16: Graph-based Methods for Natural Language Processing, pages 105–113
October 16, 2022.

the 1st edition of the Natural Language Premise Selection task, providing a detailed description of the evaluation data, and the participating systems. Moreover, we perform a detailed analysis of the behaviour of the participating systems, evaluating various aspects involved in mathematical language processing (i.e., the ability to deal with an increasing number of mathematical elements) and multi-hop inference. The best performing system achieved a MAP of 15.39, improving the performance of a TF-IDF baseline by approximately 3.0 MAP, while still leaving a large space for future improvements.

2 Natural Language Premise Selection

Given a mathematical statement s that requires a mathematical proof, and a collection (or a knowledge base) of premises $P = \{p_1, p_2, \ldots, p_{N_p}\}$, with size N_p, the task of Natural Language Premise Selection (NLPS) consists in retrieving the premises in P that are most likely to be useful for proving s.

A mathematical statement can be a definition, an axiom, a theorem, a lemma, a corollary or a conjecture. Premises are composed of universal truths and accepted truths. Definitions and axioms are *universal truths* since the mathematical community accepts them without proof. *Accepted truths* include statements that need a proof before being adopted. Theorems, lemmas and corollaries are such types of statements. These statements were, at some point, framed as a conjecture before they were proven. As such, they can be grounded on past mathematical discoveries, referencing their own supporting premises (i.e., the background knowledge that was used to prove the conjecture). This network structure of available premises can be used as a foundation in order to predict new ones. The relationship between these statements can be leveraged to build models that can better perform inference for mathematical text (Ferreira and Freitas, 2020b,a).

The NLPS task can be particularly challenging for existing Information Retrieval systems since it requires the ability to process both natural language and mathematical text (Ferreira and Freitas, 2020a; Ferreira et al., 2022). Moreover, as shown in the example in Figure 2, the retrieval of certain premises necessitates complex multi-hop inference (Ferreira and Freitas, 2020b).

Statement Type	Data Split				
	KB	Train	Dev	Test	All (Unique)
Definitions	7,077	0	0	0	7,077
Lemmas	252	134	70	69	252
Corollaries	161	113	57	57	275
Theorems	8,715	5,272	2,652	2,636	14,003
Total	16,205	5,519	2,778	2,763	21,746

Table 1: Types of mathematical statements present in PS-ProofWiki. The table shows the number divided by the data split. The last columns shows the total unique entries for each mathematical type.

3 Training and Evaluation Data

PS-ProofWiki (Ferreira and Freitas, 2020a) has a total of 21,746 different entries, composed of definitions, lemmas, corollaries and theorems, as shown in Table 1. Note that only the Knowledge Base contains definitions since definitions do not contain proofs and, consequently, do not have premises. However, definitions are often used as premises playing a fundamental role in the NLPS task. There also exists an intersection between the KB and the training set. Accordingly, we include the last column to account for all unique entries in the dataset.

Figure 3 presents a histogram with the frequency of the different number of premises. We can observe that the statements usually have a small number of premises, with $9,640$ (Around 87% of the entries in the Train/Dev/Test set) statements containing between one and five premises. The highest number of premises for one theorem is 72.

Similarly, the histogram in Figure 4 shows the frequency of the dependencies between statements, reporting how many times each statement is used as a premise. A total of 4,236 statements is connected to between one and three dependants. On average, the statements contain a total of 289 symbols (characters and mathematical symbols).

The dataset provides a specific semantic modelling challenge for natural language processing as it requires specific tokenisation and the modelling of specific discourse structures tailored towards mathematical text, such as encoding mathematical elements along with natural language, and encoding the relationship between conjectures and premises.

4 System Descriptions and Performance

Following the previous editions of the TextGraphs Shared Tasks on Multi-Hop Inference for Explanation Regeneration (Thayaparan et al., 2021; Jansen

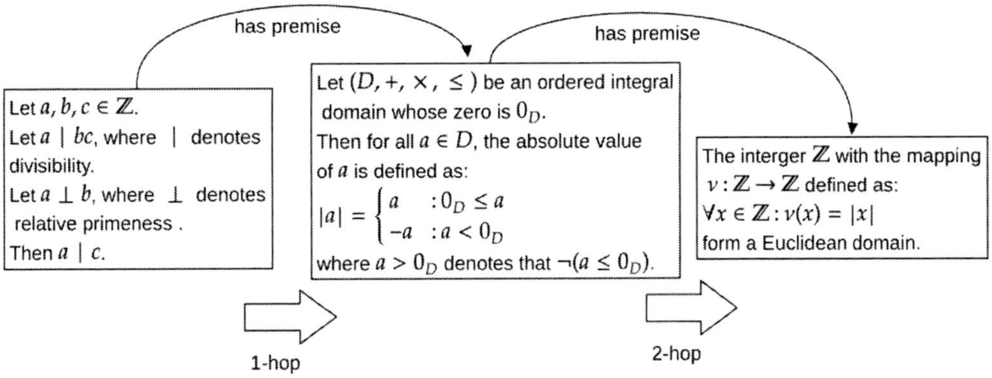

Figure 2: Example of premises requiring multi-hop inference.

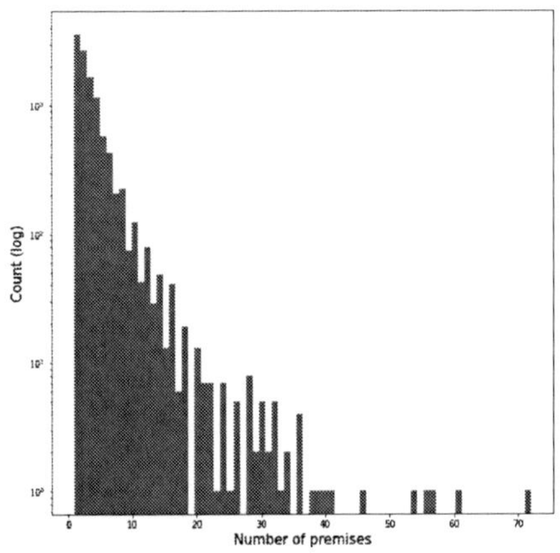

Figure 3: Distribution of the number of premises in the ProofWiki corpus. Log transformation is applied to facilitate visualisation for the y axis.

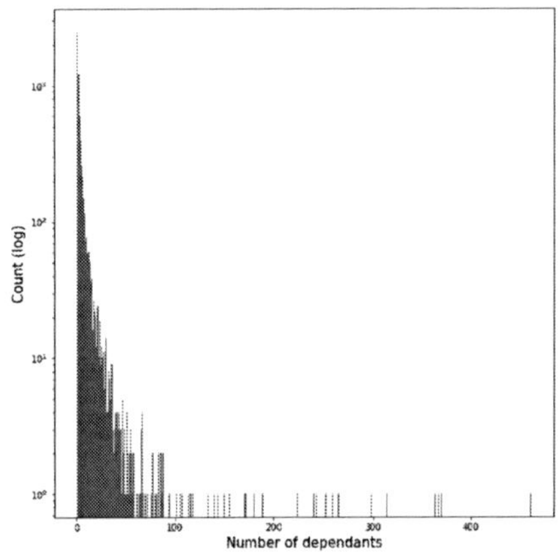

Figure 4: Number of times a statement is referred as a premise. Log transformation is applied to facilitate visualisation for the y axis.

and Ustalov, 2020, 2019), we frame Natural Language Premise Selection (NLPS) as a ranking problem. To this end, the participating systems have been evaluated using Mean Average Precision (MAP) at K, with $K = 500$. Specifically, the top 500 premises retrieved for supporting a given mathematical statement are compared against the gold premises in the corpus via MAP.

The competition has been organised on CodaLab (Pavao et al., 2022),[2] with a total of four teams submitting their solutions to the leaderboard (Tran et al., 2022; Trust et al., 2022; Kovriguina et al., 2022; Dastgheib and Asgari, 2022). Table 2 presents the overall results of the evaluation phase (test-set). In general, the shared task attracted a diverse set of submissions adopting methods spanning from state-of-the-art Transformers (Vaswani et al., 2017) to lexical-based approaches. All the participating systems improved the performance of a TF-IDF baseline, with the best performing system (IJS) achieving a MAP score of 15.39. However, the relatively low performances of the systems demonstrate that the task is still challenging for existing models, leaving large space for future improvements.

Here, we summarize the key features of the models proposed by the participating teams:

[2]https://codalab.lisn.upsaclay.fr/competitions/5692

Team Name	MAP
IJS (Tran et al., 2022)	15.39
UNLPS (Trust et al., 2022)	15.16
Kamivao (Kovriguina et al., 2022)	14.60
langml (Dastgheib and Asgari, 2022)	14.14
TF-IDF baseline	12.28

Table 2: Overall results of the 1st Shared Task on Natural Language Premise Selection (NLPS).

TF-IDF baseline. The shared task data distribution included a baseline that employs a term frequency model (TF-IDF) (see, e.g. Manning et al., 2008, Ch. 6). Specifically, the TF-IDF baseline employs sparse vector representations in combination with cosine similarity to estimate how likely a given premise in the knowledge base supports the mathematical statements provided as input. This baseline achieves a MAP score of 12.28.

IJS (Tran et al., 2022). The team investigates the task of NLPS evaluating the impact of Transformer-based contextual representations along with several similarity metrics for retrieval. Specifically, the authors propose a systematic evaluation of different pre-trained Sentence-Transformers (Reimers and Gurevych, 2019) using a bi-encoder architecture. In order to rank the premises, the authors extract the contextual representation from different Transformers, computing the similarity scores to rank how likely the sentences in the supporting knowledge base are to be a part of the set of premises for a given mathematical statement. The authors observe that the best performance are obtained via RoBERTa large (Liu et al., 2019) and Manhattan distance achieving a MAP score of 15.39.

UNLPS (Trust et al., 2022). Similar to IIJS, the team explore the usage of Sentence-Transformers (Reimers and Gurevych, 2019), employing a bi-encoder architecture for addressing the NLPS task. The team does not rely on fine-tuning techniques but, instead, adopts pre-trained Transformers to retrieve the most relevant premises via a cosine similarity score. The team demonstrated that employing the Sentence-Transformer SMPNet model, which internally adopts a pre-trained MP-Net (Song et al., 2020), yields a MAP score of 15.16.

Kamivao (Kovriguina et al., 2022). The team proposes an approach based on a mixture of dense retrieval and prompt-based methodology. Specifically, the proposed model combines a bi-encoder based on a pre-trained Sentence-Transformer (Reimers and Gurevych, 2019) (BERT (Devlin et al., 2019) and MathBERT (Peng et al., 2021)) with a GPT3 model (Brown et al., 2020) which is instructed to re-rank a set of candidate premises. In the first stage, the model uses bi-encoders and cosine similarity to retrieve a list of potentially relevant premises, while in the re-ranking stage, the authors adopt a prompt-based methodology to construct specific instructions for GPT-3. This approach achieves a MAP score of 14.60.

Iangml (Dastgheib and Asgari, 2022). The team proposes a method that relies on keywords extraction and matching to select relevant premises. The proposed approach employs a keyword extractor (Campos et al., 2020) to generate up to 20 keywords for each sentence. The team proposes and evaluates a range of similarity functions based on the extracted keyworkds through the generation of sparse embeddings. The embeddings are generated using the fastText model (Joulin et al., 2017). The scoring functions are then applied to re-rank the top 500 premises retrieved by the TF-IDF baseline. Their experiments show that the Jacardian similarity scoring function yields the best MAP performance of 14.14.

5 Detailed Analysis

In order to better evaluate and characterise the behaviour of the proposed systems beyond the aggregated MAP score, we carried out an additional analysis by partitioning the set of mathematical statements according to different categories.

Specifically, we categorise the statements in the test-set according to the total number of occurring mathematical elements (e.g., equations, variables, etc.) and the total number of gold premises. In particular, these categories allow for the evaluation of the behaviour of the systems when (a) dealing with a mixture of natural language and mathematical text and (b) retrieving premises that require multi-hop inference. The larger the number of premises supporting a given mathematical statement, in fact, the higher the number of inference steps that are likely to be required in the NLPS task.

The results of this analysis are reported in Table 3 and Table 4.

Team Name	Overall	0–5	5–10	10–20	20+
IJS	15.39	**13.89**	17.37	13.95	9.36
UNLPS	15.16	13.53	**17.43**	**14.03**	**10.08**
Kamivao	14.60	13.58	16.07	13.73	7.46
langml	14.14	12.24	16.20	13.86	7.62
TF-IDF baseline	12.28	11.27	13.29	11.70	7.15

Table 3: MAP score by number of *mathematical elements* in a mathematical statement.

Team Name	Overall	0–5	5–10	10–20	20+
IJS	15.39	**15.96**	**13.37**	**10.92**	5.89
UNLPS	15.16	15.67	13.33	10.57	5.40
Kamivao	14.60	15.05	12.84	10.03	6.76
langml	14.14	14.45	12.95	10.86	**8.02**
TF-IDF baseline	12.28	12.64	11.47	8.93	7.84

Table 4: MAP score by number of *gold premises* supporting a mathematical statement.

5.1 Number of Mathematical Elements

In order to count the number of mathematical elements in a given statement, we create apposite regular expressions leveraging the special characters used to write equations in LaTeX (e.g., "$"). Subsequently, we recompute the performance of the systems, grouping the statements in the test-set by the number of occurring mathematical elements (see Table 3).

Overall, the analysis reveals that the performances significantly decrease for all the participating systems, including the TF-IDF baseline. In addition, we observe that the second system in the overall ranking (UNLPS) is actually the most robust when dealing with an increasing number of mathematical elements. Since IJS and UNLPS employ a similar architecture based on pre-trained Sentence-Transformers (Reimers and Gurevych, 2019), the difference in results might be attributed to the specific model adopted in the experiments. UNLPS, in fact, adopts a pre-trained MPNet (Song et al., 2020) while IJS uses RoBERTa-large (Liu et al., 2019). At the same time, the overall decrease in performance confirms that additional work is still required to make Transformer-based representations able to deal with a mixture of natural language and mathematical text (Ferreira et al., 2022).

5.2 Number of Gold Premises

We perform a similar analysis by grouping the mathematical statements in the test-set according to the number of gold supporting premises. In this case, we assume that the larger the number of premises, the higher the probability of systems required to perform multi-hop inference for addressing the NLPS task (see Table 4).

Overall, a similar trend can be observed when investigating the behaviours of the systems on statements requiring an increasing number of supporting premises. The results in Table 4, in fact, show that the performances substantially decrease as the number of gold premises increases, with comparable MAP scores across different systems when considering a number of premises varying from 5 to 20. Surprisingly, when considering statements with more than 20 premises, we observe an almost entirely inverse ranking in the leaderbord, with Iangml becoming the best performing system, outperforming more complex models based on Transformers. Moreover, we observe that with 20+ premises the top 3 participating systems achieve worse performance than the TF-IDF baseline. These results indicate that pre-trained Transformers are still not robust on multi-hop inference in this context, and might suffer from a phenomenon of semantic drift similar to what previously observed in scientific explanation regeneration tasks (Jansen and Ustalov, 2019; Valentino et al., 2022, 2021).

6 Related Work

Mathematical Language Processing. Several areas of research apply Natural Language Processing for domain-specific tasks, Mathematics being one of these areas. One crucial task in this field is solving mathematical word problems, where the goal is to provide the answer to a mathematical problem written in natural language (Zhang et al., 2020; Kushman et al., 2014; Ran et al., 2019). These problems are usually self-contained and are structured in a didactic and straightforward manner, not containing complex mathematical expressions.

Some contributions focus on the representation of mathematical text and mathematical elements. Zinn (2004) proposes a representation for mathematical proofs using Discourse Representation Theory. Similarly, Ganesalingam (2013) introduces a grammar for representing informal mathematical text, while Pease et al. (2017) presents this style of text using Argumentation Theory. Such explicit representations are relevant for representing the reasoning process behind mathematical thinking. However, it is still not possible to accurately extract these representations at scale. Representations of mathematical elements are often used in the context of Mathematical Information Retrieval, used, for example, for obtaining a particular equation or expression, given a specific query. Tangent-CFT (Mansouri et al., 2019) is an embedding model that uses the subparts an expression or equation, to represent its meaning. This type of representation (Fraser et al., 2018; Zanibbi et al., 2016) often removes the expression for its original discourse, losing the textual context that can help to find a semantic representation. In this work, we focus on creating a representation that can integrate both of these aspects, natural language and mathematical elements. Similar to our work, Yuan et al. (2020) uses self-attention for mathematical elements in order to generate headlines for mathematical questions. Other relevant tasks for NLP applied to Mathematics include typing variables according to its surrounding text (Stathopoulos et al., 2018), obtaining the units of mathematical elements (Schubotz et al., 2016) and generating equations on a given topic (Yasunaga and Lafferty, 2019).

Premise Selection. Premise selection is a well-defined task in the field of Automated Theorem Proving (ATP), where proofs are encoded using a formal logical representation. Given a set of premises P, and a new conjecture c, premise selection aims to predict those premises from P that will most likely lead to an automatically constructed proof of c, where P and c are both written using a formal language. (Alemi et al., 2016) is one of the first models to use Deep Learning for premise selection in ATPs. Ferreira and Freitas (2020a) proposed an adaptation of this task, focusing on mathematical text written in natural language. A model based on Graph Neural Networks has been previously introduced for this task (Ferreira and Freitas, 2020b), however, the authors do not take into account the differences between mathematical and natural language terms, representing all statements homogeneously. The premise selection task can also be seen as an explanation reconstruction task, where premises are considered explanations for mathematical proofs.

Multi-Hop Natural Language Inference. The proposed NLPS task is related to previous work on Multi-Hop Inference and Explanation Regeneration as the set of premises retrieved by a given model can be interpreted as an explanation supporting the mathematical statement provided as input (Thayaparan et al., 2020; Xie et al., 2020; Valentino et al., 2022). Previous editions of the shared tasks series have focused on evaluating multi-hop inference in the context of science question answering (Thayaparan et al., 2021; Jansen and Ustalov, 2020, 2019). In this work, instead, we aim to assess the multi-hop inference capabilities of NLP models in a context requiring the articulation of both natural language and mathematical expressions.

7 Conclusion

Our shared task on Natural Language Premise Selection (NLPS) attracted a total of four participating teams, allowing for the evaluation of a diverse set of solutions ranging from Transformers to lexical-based approaches. The participating systems have all contributed to improving the performance of a TF-IDF baseline. The best-performing team, IJS, presented an approach based on pre-trained Sentence-Transformers, which has been shown to achieve a MAP score of 15.39. Given the challenges involved in the task, supported by the relatively low performance of state-of-the-art approaches, we hope this work will encourage future research in the field, exploring NLPS as a benchmark for testing complex inference capabilities and exploring the limit of AI and NLP models.

Acknowledgements

This work is partially funded by the SNSF project NeuMath (200021_204617).

References

Alexander A. Alemi, François Chollet, Niklas Een, Geoffrey Irving, Christian Szegedy, and Josef Urban. 2016. DeepMath - Deep Sequence Models for Premise Selection. In *Proceedings of the 30th International Conference on Neural Information Processing Systems*, NIPS 2016, pages 2243–2251, Barcelona, Spain. Curran Associates Inc.

Tom Brown et al. 2020. Language Models are Few-Shot Learners. In *Advances in Neural Information Processing Systems 33*, NeurIPS 2020, pages 1877–1901, Montréal, QC, Canada. Curran Associates, Inc.

Ricardo Campos, Vítor Mangaravite, Arian Pasquali, Alípio Jorge, Célia Nunes, and Adam Jatowt. 2020. YAKE! Keyword extraction from single documents using multiple local features. *Information Sciences*, 509:257–289.

Doratossadat Dastgheib and Ehsaneddin Asgari. 2022. Keyword-based Natural Language Premise Selection for an Automatic Mathematical Statement Proving. In *Proceedings of TextGraphs-16: Graph-based Methods for Natural Language Processing*, Gyeongju, Republic of Korea. Association for Computational Linguistics.

Jacob Devlin, Ming-Wei Chang, Kenton Lee, and Kristina Toutanova. 2019. BERT: Pre-training of Deep Bidirectional Transformers for Language Understanding. In *Proceedings of the 2019 Conference of the North American Chapter of the Association for Computational Linguistics: Human Language Technologies, Volume 1 (Long and Short Papers)*, NAACL-HLT 2019, pages 4171–4186, Minneapolis, MN, USA. Association for Computational Linguistics.

Deborah Ferreira and André Freitas. 2020a. Natural Language Premise Selection: Finding Supporting Statements for Mathematical Text. In *Proceedings of the 12th Language Resources and Evaluation Conference*, LREC 2020, pages 2175–2182, Marseille, France. European Language Resources Association.

Deborah Ferreira and André Freitas. 2020b. Premise Selection in Natural Language Mathematical Texts. In *Proceedings of the 58th Annual Meeting of the Association for Computational Linguistics*, ACL 2020, pages 7365–7374, Online. Association for Computational Linguistics.

Deborah Ferreira, Mokanarangan Thayaparan, Marco Valentino, Julia Rozanova, and Andre Freitas. 2022. To be or not to be an Integer? Encoding Variables for Mathematical Text. In *Findings of the Association for Computational Linguistics: ACL 2022*, pages 938–948, Dublin, Ireland. Association for Computational Linguistics.

Dallas Fraser, Andrew Kane, and Frank Wm. Tompa. 2018. Choosing Math Features for BM25 Ranking with Tangent-L. In *Proceedings of the ACM Symposium on Document Engineering 2018*, DocEng '18, pages 17.1–10.10, Halifax, NS, Canada. Association for Computing Machinery.

Mohan Ganesalingam. 2013. *The Language of Mathematics*, pages 17–38. Springer Berlin Heidelberg, Berlin, Heidelberg.

André Greiner-Petter, Moritz Schubotz, Fabian Müller, Corinna Breitinger, Howard Cohl, Akiko Aizawa, and Bela Gipp. 2019. Why Machines Cannot Learn Mathematics, Yet. In *Proceedings of the 4th Joint Workshop on Bibliometric-enhanced Information Retrieval and Natural Language Processing for Digital Libraries (BIRNDL 2019)*, number 2414 in CEUR Workshop Proceedings, pages 130–137, Paris, France.

Peter Jansen and Dmitry Ustalov. 2019. TextGraphs 2019 Shared Task on Multi-Hop Inference for Explanation Regeneration. In *Proceedings of the Thirteenth Workshop on Graph-Based Methods for Natural Language Processing (TextGraphs-13)*, pages 63–77, Hong Kong. Association for Computational Linguistics.

Peter Jansen and Dmitry Ustalov. 2020. TextGraphs 2020 Shared Task on Multi-Hop Inference for Explanation Regeneration. In *Proceedings of the Graph-based Methods for Natural Language Processing (TextGraphs)*, pages 85–97, Barcelona, Spain (Online). Association for Computational Linguistics.

Armand Joulin, Edouard Grave, Piotr Bojanowski, and Tomas Mikolov. 2017. Bag of Tricks for Efficient Text Classification. In *Proceedings of the 15th Conference of the European Chapter of the Association for Computational Linguistics: Volume 2, Short Papers*, EACL 2017, pages 427–431, Valencia, Spain. Association for Computational Linguistics.

Liubov Kovriguina, Roman Teucher, and Robert Wardenga. 2022. TextGraphs-16 Natural Language Premise Selection Task: Zero-Shot Premise Selection with Prompting Generative Language Models. In *Proceedings of TextGraphs-16: Graph-based Methods for Natural Language Processing*, Gyeongju, Republic of Korea. Association for Computational Linguistics.

Nate Kushman, Yoav Artzi, Luke Zettlemoyer, and Regina Barzilay. 2014. Learning to Automatically Solve Algebra Word Problems. In *Proceedings of the 52nd Annual Meeting of the Association for Computational Linguistics (Volume 1: Long Papers)*, ACL 2014, pages 271–281, Baltimore, MD, USA. Association for Computational Linguistics.

Yinhan Liu, Myle Ott, Naman Goyal, Jingfei Du, Mandar Joshi, Danqi Chen, Omer Levy, Mike Lewis, Luke Zettlemoyer, and Veselin Stoyanov. 2019. RoBERTa: A Robustly Optimized BERT Pretraining Approach.

Christopher D. Manning, Prabhakar Raghavan, and Hinrich Schütze. 2008. *Introduction to Information Retrieval*. Cambridge University Press.

Behrooz Mansouri, Shaurya Rohatgi, Douglas W. Oard, Jian Wu, C. Lee Giles, and Richard Zanibbi. 2019. Tangent-CFT: An Embedding Model for Mathematical Formulas. In *Proceedings of the 2019 ACM SIGIR International Conference on Theory of Information Retrieval*, ICTIR '19, pages 11–18, Santa Clara, CA, USA. Association for Computing Machinery.

Adrien Pavao, Isabelle Guyon, Anne-Catherine Letournel, Xavier Baró, Hugo Escalante, Sergio Escalera, Tyler Thomas, and Zhen Xu. 2022. CodaLab Competitions: An open source platform to organize scientific challenges. Technical report, LISN, CNRS, Université Paris-Saclay.

Alison Pease, John Lawrence, Katarzyna Budzynska, Joseph Corneli, and Chris Reed. 2017. Lakatos-style collaborative mathematics through dialectical, structured and abstract argumentation. *Artificial Intelligence*, 246:181–219.

Shuai Peng, Ke Yuan, Liangcai Gao, and Zhi Tang. 2021. MathBERT: A Pre-Trained Model for Mathematical Formula Understanding.

Qiu Ran, Yankai Lin, Peng Li, Jie Zhou, and Zhiyuan Liu. 2019. NumNet: Machine Reading Comprehension with Numerical Reasoning. In *Proceedings of the 2019 Conference on Empirical Methods in Natural Language Processing and the 9th International Joint Conference on Natural Language Processing*, EMNLP-IJCNLP 2019, pages 2474–2484, Hong Kong, China. Association for Computational Linguistics.

Nils Reimers and Iryna Gurevych. 2019. Sentence-BERT: Sentence Embeddings using Siamese BERT-Networks. In *Proceedings of the 2019 Conference on Empirical Methods in Natural Language Processing and the 9th International Joint Conference on Natural Language Processing*, EMNLP-IJCNLP 2019, pages 3982–3992, Hong Kong, China. Association for Computational Linguistics.

Moritz Schubotz, David Veenhuis, and Howard S. Cohl. 2016. Getting the Units Right. In *Joint Proceedings of the FM4M, MathUI, and ThEdu Workshops, Doctoral Program, and Work in Progress at the Conference on Intelligent Computer Mathematics 2016 (CICM-WS-WIP 2016)*, number 1785 in CEUR Workshop Proceedings, pages 146–156, Bialystok, Poland.

Kaitao Song, Xu Tan, Tao Qin, Jianfeng Lu, and Tie-Yan Liu. 2020. MPNet: Masked and Permuted Pre-training for Language Understanding. In *Advances in Neural Information Processing Systems 33*, NeurIPS 2020, pages 16857–16867, Montréal, QC, Canada. Curran Associates, Inc.

Yiannos Stathopoulos, Simon Baker, Marek Rei, and Simone Teufel. 2018. Variable Typing: Assigning Meaning to Variables in Mathematical Text. In *Proceedings of the 2018 Conference of the North American Chapter of the Association for Computational Linguistics: Human Language Technologies, Volume 1 (Long Papers)*, NAACL-HLT 2018, pages 303–312, New Orleans, LA, USA. Association for Computational Linguistics.

Mokanarangan Thayaparan, Marco Valentino, and André Freitas. 2020. A Survey on Explainability in Machine Reading Comprehension.

Mokanarangan Thayaparan, Marco Valentino, Peter Jansen, and Dmitry Ustalov. 2021. TextGraphs 2021 Shared Task on Multi-Hop Inference for Explanation Regeneration. In *Proceedings of the Fifteenth Workshop on Graph-Based Methods for Natural Language Processing (TextGraphs-15)*, pages 156–165, Mexico City, Mexico. Association for Computational Linguistics.

Thi Hong Hanh Tran, Matej Martinc, Antoine Doucet, and Senja Pollak. 2022. IJS at TextGraphs-16 Natural Language Premise Selection Task: Will Contextual Information Improve Natural Language Premise Selection? In *Proceedings of TextGraphs-16: Graph-based Methods for Natural Language Processing*, Gyeongju, Republic of Korea. Association for Computational Linguistics.

Paul Trust, Provia Kadusabe, Haseeb Younis, Rosane Minghim, Evangelos Milios, and Ahmed Zahran. 2022. SNLP at TextGraphs 2022 Shared Task: Unsupervised Natural Language Premise Selection in Mathematical Texts Using Sentence-MPNet. In *Proceedings of TextGraphs-16: Graph-based Methods for Natural Language Processing*, Gyeongju, Republic of Korea. Association for Computational Linguistics.

Marco Valentino, Mokanarangan Thayaparan, Deborah Ferreira, and André Freitas. 2022. Hybrid Autoregressive Inference for Scalable Multi-Hop Explanation Regeneration. *Proceedings of the AAAI Conference on Artificial Intelligence*, 36(10):11403–11411.

Marco Valentino, Mokanarangan Thayaparan, and André Freitas. 2021. Unification-based Reconstruction of Multi-hop Explanations for Science Questions. In *Proceedings of the 16th Conference of the European Chapter of the Association for Computational Linguistics: Main Volume*, EACL 2021, pages 200–211, Online. Association for Computational Linguistics.

Ashish Vaswani, Noam Shazeer, Niki Parmar, Jakob Uszkoreit, Llion Jones, Aidan N. Gomez, Łukasz Kaiser, and Illia Polosukhin. 2017. Attention Is All You Need. In *Advances in Neural Information Processing Systems 30*, NIPS 2017, pages 6000–6010, Vancouver, BC, Canada. Curran Associates, Inc.

Sean Welleck, Jiacheng Liu, Ronan Le Bras, Hannaneh Hajishirzi, Yejin Choi, and Kyunghyun Cho. 2021. NaturalProofs: Mathematical Theorem Proving in Natural Language. In *Proceedings of the Neural Information Processing Systems Track on Datasets and Benchmarks*.

Zhengnan Xie, Sebastian Thiem, Jaycie Martin, Elizabeth Wainwright, Steven Marmorstein, and Peter Jansen. 2020. WorldTree V2: A Corpus of Science-Domain Structured Explanations and Inference Patterns supporting Multi-Hop Inference. In *Proceedings of the 12th Conference on Language Resources and Evaluation*, LREC 2020, pages 5456–5473, Marseille, France. European Language Resources Association (ELRA).

Michihiro Yasunaga and John D. Lafferty. 2019. TopicEq: A Joint Topic and Mathematical Equation Model for Scientific Texts. *Proceedings of the AAAI Conference on Artificial Intelligence*, 33(01):7394–7401.

Ke Yuan, Dafang He, Zhuoren Jiang, Liangcai Gao, Zhi Tang, and C. Lee Giles. 2020. Automatic Generation of Headlines for Online Math Questions. *Proceedings of the AAAI Conference on Artificial Intelligence*, 34(05):9490–9497.

Richard Zanibbi, Kenny Davila, Andrew Kane, and Frank Wm. Tompa. 2016. Multi-Stage Math Formula Search: Using Appearance-Based Similarity Metrics at Scale. In *Proceedings of the 39th International ACM SIGIR Conference on Research and Development in Information Retrieval*, SIGIR '16, pages 145–154, Pisa, Italy. Association for Computing Machinery.

Jipeng Zhang, Lei Wang, Roy Ka-Wei Lee, Yi Bin, Yan Wang, Jie Shao, and Ee-Peng Lim. 2020. Graph-to-Tree Learning for Solving Math Word Problems. In *Proceedings of the 58th Annual Meeting of the Association for Computational Linguistics*, ACL 2020, pages 3928–3937, Online. Association for Computational Linguistics.

Claus Zinn. 2004. *Understanding Informal Mathematical Discourse*. Ph.D. thesis, Universität Erlangen-Nürnberg, Institut für Informatik.

IJS at TextGraphs-16 Natural Language Premise Selection Task: Will Contextual Information Improve Natural Language Premise Selection?

Hanh Thi Hong TRAN[1,2,3], **Matej MARTINC**[1], **Antoine DOUCET**[3], **Senja POLLAK**[1]
[1]Jožef Stefan Institute, Slovenia
[2]Jozef Stefan International Postgraduate School, Slovenia
[3]University of La Rochelle, France

Abstract

Natural Language Premise Selection (NLPS) is a mathematical Natural Language Processing (NLP) task that retrieves a set of useful relevant premises to support the end-user finding the proof for a particular statement. In this paper, we evaluate the impact of Transformer-based contextual information and different fundamental similarity scores towards NLPS. The results demonstrate that the contextual representation is better at capturing meaningful information despite not being pretrained on mathematical background in comparison with the statistical approach (e.g., the TF-IDF) with a boost of around 3.00% MAP@500. Our code is publicly available at https://github.com/honghanhh/premise-selection.

Keywords: *Premise selection, NLPS, contextual information, Transformers.*

1 Introduction

Natural Language Premise Selection (NLPS) (Ferreira and Freitas, 2020a), inspired by the field of Automated Theorem Proving, is a mathematical NLP task that retrieves a set of useful relevant premises. Given a mathematical statement written in natural language as the input, NLPS systems predict the relevant premises that could support an end-user finding a proof for that mathematical statement.

Mathematically, NLPS task can be defined as:

Definition 1.1. *Given a new mathematical statement s, that requires a mathematical proof, and a collection (or a knowledge base) of premises $P = p_1, p_2, \ldots, p_{Np}$, with size Np, retrieve the premises in P that are most likely to be useful for proving s.*

The premises often include supporting definitions and propositions, which can act as explanations for the proof process. Figure 1 presents examples of 2 premises that support a given mathematical statement or theorem.

Theorem

> For every integer n such that $n > 1$, n can be expressed as the product of one or more primes, uniquely up to the order in which they appear.

Proof

> In Integer is Expressible as Product of Primes it is proved that every integer n such that $n > 1$, n can be expressed as the product of one or more primes.
>
> In Prime Decomposition of Integer is Unique, it is proved that this prime decomposition is unique up to the order of the factors.

Figure 1: Example premises supporting a given theorem (Ferreira and Freitas, 2020a).

Most of the existing systems focus on manual feature engineering or statistical approaches to extract meaningful mathematical knowledge, with one exception being the study by Ferreira and Freitas (2020b), where they tackle the task by employing Deep Convolutional Graph Neural Networks (DCGNN) on graph representations. The state of the art models for NLP such as BERT (Devlin et al., 2016) are not fully explored under the assumption that they do not encode the intricate mathematical background knowledge needed to reason over mathematical discourse.

The 1st Shared Task on Natural Language Premise Selection (Valentino et al., 2022), organized as part of the TextGraphs 2022 workshop, presented one of the first opportunities to systematically compare different approaches towards a NLPS task in an Information Retrieval setting, by adopting PS-ProofWiki (Premise Selection-ProofWiki) dataset (Ferreira and Freitas, 2020a). This dataset can be considered as the baseline corpus for our specific shared task.

The contributions of this paper can be summarised as follows:

- An empirical evaluation of several contextual representations relying on Transformer-based language models;

Proceedings of TextGraphs-16: Graph-based Methods for Natural Language Processing, pages 114–118
October 16, 2022.

- Evaluation of the performance of different similarity scores, including Cosine, Euclidean, and Manhattan score on the NLPS task.

This paper is organised as follows: Section 2 presents the related work in premise selection. Next, we introduce our methodology, experimental setup and evaluation metrics in Section 3. The corresponding results are presented in Section 4. Finally, we conclude our work and suggest future directions in Section 5.

2 Related work

In this section, we present the related research in NLP applied to the NLPS task in the domain of Automated Theorem Proving.

The research was first introduced by Alama et al. (2014), who employed corpus analysis and kernel-based methods, in order to showcase the usefulness of automatic premise selection systems for proving the conjectures in the field of Automated Theorem Proving (ATP). Few years later, Irving et al. (2016) proposed a neural deepmath-deep sequence architecture for premise selection using formal statements from the Mizar corpus, which solved 67.90% of the conjectures present in the Mathematical Mizar Library. Other machine learning based approaches have also been investigated for the task at hand (e.g. KNN (Gauthier and Kaliszyk, 2015), Random Forest (Färber and Kaliszyk, 2015), to mention a few).

Similar to the previous research, (Ferreira and Freitas, 2021) formulate this problem as a pairwise relevance classification problem and present STAR, a cross-modal representation for mathematical statements with two layers of self-attention, one for each language modality present in the mathematical text.

Recently, Ferreira and Freitas (2020a) introduced a new systematic formulation of the task under the name Natural Language Premise Selection (NLPS) and published a new evaluation corpus called NL-PS. They propose two baseline approaches, using TF-IDF and PV-DBOW (Le and Mikolov, 2014). Additionally, they also suggested to model the task as a pairwise relevance classification problem and tackled it by employing neural contextual representations, namely BERT and SciBERT (Beltagy et al., 2019).

While the previous work focused on capturing either content (local) or structural dependencies (global) across natural language mathematical statements, Ferreira and Freitas (2020b) were the first to consider NLPS as a link prediction problem using Deep Convolutional Graph Neural Networks (DCGNN), with the aim of capturing both local and global information. Their study demonstrates the capability of graph embeddings to capture structural and content elements of mathematical statements.

3 Methodology

3.1 Data

The experiments are conducted on PS-ProofWiki (so-called Premise Selection-ProofWiki) dataset (Ferreira and Freitas, 2020a), which contains 3 subsets: training set, development set, and test set. Each mentioned subset includes a list of mathematical statements and their relevant premises. The number of instances in each subset are presented in Table 1. Besides, there is a knowledge base supporting these statements, which contains approximately 16,205 premises.

Subsets	Amount
Training set	5,519
Development set	2,778
Test set	2,763

Table 1: The number of examples in PS-ProofWiki's subsets.

Initially, the dataset was used for evaluating semantic representations (e.g., textual entailment and inference for mathematics (Ferreira and Freitas, 2020a), embeddings (Ferreira and Freitas, 2021), or mathematical discourse (Ferreira et al., 2022)). Regarding our research, we adopt the dataset for NLPS task with the aim to retrieve the set of relevant premises for a given statement in the test set by ranking the sentences contained in the supporting knowledge base.

3.2 Methods

Our research focuses on the impact of contextual information from Transformer-based language models compared with the statistical approaches (baselines) towards NLPS task. For simplification and better comparison, we extract contextual representations from different Transformer-based language models and compute several similarity scores to rank how likely the sentences in the knowledge base are a part of the set of premises for a given mathematical statement. The overall workflow is presented in Figure 2.

We employ several Transformer-based models, including PatentSBERTa (Bekamiri et al., 2022) (*PatentSBERTa*), T5-Large (Raffel et al., 2020) (*gtr-t5-large* and *sentence-t5-large*), RoBERTA-Large (Liu et al., 2019) (*all_datasets_v3_roberta-large*), Mpnet-Base (Song et al., 2020) (*all-mpnet-base-v2* and *all-mpnet-base-v_outcome_sim*), MiniLM (Wang et al., 2020) (*all-MiniLM-L6-v2* and *ll-MiniLM-L12-v2*). The models were obtained from the Hugging Face library[1] and were chosen according to the number of downloads and likes criteria.

Note that all the chosen models share the same pretraining purpose: they aim to train sentence embedding models on very large textual datasets using a self-supervised learning objective. As sentence Transformer models, they map the sentences and paragraphs to a dense vector space. Thus, we encoded the statements and premises into vector representations and then used different similarity metrics to calculate the similarity between a specific premise and the corresponding statement. The obtained similarity scores are afterwards used for ranking the premises in a descending order. We keep top 500 most relevant premises for each statement. We compare three similarity metrics, namely Cosine, Euclidean, and Manhattan similarity. All the experiments have been ran on a A100-PCIE-40GB GPU.

3.3 Evaluation metrics

For each model, we retrieve the top 500 premises from the knowledge base that support a given statement. We use Mean Average Precision at K (MAP@K) with K = 500 for the evaluation. This evaluation metric has also been used in the related work (Ferreira and Freitas, 2020a), thus our results are directly comparable to the state of the art methods.

4 Results

In this Section, we evaluate the suitability of different contextual representations of premises from the knowledge base for retrieving the top relevant premises for a given statement in the test set. We also compare the obtained results with the results of the shared task baseline (Valentino et al., 2022).

[1]https://huggingface.co/

Table 2 presents the performance of contextual representations extracted from different Transformer-based pretrained language models using Cosine similarity as the similarity metric. The shared task baseline to which we compare our approaches uses a simple term frequency model (TF-IDF) to rank how likely the sentences (premises) in the knowledge base are a part of the set of premises for a given mathematical statement.

Representation	MAP@500
sentence-t5-large	0.134110
gtr-t5-large	0.139367
all-mpnet-base-v_outcome_sim	0.144706
PatentSBERTa	0.146141
all-MiniLM-L6-v2	0.146995
all-mpnet-base-v2	0.151724
all-MiniLM-L12-v2	0.152427
all_datasets_v3_roberta-large	**0.153897**
Baseline	0.122800

Table 2: Performance of different representations on the test data using Cosine similarity score.

The results demonstrate that by employing Transformer-based models we can outperform the statistical baseline by a relatively large margin in terms of the MAP@500 evaluation metric. The best contextual representation for the task at hand was obtained by employing the large version of RoBERTa. Using this model, we can improve on the baseline performance by 3.11 percentage points. All tested contextual representations manage to outperform the baseline, with the performance improvement ranging from about 1.00 to 3.00 percentage points in terms of MAP@500. This indicates that contextual representations from Transformer-based language models are capable of encoding meaningful information from intricate mathematical background knowledge despite not being pretrained on domain-specific mathematical texts.

Similarity score	MAP@500
Cosine	0.153897
Euclidean	0.153896
Manhattan	**0.153902**

Table 3: Similarity score performance on the test data using RoBERTa embeddings

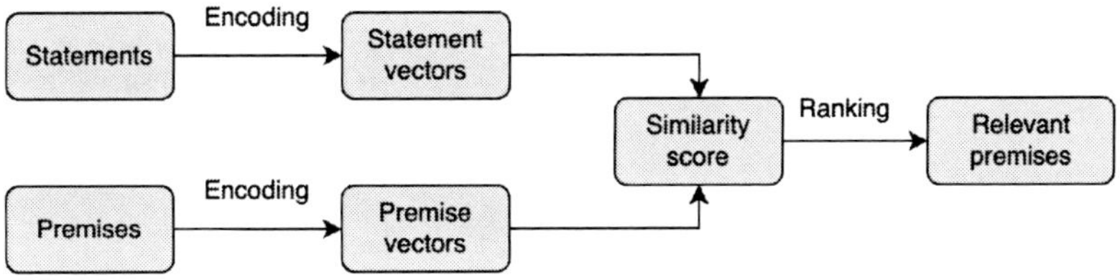

Figure 2: Our general workflow.

Using the contextual representations obtained from our best model, i.e. the large version of RoBERTa, we also evaluate three different similarity scores used for measuring similarity between premise and statement representations, namely Cosine, Euclidean, and Manhattan similarities. The results presented in Table 3 show that Manhattan similarity works slightly better than the other two similarity measures, although the difference is marginal in terms of MAP@500.

Teams	MAP@500	Ranking
IJS	0.1539	1
PaulTrust	0.1516	2
kamivao	0.1460	3
langml	0.1414	4
Organizers	0.1228	5

Table 4: Ranking on the shared task leaderboard.

Table 4 presents comparison between our proposed approach and the approaches proposed by other teams participating in the shared task in terms of rank and MAP@500. As can be seen, our system outperforms all others. Regarding the reproducibility and complexity, our approach uses a simple paradigm that is easy to reproduce and scale to large knowledge bases, but nevertheless offers a relatively efficient retrieval of premises.

5 Conclusion

In this paper, we have investigated the performance of contextual representations towards the task of Natural Language Premise Selection. We also evaluated the impact of different similarity scores. By using the contextual information obtained from the pretrained Transformer-based models in order to obtain premise and statement representations, we manage to outperform the baseline statistical approach using TF-IDF (the baseline) by a decent margin of around 3 percentage points in terms of MAP@500. These findings serve as a good initiative to explore the potential of using language models' for the NLPS task further. We also showed that by using the Manhattan distance for measuring similarity between representations, we can improve the performance by a small margin.

There remains a lot of room for improvement. In the future, we would like to investigate the effect of different mathematical representations on the performance of the model, e.g., by feeding the model graph representations. Combinations of contextual and graph representations will also be explored.

6 Acknowledgements

The work was partially supported by the Slovenian Research Agency (ARRS) core research programme Knowledge Technologies (P2-0103) and the project CANDAS (J6-2581). The first author was partly funded by Region Nouvelle Acquitaine. This work has also been supported by the TERMITRAD (2020-2019-8510010) project funded by the Nouvelle-Aquitaine Region, France.

References

Jesse Alama, Tom Heskes, Daniel Kühlwein, Evgeni Tsivtsivadze, and Josef Urban. 2014. Premise selection for mathematics by corpus analysis and kernel methods. *Journal of automated reasoning*, 52(2):191–213.

Hamid Bekamiri, Daniel S Hain, and Roman Jurowetzki. 2022. Patentsberta: A deep nlp based hybrid model for patent distance and classification using augmented sbert. *Technological Forecasting and Social Change*.

Iz Beltagy, Kyle Lo, and Arman Cohan. 2019. Scibert: A pretrained language model for scientific text. *arXiv preprint arXiv:1903.10676*.

Jacob Devlin, Ming-Wei Chang, Kenton Lee, and Kristina Toutanova. 2016. Bert: Bidirectional encoder representations from transformers.

Michael Färber and Cezary Kaliszyk. 2015. Random forests for premise selection. In *International Symposium on Frontiers of Combining Systems*, pages 325–340. Springer.

Deborah Ferreira and André Freitas. 2020a. Natural language premise selection: Finding supporting statements for mathematical text. *arXiv preprint arXiv:2004.14959*.

Deborah Ferreira and André Freitas. 2020b. Premise selection in natural language mathematical texts. In *Proceedings of the 58th Annual Meeting of the Association for Computational Linguistics*, pages 7365–7374.

Deborah Ferreira and André Freitas. 2021. Star: Cross-modal [sta] tement [r] epresentation for selecting relevant mathematical premises. In *Proceedings of the 16th Conference of the European Chapter of the Association for Computational Linguistics: Main Volume*, pages 3234–3243.

Deborah Ferreira, Mokanarangan Thayaparan, Marco Valentino, Julia Rozanova, and André Freitas. 2022. To be or not to be an integer? encoding variables for mathematical text. In *Findings of the Association for Computational Linguistics: ACL 2022*, pages 938–948.

Thibault Gauthier and Cezary Kaliszyk. 2015. Premise selection and external provers for hol4. In *Proceedings of the 2015 Conference on Certified Programs and Proofs*, pages 49–57.

Geoffrey Irving, Christian Szegedy, Alexander A Alemi, Niklas Eén, François Chollet, and Josef Urban. 2016. Deepmath-deep sequence models for premise selection. *Advances in neural information processing systems*, 29.

Quoc Le and Tomas Mikolov. 2014. Distributed representations of sentences and documents. In *International conference on machine learning*, pages 1188–1196. PMLR.

Yinhan Liu, Myle Ott, Naman Goyal, Jingfei Du, Mandar Joshi, Danqi Chen, Omer Levy, Mike Lewis, Luke Zettlemoyer, and Veselin Stoyanov. 2019. Roberta: A robustly optimized bert pretraining approach. *arXiv preprint arXiv:1907.11692*.

Colin Raffel, Noam Shazeer, Adam Roberts, Katherine Lee, Sharan Narang, Michael Matena, Yanqi Zhou, Wei Li, Peter J Liu, et al. 2020. Exploring the limits of transfer learning with a unified text-to-text transformer. *J. Mach. Learn. Res.*, 21(140):1–67.

Kaitao Song, Xu Tan, Tao Qin, Jianfeng Lu, and Tie-Yan Liu. 2020. Mpnet: Masked and permuted pre-training for language understanding. *Advances in Neural Information Processing Systems*, 33:16857–16867.

Marco Valentino, Deborah Ferreira, Mokanarangan Thayaparan, André Freitas, and Dmitry Ustalov. 2022. Textgraphs 2022 shared task on natural language premise selection. In *Proceedings of the Sixteenth Workshop on Graph-Based Methods for Natural Language Processing (TextGraphs-16)*. Association for Computational Linguistics.

Wenhui Wang, Furu Wei, Li Dong, Hangbo Bao, Nan Yang, and Ming Zhou. 2020. Minilm: Deep self-attention distillation for task-agnostic compression of pre-trained transformers. *Advances in Neural Information Processing Systems*, 33:5776–5788.

UNLPS at TextGraphs-16 Natural Language Premise Selection Task: Unsupervised Natural Language Premise Selection in Mathematical Text using Sentence-MPNet

Paul Trust
University College Cork

Provia Kadusabe
Worldquant University

Haseeb Younis
University College Cork

Rosane Minghim
University College Cork

Ahmed Zahran
University College Cork

Evangelos Millos
Dalhousie University

Abstract

This paper describes our system for the submission to the TextGraphs 2022 shared task at COLING 2022: Natural Language Premise Selection (NLPS) from mathematical texts. The task of NLPS regards selecting mathematical statements called premises in a knowledge base written in natural language and mathematical formulae that are most likely to be used to achieve a particular mathematical proof. We formulated this solution as an unsupervised semantic similarity task by first obtaining contextualized embeddings of both the premises and mathematical proofs using sentence transformers. We then obtained the cosine similarity between these embeddings and then selected premises with the highest cosine scores as the most probable. Our system improves over the baseline system that uses bag of words models based on term frequency inverse document frequency in terms of mean average precision (MAP) by about 23.5% (0.1516 versus 0.1228).

1 Introduction

Deep learning methods have achieved state of the art performance across several natural language processing (NLP) tasks in a wide variety of applications in several fields. Despite the importance of the field of mathematics and its contribution to scientific discovery, the application of NLP to mathematical text is still under-explored (Ferreira and Freitas, 2020a).

The task of natural language premise selection in mathematical text is a novel application of NLP in the field of mathematics. It involves selecting mathematical statements (premises) which are written in natural language and mathematical formulae that are most likely to be useful in proving a given conjecture or mathematical proof from a knowledge base.

More formally, given a set of premises P and a new conjecture c, all written in a combination of free text and mathematical formulae, Natural Language Premise Selection (NLPS) aims to select premises from P that will be helpful in proving a conjecture or proof c (Ferreira and Freitas, 2021). This is not a trivial task since it involves comprehending mathematical text, which in turn requires understanding of distinctive structure, discourse, and dependencies within text.

Computational approaches have been proposed to solve this task. For example, Ferreira (2021) used a graph neural network trained in a supervised learning approach to extract the most relevant premises (Ferreira and Freitas, 2020b). In this work we formulate the Natural Language Premise Selection task as an unsupervised semantic similarity task by retrieving premises that have a higher cosine similarity score with the given conjecture or proof of interest. A straightforward way to solve the task would have been to encode the premises and conjectures using word embeddings, and then perform cosine similarity to obtain the most relevant premises as those with the highest cosine score. However, this naive approach requires that both sentences are fed into the neural network, which causes a massive computational overhead. Additionally, for better performance fine tuning or pretraining the models on downstream sentence pairs may be necessary (Devlin et al., 2019), and that is computationally expensive.

In this work, we propose to use SMPNet (Sentence Masked and Permuted Language Modeling), a computationally efficient and effective sentence transformer, which is a modification of the pre-trained MPNet (Song et al., 2020a) that uses Siamese and triplet network structure to derive semantically meaningful sentence embeddings that were used for this task. MPNet (Song et al., 2020a) is a variant of transformer models (Vaswani et al., 2017) that leverages the advantages of BERT (Bidirectional Encoder Representations from Transformers) (Devlin et al., 2019) and XLNet (Yang et al.,

Proceedings of TextGraphs-16: Graph-based Methods for Natural Language Processing, pages 119–123
October 16, 2022.

2019) (Generalized Autoregressive Pretraining for Language Understanding) while avoiding their limitations.

2 Related work

2.1 Natural Language Premise Selection

The applications of natural language processing to mathematical text is still an under-explored area despite its great potential. The following are some of the key previous work on natural language premise selection. (Ferreira and Freitas, 2020b) formulates the task of premise selection from mathematical text as a link prediction problem using a deep convolution neural network. (Ferreira and Freitas, 2021) proposes a cross-model attention to learn mathematical text for natural language premise selection.

Our work is different from the previous approaches in that we focus on unsupervised learning approach using sentence transformers based on MPNet. This is an attempt to circumvent the labeling issue, which is a hard one for mathematical text, as well as improve the performance of the baseline methods mentioned.

2.2 Text Representation

Text data in most cases need to be converted into numerical values to be able to perform any meaningful machine learning operations. The form in which text is encoded directly influences the performance of models on downstream tasks. The traditional way to represent text is count-based approaches (bag of words). Bag of words approaches (Ramos et al., 2003) represent text based on the frequency of occurrence of terms in a document. The challenges with these approaches is that they sometimes do not capture any notion of similarity among semantically related words.

Static word embedding approaches that represent words as outputs of a neural network, such as word2vec (Mikolov et al., 2013) improved word representations since it was very easy to retrieve the most semantically related words for a given target word. The key weakness of these approaches is that the context in which the word is used is not captured. That means that a word has the same vector representation regardless the context in which it is used.

Contextualized language representations (Peters et al., 2018; Devlin et al., 2019) captures the context in which words are used improving performance on downstream tasks. The challenges with naive contextualized representations is that they are are not adapted for semantic similarity tasks.

Sentence embeddings (Reimers and Gurevych, 2019) modify contextualized embeddings by combining word embeddings in a sentence through a pooling strategy. They are additionally pre-trained and fine-tuned on a large corpus of sentence pairs making them ideal for semantic similarity tasks.

3 Methodology

Consider a knowledge base K from which we retrieve a collection of N mathematical premises $P = \{p_1, ..., p_N\}$ written in natural language. We would like to retrieve the premises P in K that are most likely to be useful in proving a mathematical statement or conjecture $c \in \{c_1, ...c_M\}$. We formulate this task as a semantic similarity task by retrieving premises P in K that were semantically close to a given statement or conjecture c.

3.1 Embedding Construction

The organizers of the shared task on Natural Language Premise Selection released a baseline method alongside the data, which uses a term-frequency inverse document frequency (TF-IDF) model to find the semantically related premises from a knowledge base given a mathematical conjecture, which is used to compare with our method.

3.1.1 Bag of words Baseline (TF-IDF)

TF-IDF (Term Frequency Inverse Document frequency) is a combination of two word statistics: term frequency, which is a measure of how many times a word appears in a document and Inverse Document frequency (IDF), which is a measure of whether a term is common in a given document (Ramos et al., 2003).

3.1.2 BERT

BERT (Devlin et al., 2019) is a transformer model(Vaswani et al., 2017) that was pre-trained in a bi-directional context with two objectives: masked language modeling and next sentence prediction using the bookcorpus (800 million words) and English wikipedia (2,500 million words). Additionally, the trained model can be fine-tuned for downstream tasks. Word embeddings are extracted from the last layers of the network.

3.1.3 SBERT

SBERT (Sentence-BERT) (Reimers and Gurevych, 2019) is a modification of the pre-trained BERT networks using Siamese and triplet networks, which make it able to derive semantically meaningful sentence embeddings. This model was trained using Stanford Natural Language Inference(SNLI) and Multi-Genre Natural Language Inference (MNLI) datasets. SNLI contained $570,000$ annotated sentence pairs and MNLI contained 430000 annotated sentence pairs.

3.1.4 SMPNet

SPMNet is a sentence transformer that uses a pre-trained MPNet model and fine-tuned on a large and diverse dataset of 1 billion sentence pairs using a contrastive learning objective. In our experiments, we particularly used the version named "all-mpnet-base-v2" which maps sentences and paragraphs to a 768 dimensional dense vector space (Reimers and Gurevych, 2019).

The contextualized representations of the premises and mathematical statements were obtained using sentence embeddings with SPMNet (Reimers and Gurevych, 2019). Let the obtained sentence embeddings for mathematical premises be P_E and those for conjectures be C_E.

3.2 Premise Selection

To identify the most important premises given a mathematical conjecture, we calculate the cosine similarity between the embeddings of the mathematical conjectures C_E and those of the mathematical premises P_E as follows:

$$CosineSimilarity(P_E, C_E) = \frac{P_E * C_E}{||P_{E]}|| * ||C_E||} \quad (1)$$

To retrieve the most important premises from knowledge base K for proving a conjecture C, we rank the premises according to the cosine similarity scores and select those premises that had the highest cosine similarity scores with the given mathematical conjectures

4 Experiments and Results

4.1 Datasets

The dataset used for experiments in this paper was provided by the organizers of the shared task on Natural Language Premise Selection organized at TextGraphs-16, a workshop on Graph theory and natural language processing at EMNLP 2022 (Valentino et al., 2022).

The dataset is composed of a training set ($5,519$ instances), a development set ($2,778$ instances), and a test set ($2,763$ instances), each including a list of mathematical statements and their relevant premises. The knowledge base supporting these statements contains approximately $16,205$ premises (Valentino et al., 2022).

4.2 Evaluation and Experimental setup

Our proposed model was compared with the bag of words baseline and other models using Mean Average Precision (MAP). MAP is computed as follows:

$$MAP = \frac{\sum_{i=1}^{N} AvgP(S_i)}{N} \quad (2)$$

where N is the total number of statements, S_i is the $i-$th mathematical statements and $AvgP(S_i)$ is the average precision. The test set was hosted on codalab (Valentino et al., 2022) by the organizers of the shared task.

We used Sentence-Transformers library [1] (Reimers and Gurevych, 2019) for computing sentence embedding for SBERT and SMPNet, bag of words baseline was implemented using sklearn package [2] (Pedregosa et al., 2011) and BERT word embeddings were obtained using the huggingface [3] library (Wolf et al., 2019). Our code used for the experiments can be found on `https://github.com/TrustPaul/Premise-selection-coling.git`

4.3 Discussion

Table 1 shows the results of our proposed approach (SPMNet) and the baseline models. Our approach (SPMNet) achieves mean average precision (MAP) of 0.151638 which is about 23% above the baseline comparison method of bag of words, which achieved MAP of 0.1228.

Additionally, we performed experimental comparison with SBERT, which is also a sentence transformer but with BERT as an underlying transformer. Experiment results from the Table 1 reveal that SBERT also outperforms the baseline bag-of-words model but is outperformed by SMPNet. We hypothesize that this is due to the impact of the underlying

[1] `https://www.sbert.net/`
[2] `https://scikit-learn.org/`
[3] `https://huggingface.co/`

Model	Mean Average Precision (MAP)
TF-IDF (Baseline)	0.1228
BERT Word Embedding	0.1109
Sentence BERT	0.1465
Sentence MPNet (Ours)	**0.1516**

Table 1: Mean average Precision (MAP) for models used in our experiments. TF-IDF stands for Term Frequency-Inverse Document Frequency which is a bag of words baseline, BERT stands for Bidirectional Encoder Representations from Transformers and MPNet represents Masked and Permuted Pre-training for Language Understanding

transformer model used to generate sentence embeddings, since MPNet is often a better performing model compared to BERT and also because SPMNet was fine-tuned on a larger dataset compared SBERT (1 billion sentence pairs versus 570,000 sentence pairs)(Song et al., 2020b).

Contrary to our expectations, naive word embeddings obtained by BERT are outperformed even by the bag-of-words baseline model. This re-enforces the role played by the pre-training procedure and domain specific data employed in sentence transformers for semantic similarity tasks (Reimers and Gurevych, 2019).

5 Conclusion

In this work, we introduce an approach (SPMnet) for natural language premise selection, which is a task that involves finding the relevant theorems, axioms and definitions in natural language mathematical texts. Our proposed approach uses sentence embeddings based on the state-of-the-art transformer MPNet (Masked and Permuted Language Modeling) generating high quality embeddings that we used for retrieving the most important premises for a given mathematical conjecture. The results from our experiment show that the proposed approach (SPMNet) outperforms the baseline method (TF-IDF) by 0.028838 in mean average precision (MAP) which is a 23.5% improvement.

6 Acknowledgements

We thank Science Foundation Ireland (SFI) Center for Research Training in Advanced Networks and Future communications at University College Cork for funding this research and Irish Centre for High-End Computing (ICHEC) for providing access to computing power for running some of our experiments.

References

Jacob Devlin, Ming-Wei Chang, Kenton Lee, and Kristina Toutanova. 2019. BERT: Pre-training of deep bidirectional transformers for language understanding. In *Proceedings of the 2019 Conference of the North American Chapter of the Association for Computational Linguistics: Human Language Technologies, Volume 1 (Long and Short Papers)*, pages 4171–4186, Minneapolis, Minnesota. Association for Computational Linguistics.

Deborah Ferreira and André Freitas. 2020a. Natural language premise selection: Finding supporting statements for mathematical text. In *Proceedings of the 12th Language Resources and Evaluation Conference*, pages 2175–2182, Marseille, France. European Language Resources Association.

Deborah Ferreira and André Freitas. 2020b. Premise selection in natural language mathematical texts. In *Proceedings of the 58th Annual Meeting of the Association for Computational Linguistics*, pages 7365–7374, Online. Association for Computational Linguistics.

Deborah Ferreira and André Freitas. 2021. STAR: Cross-modal [STA]tement [R]epresentation for selecting relevant mathematical premises. In *Proceedings of the 16th Conference of the European Chapter of the Association for Computational Linguistics: Main Volume*, pages 3234–3243, Online. Association for Computational Linguistics.

Tomas Mikolov, Kai Chen, Greg Corrado, and Jeffrey Dean. 2013. Efficient estimation of word representations in vector space. *arXiv preprint arXiv:1301.3781*.

Fabian Pedregosa, Gaël Varoquaux, Alexandre Gramfort, Vincent Michel, Bertrand Thirion, Olivier Grisel, Mathieu Blondel, Peter Prettenhofer, Ron Weiss, Vincent Dubourg, et al. 2011. Scikit-learn: Machine learning in python. *the Journal of machine Learning research*, 12:2825–2830.

Matthew E. Peters, Mark Neumann, Mohit Iyyer, Matt Gardner, Christopher Clark, Kenton Lee, and Luke Zettlemoyer. 2018. Deep contextualized word representations. In *Proceedings of the 2018 Conference of the North American Chapter of the Association for Computational Linguistics: Human Language Technologies, Volume 1 (Long Papers)*, pages 2227–2237,

New Orleans, Louisiana. Association for Computational Linguistics.

Juan Ramos et al. 2003. Using tf-idf to determine word relevance in document queries. In *Proceedings of the first instructional conference on machine learning*, volume 242, pages 29–48. Citeseer.

Nils Reimers and Iryna Gurevych. 2019. Sentence-bert: Sentence embeddings using siamese bert-networks. In *Proceedings of the 2019 Conference on Empirical Methods in Natural Language Processing*. Association for Computational Linguistics.

Kaitao Song, Xu Tan, Tao Qin, Jianfeng Lu, and Tie-Yan Liu. 2020a. Mpnet: Masked and permuted pre-training for language understanding. *Advances in Neural Information Processing Systems*, 33:16857–16867.

Kaitao Song, Xu Tan, Tao Qin, Jianfeng Lu, and Tie-Yan Liu. 2020b. Mpnet: Masked and permuted pre-training for language understanding. In *Advances in Neural Information Processing Systems*, volume 33, pages 16857–16867. Curran Associates, Inc.

Marco Valentino, Deborah Ferreira, Mokanarangan Thayaparan, André Freitas, and Dmitry Ustalov. 2022. Textgraphs 2022 shared task on natural language premise selection. In *Proceedings of the Sixteenth Workshop on Graph-Based Methods for Natural Language Processing (TextGraphs-16)*. Association for Computational Linguistics.

Ashish Vaswani, Noam Shazeer, Niki Parmar, Jakob Uszkoreit, Llion Jones, Aidan N Gomez, Łukasz Kaiser, and Illia Polosukhin. 2017. Attention is all you need. *Advances in neural information processing systems*, 30.

Thomas Wolf, Lysandre Debut, Victor Sanh, Julien Chaumond, Clement Delangue, Anthony Moi, Pierric Cistac, Tim Rault, Rémi Louf, Morgan Funtowicz, et al. 2019. Huggingface's transformers: State-of-the-art natural language processing. *arXiv preprint arXiv:1910.03771*.

Zhilin Yang, Zihang Dai, Yiming Yang, Jaime Carbonell, Russ R Salakhutdinov, and Quoc V Le. 2019. Xlnet: Generalized autoregressive pretraining for language understanding. *Advances in neural information processing systems*, 32.

Keyword-based Natural Language Premise Selection for an Automatic Mathematical Statement Proving

Doratossadat Dastgheib[†] and **Ehsaneddin Asgari**[*]
[†] Language Processing and Digital Humanities Lab, Tehran, Iran.
[†] Department of Computer and Data Science, Shahid Beheshti University, Tehran, Iran.
[*] NLP Expert Center, Data:Lab, Volkswagen AG, Munich, Germany
d_dastgheib@sbu.ac.ir, asgari@berkeley.edu

Abstract

Extraction of supportive premises for a mathematical problem can contribute to profound success in improving automatic reasoning systems. One bottleneck in automated theorem proving is the lack of a proper semantic information retrieval system for mathematical texts. In this paper, we show the effect of keyword extraction in the natural language premise selection (NLPS) shared task proposed in TextGraph-16 that seeks to select the most relevant sentences supporting a given mathematical statement.

1 Introduction

A mathematical statement requires a collection of appropriate definitions, previously proved statements, and inference rules to be proved. The automatic reasoning field deals with computing systems automating proof procedures and proof checking. One of the considerations in implementing automatic deduction and artificial intelligence approaches is restricting the proof search space and preventing the automatic prover from pursuing unfruitful reasoning paths. A dual aspect of search is looking for previous results that could be useful in proof completion (Portoraro, 2021).

Premise selection was initially introduced in (Blanchette et al., 2016) as a task to select a part of a formal library that improves the chance that an automatic prover can prove a mathematical conjecture. In (Irving et al., 2016), neural network-based premise selectors were applied for the first time, and (Ferreira and Freitas, 2021) reformulated the problem as a pairwise relevance classification problem.

Similar challenges in mathematical context have been proposed, such as ARQMATH (Zanibbi et al., 2020) seeking an answers retriever and ranker for a given mathematical question. An answer retriever system mainly needs to consider mathematical text similarities. However, the premise selector task also requires a mathematical concept understanding component.

In this study, we work on the shared-task introduced by the 16th Workshop on Graph-Based Natural Language Processing (Valentino et al., 2022) on natural language premise selection. In this task, the teams are given a collection of mathematical statements in natural language and the goal is to retrieve supportive premises from a knowledge-base that can prove certain statements.

In this study we look into the effectiveness of keyword extraction in selecting premises for proving each statement outperforms the TF-IDF-based baseline.

2 Approach

2.1 Data Description

The dataset used in this task is a collection of mathematical statements and their premises extracted from ProofWiki, available in (Ferreira and Freitas, 2020). Each statement in the dataset is expressed in natural language, and the formulas are in LaTeX format. An overview of the dataset can be found in Table 1. The collection contains 21614, statements spanning 1227949, tokens in total.

2.2 Preprocessing

For data cleaning, we perform specific preprocessing steps, e.g., removing LaTeXcommands such as `begin` that describe a part of a formula in the sentence from the texts of statements. We perform this step to avoid their extractions as keywords in the next part of the pipeline. Then using an automatic keyword extractor (Campos et al., 2020), we generate up to 20 keywords for each sentence. Table 1 provides sample keywords for an example statement.

Embedding. To compare the semantic and context similarity of keywords, we also produce all keywords embeddings using fastText embedding pretrained on Wikipedia (Joulin et al., 2016).

Proceedings of TextGraphs-16: Graph-based Methods for Natural Language Processing, pages 124–126
October 16, 2022.

	Train	Dev	Test	Knowledge Base
Instance Number	5519	2778	2763	16205
Statement Example	Let $Q_n = \langle a_j \rangle_{0 \le j \le n}$ be a geometric sequence of length n consisting of positive integers only. Let a_1 and a_n be coprime. Then the jth term of Q_n is given by: $a_j = q^j p^{n-j}$			
Premise Example	Let $\langle x_n \rangle$ be a geometric sequence in $\mathbb{R}$ defined as $x_n = ar^n$ for $n = 0, 1, 2, 3, \dots$ The parameter: $r \in \mathbb{R} : r \neq 0$ is called the common ratio of $\langle x_n \rangle$.			
Statement Keywords	sequence, length, consisting, geometric, positive, integers, coprime, term			**Premise Keywords**: sequence, defined, geometric, parameter, called, common, ratio

Table 1: Overview of available dataset for retrieving supportive premises along with an example statement and one of its premises with their respective extracted keywords.

2.3 Retrieval Approach

The retrieval system should assign a score between the statements and their candidate premises. For sentences S_1, S_2 in dataset (coming from statement or premises) we extract the keyword sets KS_1, and KS_2 respectively. We define our suggested schemes for scoring as follows:

1. **Keyword Jaccardian Similarity.** The intersection cardinality over union cardinality of extracted keywords from the statement and the candidate premise:
$$Score(KS_1, KS_2) = \frac{|KS_1 \cap KS_2|}{|KS_1 \cup KS_2|}$$
2. **Keyword Affecting Relevance Score.** We measure the affecting relevance scores of keywords in the intersection keywords set:
$$Score(KS_1, KS_2) = \sum_{k_i \in KS_1 \cap KS_2} (1 - r_{i_1}) \times (1 - r_{i_2})$$
where r_{i_1} and r_{i_2} are keyword scores for keyword k_i in the sentences S_1 and S_2 respectively.
3. **Keyword Embedding Similarity.** Sum of cosine similarity of embeddings in two keyword sets:
$$Score(KS_1, KS_2) = \sum_{k_1 \in KS_1, k_2 \in KS_2} \textbf{cos-sim}(k_1, k_2)$$

We select the premises with maximum scores as the ultimate premise for each statement.

2.4 Evaluation

The systems are supposed to rank the sentences in the knowledge base premises for a given mathematical statement. We evaluate our NLPS system using Mean Average Precision (MAP) for 500 top premises retrieved from the knowledge base and introduced the term frequency (TF-IDF) model as a baseline.

3 Results

The results achieved using methods described in the previous section compared to the baseline score are presented in Table 2. Keyword-based approaches performed reasonably well in retrieving premises for given mathematical statements and outperformed the TF-IDF-based baseline. However, the embedding-based approach did not achieve competitive performance. One reason can be the ambiguity in the fixed embeddings as fastText.

4 Conclusions

In this paper, we checked the effectiveness of keyword extraction of mathematical statements for premise selection shared task NLPS and considered three keyword scoring schemas. Given statements,

Method	Dev	Test
Base line	0.1239	0.1228
Jaccardian Sim.	**0.1364**	**0.1414**
Affected Rel.	0.1256	0.129
Embedding Sim.	0.0539	0.05

Table 2: Mean Average Precision (MAP) socre for of our proposed methods in comparison with the tf-idf baseline.

we scored the keywords extracted for each statement and selected supportive sentences. Results show that keywords of statements can be effectively used in selecting relevant premises.

References

Jasmin C. Blanchette, Cezary Kaliszyk, Lawrence C. Paulson, and Josef Urban. 2016. Hammering towards qed. *Journal of Formalized Reasoning*, 9(1):101–148.

Ricardo Campos, Vítor Mangaravite, Arian Pasquali, Alípio Jorge, Célia Nunes, and Adam Jatowt. 2020. Yake! keyword extraction from single documents using multiple local features. *Information Sciences*, 509:257–289.

Deborah Ferreira and André Freitas. 2020. Natural language premise selection: Finding supporting statements for mathematical text. In *Proceedings of the 12th Language Resources and Evaluation Conference*, pages 2175–2182, Marseille, France. European Language Resources Association.

Deborah Ferreira and André Freitas. 2021. STAR: Cross-modal [STA]tement [R]epresentation for selecting relevant mathematical premises. In *Proceedings of the 16th Conference of the European Chapter of the Association for Computational Linguistics: Main Volume*, pages 3234–3243, Online. Association for Computational Linguistics.

Geoffrey Irving, Christian Szegedy, Alexander A Alemi, Niklas Een, Francois Chollet, and Josef Urban. 2016. Deepmath - deep sequence models for premise selection. In *Advances in Neural Information Processing Systems*, volume 29. Curran Associates, Inc.

Armand Joulin, Edouard Grave, Piotr Bojanowski, and Tomas Mikolov. 2016. Bag of tricks for efficient text classification. *arXiv preprint arXiv:1607.01759*.

Frederic Portoraro. 2021. Automated Reasoning. In Edward N. Zalta, editor, *The Stanford Encyclopedia of Philosophy*, Fall 2021 edition. Metaphysics Research Lab, Stanford University.

Marco Valentino, Deborah Ferreira, Mokanarangan Thayaparan, André Freitas, and Dmitry Ustalov. 2022. Textgraphs 2022 shared task on natural language premise selection. In *Proceedings of the Sixteenth Workshop on Graph-Based Methods for Natural Language Processing (TextGraphs-16)*. Association for Computational Linguistics.

Richard Zanibbi, Douglas W. Oard, Anurag Agarwal, and Behrooz Mansouri. 2020. Overview of arqmath 2020: Clef lab on answer retrieval for questions on math. In *Experimental IR Meets Multilinguality, Multimodality, and Interaction: 11th International Conference of the CLEF Association, CLEF 2020, Thessaloniki, Greece, September 22–25, 2020, Proceedings*, page 169–193, Berlin, Heidelberg. Springer-Verlag.

TextGraphs-16 Natural Language Premise Selection Task: Zero-Shot Premise Selection with Prompting Generative Language Models

Liubov Kovriguina[1], **Roman Teucher**[1],
Robert Wardenga[2]
[1]Fraunhofer IAIS Dresden, [2]InfAI Leipzig
{liubov.kovriguina,roman.teucher}@iais.fraunhofer.de
{wardenga}@infai.org

Abstract

Automated theorem proving can benefit a lot from methods employed in natural language processing, knowledge graphs and information retrieval: this non-trivial task combines formal languages understanding, reasoning, similarity search. We tackle this task by enhancing semantic similarity ranking with prompt engineering, which has become a new paradigm in natural language understanding. None of our approaches requires additional training. Despite encouraging results reported by prompt engineering approaches for a range of NLP tasks, for the premise selection task vanilla re-ranking by prompting GPT-3 doesn't outperform semantic similarity ranking with SBERT, but merging of the both rankings shows better results.

1 Introduction

The recently proposed task of Natural Language Premise Selection for mathematical statements (Ferreira and Freitas, 2020a) follows in line with tasks such as Mathematical Information Retrieval (Líška et al., 2011) and Mathematical Formula Understanding (e.g. (Peng et al., 2021)). Those tasks share the common objective to improve the processing and understanding of mathematical statements, which are a significant part of scientific information. On the other hand, with the advent of the attention mechanism (Vaswani et al., 2017) pretrained and fine-tuned Transformers, such as BERT (see (Devlin et al., 2018)), GPT-3 ((Brown et al., 2020b)) etc. were able to improve state of the art results for many Natural Language Task. In this short paper we investigate the use of Transformers for the Natural Language Premise Selection in the context of mathematical statements within the 1st Shared Task Natural Language Premise Selection at TextGraphs2022 Workshop(Valentino et al., 2022). We propose embedding the knowledge base with a BERT style transformer to obtain dense embedding of the statement in the knowledge base. By computing similarity of a given statement with the knowledge base we then obtain relevant candidates from the knowledge base that can be fed into a large Language model, such as GPT-3, to rank the candidates according to their importance to the given statement. We look at two structurally different transformers to compute the embeddings. 1. Sentence BERT (Reimers and Gurevych, 2019) and 2. MathBERT (Peng et al., 2021). The final ranking of the premises is done with GPT-3 using the OpenAI playground. As this approach does not require further training of the Transformer models and only uses the inherent knowledge it falls under the regime of Zero-shot Learning.

2 Related work

Transformer Models are large and deep neural network based on the attention mechanism (see (Vaswani et al., 2017)) that where pretrained originally with general Language Processing and Understanding tasks in mind (see (Vaswani et al., 2017), (Devlin et al., 2018), (Brown et al., 2020b), (Reimers and Gurevych, 2019)). Recently Transformers have been applied to tasks apart from Natural Language Processing and Generation. Models designed specifically for mathematical task can be found in (Shen et al., 2021) and (Peng et al., 2021).

Premise Selection (Ferreira and Freitas, 2020a) can be viewed as a precursor for Automated Theorem Proving (Alama et al., 2014). Automated Theorem Proving has a long history (Anderson, 1973) and is recently being tackled with approaches using Deep Neural Networks (e.g. (Ferreira and Freitas, 2020b), (Irving et al., 2016) and also (Polu and Sutskever, 2020)).

The approach in this paper is inspired by RETRO (Borgeaud et al., 2021) – a model that is able to reference a large knowledge base to solve general language tasks, by using a transformer on top of a frozen BERT retriever – and recent successes in prompt engineering for very large Language Mod-

Proceedings of TextGraphs-16: Graph-based Methods for Natural Language Processing, pages 127–132
October 16, 2022.

els (Brown et al., 2020b).

3 Dataset Description

The organizers provide a dataset [1] with a tf-idf baseline (Valentino et al., 2022). Provided data consist of training, validation and test sets and a knowledge base. Each sample in the training and development sets includes *id*, *theorem text* and list of relevant *premise id's*. Texts of theorems and premises are represented in LaTeX markup. Dataset statistics are shown in Table 1. The knowledge base comprises 16205 premises.

4 Approach description

The central approach, which we have designed and evaluated for the premise selection task is **leveraging prompting methods for re-ranking**. Overall idea of it is to generate a primary ranking and further improve it by prompting generative language model with an instruction and top-k candidates from the primary ranking.

Prompt-based learning in a new paradigm in natural language processing. "Unlike traditional supervised learning, which trains a model to take in an input x and predict an output y as $P(y|x)$, prompt-based learning is based on language models that model the probability of text directly"(Liu et al., 2021). During prompt-based learning the original input x is modified using a template into a textual string prompt x' that has some unfilled slots (i.e., for model's answer), and then the language model is used for generating sequence completing the template. Due to multitasking abilities of generative language models to perform well on a wide range of tasks, there has appeared a bunch of prompt engineering approaches (prompt sharing, decomposition, noising, etc.), i.e. authors of the survey in (Liu et al., 2021) propose a typology including above 50 approaches.

For the primary ranking we have implemented two unsupervised approaches without model fine-tuning on train or validation sets: first uses sentence transformers (see Section 4.1) and second one uses MathBERT[2] (see Section 4.2) for embedding premise and theorems. Both approaches score premises by computing cosine similarity between the text of premise and text of theorem.

For re-ranking with prompt engineering we create prompts containing top-10 candidates from primary ranking and feed them to the GPT-3 model(Brown et al., 2020a) via OpenAI Playground[3], model *text-davinci-002*. Details of the approach are provided in sec. 4.3 and Appendix.

4.1 Ranking with Sentence Transformers

Sentence transformers (Sentence-BERT, SBERT) is an approach proposed in (Reimers and Gurevych, 2019) with implementation available at Gitlab[4]. It is "a modification of the pretrained BERT network that uses siamese and triplet network structures to derive semantically meaningful sentence embeddings that can be compared using cosine-similarity"(Reimers and Gurevych, 2019). Authors of SBERT add a pooling operation to the output of BERT / RoBERTa to derive a fixed sized sentence embedding and experiment with three pooling strategies: using the output of the CLS-token,computing the mean of all output vectors (MEAN-strategy), and computing a max-over-time of the output vectors (MAX-strategy). In our experiments we used the default MEAN configuration.

During encoding of the texts of premises and theorems maximal length of input sequence was set to 90 tokens, that affect less than 10% of theorems in input data (see Table 1). Cosine similarity was computing using the built-in function in sentence transformers library[5]. This approach participated in evaluation phase and was ranked third among the shared task approaches (see Table 2, name **Ranking-SBERT**).

4.2 Ranking with MathBERT

There are a couple of Transformer models pre-trained on Mathematical Text. Most notably MathBERT-EDU (Shen et al., 2021) and MathBERT (Peng et al., 2021). While the first is constructed for General NLP Tasks in Mathematics Education the latter focuses on Mathematical Formula Understanding. With MathBERT the authors include two pretraining tasks specifically designed to 1. relate a formula to its surrounding context (called Context Correspondence Prediction) and 2. relate parts of a formula to each other (Masked Substructure Prediction). Thus MathBERT is par-

[1] https://github.com/ai-systems/tg2022task_premise_retrieval
[2] https://huggingface.co/tbs17/MathBERT
[3] https://beta.openai.com/playground
[4] https://github.com/UKPLab/sentence-transformers
[5] https://www.sbert.net/docs/package_reference/util.html

Split	Train	Validation	Test
number of samples	8,438	2,779	2,712
average number of tokens per sample	42,65	42,81	43,01
long samples (>90 tokens) ratio	0,06	0,06	0,07

Table 1: Statistics of the training, validation, and test sets.

ticularly suitable to produce embeddings of the Knowledge base. Unfortunately The weights and source code are not available at the time of writing this article. We therefore experiment with embeddings computed using MathBERT-EDU.

Following the embedding of the knowledge base and the given statement we compute the similarity with FAISS (Johnson et al., 2019).

4.3 Re-ranking SBERT with Prompting GPT-3

This approach combines better performing **Ranking-SBERT** with **Prompting GPT-3**. The overall pipeline is shown in Fig. 1 We select top-10 candidates and design two prompt templates (see Appendix). **Prompt template a)** instructs the model to rank the premises by its relevance with the instruction *Rank premise IDs in the Knowledge by its relevance for the theorem. IDs of the most relevant premises appear first.* and **Prompt template b)** asks the model to select the most relevant premise ID: *Select most relevant premise ID for the given theorem.* None of the prompt templates includes a "helping" example. Both prompts performed reasonable in manual experiments, but **Prompt template a)** was chosen for implementation as the one with a higher possible impact on primary ranking.

5 Experiments

GPT-like models, despite impressive performance on many NLP tasks under the zero-shot and few-shot setup, are not capable of long-term memory. During re-ranking, the model may favor last seen premises and "forget" the relevant ones, that were presented (ranked) first in the original ranking.

We have implemented three simple experiments to estimate how the order of the premises in the prompt influences the GPT-3 generated ranking. Results are provided in Table2.

Experiment 1. Favoring the "last seen premise". In this experiment, we checked, whether GPT-3 favours "last seen" (and, probably, irrelevant) premise in the end of the prompt to more relevant ones in the middle of the prompt. For this reason, premises with ranks 1 and 2 were swapped in the ranking obtained from GPT-3. Since the Mean Average Precision (MAP) decreased, it is possible to say, that GPT-3 at least relies on the meaning of premises while re-ranking.

Experiment 2A. "Forgetting" a relevant premise. In this experiment, the premise id with rank 1 in Ranking-SBERT was moved closer to the ranking head in GPT-3 ranking (to rank 3). It slightly improved the GPT-3 ranking, but hasn't outperformed Ranking-SBERT approach.

Experiment 2B. "Forgetting" a relevant premise. In this experiment, a merged ranking was created by inserting the premise with rank 1 from Ranking-SBERT, to the re-ranked results from GPT-3. This has resulted in major improvement and has shown, that GPT-3 struggles with memorizing relevant information and tends to increase the rank of relevant premises, if they appear at the beginning of a long sequence.

6 Results and Error Analysis

Results of approaches, described in Section 4, are summarized in Table 2. For single rankings, best results were shown by **Ranking-SBERT**. **Re-ranking SBERT with Prompting GPT-3** approach performed slightly worse. However, merging these two rankings has led to the improved result (see Experiment 2B).

The results in the table steer towards the actively discussed question, have large language models (not only GPT-like) actually learned to do reasoning, or have they only memorized training examples (Li et al., 2021; Si et al., 2020), see also [6], [7]. Despite its game-changing performance for many NLP tasks, GPT-3 doesn't outperform SBERT for the natural language premise selection task, where reasoning based on a large knowledge base is required.

[6] `https://jens-lehmann.org/blog/neural-language-models/`

[7] `https://lambdalabs.com/blog/demystifying-gpt-3/`

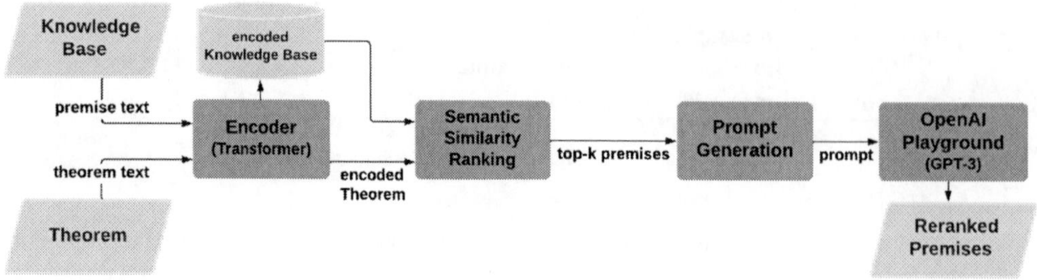

Figure 1: Premise Re-ranking with Prompts Template Design

Approach /Accuracy	Train	Validation	Test	Phase
Ranking-SBERT	n/a	n/a	**0,1460**	evaluation
Ranking-MathBERT-EDU	n/a	n/a	0.0609	post-competition
Re-ranking SBERT with Prompting GPT-3	n/a	n/a	0,1423	evaluation
Experiment 1. Favouring last seen item	n/a	n/a	0,1262	post-competition
Experiment 2A. Merged ranking	n/a	n/a	0,1450	post-competition
Experiment 2B. Merged ranking	n/a	n/a	**0,1497**	post-competition

Table 2: Approaches performance and experiments

Moreover, analysis of the GPT-3 generation output shows that the model occasionally repeated premise ids, omitted premise ids or "hallucinated" ids with comparable length during generation (total 16,5% of all premises). This erroneous output was not taken into account during re-ranking: it means, that for each sample there is a different portion of premises, re-ranked by GPT-3.

Prompt design should be implemented carefully, because GPT-3 tends to rely on the order of premises in the prompt, as well as on its meaning. Although the model doesn't really favor the last seen information in the prompt, it suffers from forgetting relevant information, if it was presented at the beginning of the prompt. This can be handled, for example by randomly shuffling elements subjected to re-ranking by GPT-3.

Overall, re-ranking by prompting generative language models, in a vanilla setup, does not improve similarity-based ranking, although merging these two rankings brings a better result.

7 Limitations and Future Work

While the approach presented here requires conceptually low resources compared to fine-tuning to the given training data, the use of GPT-3 comes with a significant cost (with the most capable model costing up to $0.02 for 1000 tokens). Furthermore, mathematical formulas are non-typical input for training general language models and hence tokenization might be less accurate thus also reducing the capability of the transformer models used for pre-ranking as they come with a maximum sequence length (512 for SBERT, MathBERT-EDU and MathBERT).

Performance of the proposed similarity ranking and prompt engineering approach, and available results from the shared task leaderboard show, that automated theorem proving is a hard task for NLU methods. LaTeXmarkup remains a hard type of input for encoders, that could possibly be overcome by using language models that have been pre-trained on LaTeX(e.g. MathBERT) or input-agnostic models, such as Perceiver. Furthermore, transformation of formulas into typesetting invariant representations should be investigated. Especially the representation of formulas as Operator Trees or translation to natural language might be beneficial in combination with general Language Models.

References

Jesse Alama, Tom Heskes, Daniel Kühlwein, Evgeni Tsivtsivadze, Josef Urban, J Alama, T Heskes, · D Kühlwein, · E Tsivtsivadze, and · J Urban. 2014. Premise selection for mathematics by corpus analysis and kernel methods. *J Autom Reasoning*, 52:191–213.

Robert B. Anderson. 1973. Symbolic logic and mechanical theorem proving.

Sebastian Borgeaud, Arthur Mensch, Jordan Hoffmann, Trevor Cai, Eliza Rutherford, Katie Millican, George van den Driessche, Jean-Baptiste Lespiau, Bogdan Damoc, Aidan Clark, Diego de Las Casas, Aurelia Guy, Jacob Menick, Roman Ring, Tom Hennigan, Saffron Huang, Loren Maggiore, Chris Jones, Albin Cassirer, Andy Brock, Michela Paganini, Geoffrey Irving, Oriol Vinyals, Simon Osindero, Karen Simonyan, Jack W. Rae, Erich Elsen, and Laurent Sifre. 2021. Improving language models by retrieving from trillions of tokens. *CoRR*, abs/2112.04426.

Tom Brown, Benjamin Mann, Nick Ryder, Melanie Subbiah, Jared D Kaplan, Prafulla Dhariwal, Arvind Neelakantan, Pranav Shyam, Girish Sastry, Amanda Askell, et al. 2020a. Language models are few-shot learners. *Advances in neural information processing systems*, 33:1877–1901.

Tom B. Brown, Benjamin Mann, Nick Ryder, Melanie Subbiah, Jared Kaplan, Prafulla Dhariwal, Arvind Neelakantan, Pranav Shyam, Girish Sastry, Amanda Askell, Sandhini Agarwal, Ariel Herbert-Voss, Gretchen Krueger, Tom Henighan, Rewon Child, Aditya Ramesh, Daniel M. Ziegler, Jeffrey Wu, Clemens Winter, Christopher Hesse, Mark Chen, Eric Sigler, Mateusz Litwin, Scott Gray, Benjamin Chess, Jack Clark, Christopher Berner, Sam McCandlish, Alec Radford, Ilya Sutskever, and Dario Amodei. 2020b. Language models are few-shot learners. *CoRR*, abs/2005.14165.

Jacob Devlin, Ming-Wei Chang, Kenton Lee, and Kristina Toutanova. 2018. BERT: pre-training of deep bidirectional transformers for language understanding. *CoRR*, abs/1810.04805.

Deborah Ferreira and André Freitas. 2020a. Natural language premise selection: Finding supporting statements for mathematical text. In *Proceedings of the 12th Language Resources and Evaluation Conference*, pages 2175–2182, Marseille, France. European Language Resources Association.

Deborah Ferreira and André Freitas. 2020b. Premise selection in natural language mathematical texts. In *Proceedings of the 58th Annual Meeting of the Association for Computational Linguistics*, pages 7365–7374, Online. Association for Computational Linguistics.

Geoffrey Irving, Christian Szegedy, Alexander A Alemi, Niklas Een, Francois Chollet, and Josef Urban. 2016. Deepmath - deep sequence models for premise selection. In *Advances in Neural Information Processing Systems*, volume 29. Curran Associates, Inc.

Jeff Johnson, Matthijs Douze, and Hervé Jégou. 2019. Billion-scale similarity search with GPUs. *IEEE Transactions on Big Data*, 7(3):535–547.

Xiang Lorraine Li, Adhiguna Kuncoro, Cyprien de Masson d'Autume, Phil Blunsom, and Aida Nematzadeh. 2021. Do language models learn commonsense knowledge?

Martin Líška, Petr Sojka, Michal Růžička, and Petr Mravec. 2011. Web interface and collection for mathematical retrieval: Webmias and mrec.

Pengfei Liu, Weizhe Yuan, Jinlan Fu, Zhengbao Jiang, Hiroaki Hayashi, and Graham Neubig. 2021. Pre-train, prompt, and predict: A systematic survey of prompting methods in natural language processing. *arXiv preprint arXiv:2107.13586*.

Shuai Peng, Ke Yuan, Liangcai Gao, and Zhi Tang. 2021. Mathbert: A pre-trained model for mathematical formula understanding. *CoRR*, abs/2105.00377.

Stanislas Polu and Ilya Sutskever. 2020. Generative language modeling for automated theorem proving. *CoRR*, abs/2009.03393.

Nils Reimers and Iryna Gurevych. 2019. Sentence-bert: Sentence embeddings using siamese bert-networks. *arXiv preprint arXiv:1908.10084*.

Jia Tracy Shen, Michiharu Yamashita, Ethan Prihar, Neil T. Heffernan, Xintao Wu, and Dongwon Lee. 2021. Mathbert: A pre-trained language model for general NLP tasks in mathematics education. *CoRR*, abs/2106.07340.

Chenglei Si, Ziqing Yang, Yiming Cui, Wentao Ma, Ting Liu, and Shijin Wang. 2020. Benchmarking robustness of machine reading comprehension models.

Marco Valentino, Deborah Ferreira, Mokanarangan Thayaparan, André Freitas, and Dmitry Ustalov. 2022. Textgraphs 2022 shared task on natural language premise selection. In *Proceedings of the Sixteenth Workshop on Graph-Based Methods for Natural Language Processing (TextGraphs-16)*. Association for Computational Linguistics.

Ashish Vaswani, Noam Shazeer, Niki Parmar, Jakob Uszkoreit, Llion Jones, Aidan N Gomez, Ł ukasz Kaiser, and Illia Polosukhin. 2017. Attention is all you need. In *Advances in Neural Information Processing Systems*, volume 30. Curran Associates, Inc.

Parameter name	Value
max_new_tokens	300
temperature	0.7
top_p	1
openai_frequency_penalty	0.0
openai_ presence_penalty	0.0
openai_stop_sequences	[ ]
n_responses	1

Table 3: GPT-3 Model parameters.

A Appendix

A.1 Experiment details and Parameters

The parameters for OpenAIs GPT-3 model in the OpenAI API have been chosen according to Table 3.

Author Index

Aksenova, Anna, 77
Asgari, Ehsaneddin, 124

Cheng, Yuchang, 25
Constant, Mathieu, 70

Dastgheib, Doratossadat, 124
Dong, MeiXing, 60
Doucet, Antoine, 114

Feng, Xincan, 25
Ferreira, Deborah, 105
Flek, Lucie, 89
Freitas, André, 105

Gavrishina, Ekaterina, 77
Geiss, Henri-Jacques, 89
Gokhan, Tuba, 44

Héja, Enikő, 35

Kadusabe, Provia, 119
Kovriguina, Liubov, 127
Kutuzov, Andrey, 77

Lee, Mark, 44
Ligeti-Nagy, Noémi, 35

Martinc, Matej, 114
Martínez, Javier, 1
Mihalcea, Rada, 60
Milios, Evangelos, 119
Minghim, Rosane, 119
Montero, David, 1

Nikishina, Irina, 11

Ollinger, Sandrine, 70

Panchenko, Alexander, 11
Plepi, Joan, 89
Pollak, Senja, 114

Qu, Zhi, 25

Rykov, Elisei, 77

Sakketou, Flora, 89
Sinha, Aman, 70
Smith, Phillip, 44

Teucher, Roman, 127
Thayaparan, Mokanarangan, 105
Tran, Thi Hong Hanh, 114
Trust, Paul, 119
Tutubalina, Elena, 11

Ustalov, Dmitry, 105

Vakhitova, Alsu, 11
Valentino, Marco, 105

Wardenga, Robert, 127
Watanabe, Taro, 25
Wold, Sondre, 54

Xu, Xueming, 60

Yebes, Javier, 1
Younis, Haseeb, 119
Yugami, Nobuhiro, 25

Zahran, Ahmed, 119